Robert Hebert Quick

Essays on Educational Reformers

Robert Hebert Quick

Essays on Educational Reformers

ISBN/EAN: 9783337295967

Printed in Europe, USA, Canada, Australia, Japan

Cover: Foto ©Thomas Meinert / pixelio.de

More available books at **www.hansebooks.com**

EDUCATIONAL REFORMERS.

READING-CLUB BOOKS ON TEACHING.

The growth of State Reading-Circles among teachers within the past year or two has been a marvel. The following are the books on Pedagogy recently adopted; and these editions have been prepared with Notes, Analyses, etc., *expressly to meet this demand.*

Sully's Psychology, abridged and annotated with Review, Test, and Examination Exercises, and Pedagogical References, by J. A. Reinhart, Ph.D. 16mo, pp. 373.... $1.50

Tate's Philosophy of Education, only complete edition. Pp. 330 .... 1.50

Payne's Lectures on Education, indexed and analyzed. Pp. 281 .... 1.00

Quick's Educational Reformers. 1886 Edition............ 1.50

DeGraff"s School-Room Guide, the standard work on *Practice.* Pp. 449 .... 1.50

Hoose's Province of Methods in Teaching. Pp. 376........ 1.00

The above volumes are uniform in binding.

Payne's Lectures. Complete edition. 8vo, pp. 385.......... 1.50

Fitch's Lectures on Teaching. 12mo, pp. 437............. 1.25

Page's Theory and Practice of Teaching. 12mo, pp. 422.... 1.25

Johonnot's Principles and Practice of Teaching. Pp. 395.. 1.50

Partridge's Quincy Methods. 12mo, pp. 660............... 1.50

Parker's Talks on Teaching. 16mo, pp. 182............... 1.00

On some of these books Special Prices are made to members of certain Reading Circles. In all such cases our rates for our own superior editions are the same as the lowest offered for any edition of the books.

ON

Educational Reformers.

BY

ROBERT HEBERT QUICK,

M.A. TRIN. COLL. CAM., LATE SECOND MASTER IN THE SURREY
COUNTY SCHOOL, AND FORMERLY CURATE OF
ST. MARK'S WHITECHAPEL.

READING-CLUB EDITION.

SYRACUSE, N. Y.:
C. W. BARDEEN, PUBLISHER.
1886.

PUBLISHER'S NOTE.

The plates from which this work has hitherto been issued having become so worn as to necessitate renewal, I have made the page uniform with the "Reading-Club" editions of Sully's "Outlines of Psychology with special reference to the Theory of Education," Tate's "Philosophy of Education," Payne's "Science and Art of Education," DeGraff's "School-Room Guide," etc.

I have also inserted in brackets translations of the many Latin, French, and German quotations. Prof. Quick wrote for the English schoolmaster, who is usually a university graduate, little thinking that the book would be purchased in thousands by the common-school teachers of America. These passages in foreign tongues have heretofore made many paragraphs unintelligible to these readers, who will appreciate the fact that this edition may be understood from preface to finis by those who have no other language than English.

The Index is entirely new and much fuller than in former editions. Especial pains has been taken to facilitate ready comparison of different views upon the same subject, and especially to indicate the passages where reference is made to the influence of one reformer upon others who followed him.

I have also added a few bibliographical notes, and in general it may be said that everything in brackets [ ] is an addition of mine to the matter of previous editions.

SYRACUSE, N. Y., March 15, 1886.

PREFACE.

"It is clear that in whatever it is our duty to act, those matters also it is our duty to study." These words of Dr. Arnold's seem to me incontrovertible. So a sense of duty, as well as fondness for the subject, has led me to devote a period of leisure to the study of *Education*, in the practice of which I have been for some years engaged.

There are countries where it would be considered a truism that a teacher in order to exercise his profession intelligently should know something about the chief authorities in it. Here, however, I suppose such an assertion will seem paradoxical; but there is a good deal to be said in defense of it. De Quincy has pointed out that a man who takes up any pursuit without knowing what advances others have made in it, works at a great disadvantage. He does not apply his strength in the right direction, he troubles himself about small matters and neglects great, he falls into errors that have long since been exploded. An educator is, I think, liable to these dangers if he brings to his task no knowledge but that which he learnt for the tripos, and no skill but that which he acquired in the cricket-ground or on the river. If his pupils are placed entirely in his hands, his work is one of great difficulty, with heavy penalties attached to all blundering in it; though here, as in the case of the ignorant doctor and careless architect, the penalties, unfortunately, are paid by his victims. If (as more commonly happens) he has simply to give a class prescribed instruction, his smaller scope of action limits proportionally the mischief that may ensue; but even then it is obviously desirable that his teaching should be as good as possible, and he is not likely to employ the best methods if he invents as he goes along, or simply falls back on his rememberance of how he was taught himself, perhaps in very different circumstances. I venture to think, therefore, that practical men in education, as in most other things, may derive benefit from the knowledge of what has already been said and done by the leading men engaged in it, both past and present.

All study of this kind, however is very much impeded by want of books. "Good books are in German," says Profesor Seeley. I have found that on the history of Education, not only *good* books, but *all* books are in German, or some other foreign language.*

---

* When the greater part of this volume was already written, Mr. Parker published his sketch of the history of Classical Education (*Essays on a Liberal Education*, edited by Farrar). He seems to me to have been very successful in bringing out the most important features of his subject, but his essay necessarily shows marks of over-compression. Two volumes have also lately appeared on *Christian Schools and Scholars* (Longmans, 1867). Here we have a good deal of information which we want, and also, as it seems to me, a good deal which we do not want. The

I have, therefore, thought it worth while to publish a few such imperfect sketches as these, with which the reader can hardly be less satisfied than the author. They may, however, prove useful till they give place to a better book.

Several of the following essays are nothing more than compilations. Indeed a hostile critic might assert that I had used the scissors with the energy of Mr. Timbs and without his discretion. The reader, however, will probably agree with me that I have done wisely in putting before him the opinions of great writers in their own language. Where I am simply acting as reporter, the author's own way of expressing himself is obviously the best; and if, following the example of the gypsies and Sir Fretful Plagiary, I had disfigured other people's offspring to make them pass for my own, success would have been fatal to the purpose I have steadily kept in view. The sources of original ideas in any subject, as the student is well aware, are few,* but for irrigation we re-

---

work characteristically opens with a 10th century description of the personal appearance of St. Mark when he landed at Alexandria. The author treats only of the times which preceded the Council of Trent. A very interesting account of early English education has been given by Mr. Furnivall, in the 2d and 3d numbers of the *Quarterly Journal of Education* (1867).

*Study of the old authors proves that the utterances of some of our most conspicuous reformers—of Mr. Lowe and Mr. Farrar, for instance—do not give much evidence of originality, as no doubt those gentlemen would readily acknowledge.

quire troughs as well as water-springs, and these essays are intended to serve in the humbler capacity.

A word about the incomplete handling of my subjects. I have not attempted to treat any subject completely or even with anything like completeness. In giving a sketch of the opinions of an author, one of two methods must be adopted; we may give an epitome of all that he has said, or by confining ourselves to his most valuable and characteristic opinions, may gain space to give these fully. As I detest epitomes I have adopted the latter method exclusively, but I may sometimes have failed in selecting an author's most characteristic principles; and probably no two readers of a book would entirely agree as to what was most valuable in it: so my account must remain, after all, but a poor substitute for the author himself.

For the part of a critic I have at least one qualification—practical acquaintance with the subject. As boy or master, I have been connected with no less than eleven schools, and my perception of the blunders of other teachers is derived mainly from the remembrance of my own. Some of my mistakes have been brought home to me by reading works on education, even those with which I do not in the main agree. Perhaps there are teachers who on looking through the following pages may meet with a similar experience.

Had the essays been written in the order in which they

stand, a good deal of repetition might have been avoided, but this repetition has at least the advantage of bringing out points which seem to me important; and as no one will read the book as carefully as I have done, I hope no one will be as conscious of this and other blemishes in it.

I much regret that in a work which is nothing if it is not practically useful, I have so often neglected to mark the exact place from which quotations are taken. I have myself paid the penalty of this carelessness in the trouble it has cost me to verify passages which seemed inaccurate.

The authority I have had recourse to most frequently is Raumer (*Geschichte der Pædagogik*). In his first two volumes he gives an account of the chief men connected with education, from Dante to Pestalozzi. The third volume contains essays on various parts of education, and the fourth is devoted to German Universities. There is an English translation published in America, of the fourth volume only. I confess to a great partiality for Raumer—a partiality which is not shared by a Saturday Reviewer and by other competent authorities in this country. But surely a German author who is not profound, and is almost perspicuous, has some claim on the gratitude of English readers, if he gives information which we cannot get in our own language. To Raumer I am indebted for all that I have written about Ratich, and almost all about Basedow. Elsewhere his history has been used, though not to the same extent.

C. A. Schmid's *Encyclopædie des Erziehungs und Unterrichtswesens* is a vast mine of information on everything connected with education. The work is still in progress. The part containg *Rousseau* has only just reached me. I should have been glad of it when I was giving an account of the *Emile*, as Raumer was of little use to me.

Those for whom Schmid is too diffuse and expensive will find Carl Gottlob Hergang's *Pædagogische Realencyclopædie* useful. This is in two thick volumes, and costs, to the best of my memory, about eighteen shillings. It was finished in 1847.

The best sketch I have met with of the general history of education is in the article on *Pædagogik* in *Meyer's Conversations-Lexicon*. I wish some one would translate this article; and I should be glad to draw the attention of the editor of an educational periodical, say the *Museum* or the *Quarterly Journal of Education*, to it.

I have come upon references to many other works on the History of Education, but of these the only ones I have seen are Theodore Fritz's *Esquissse d'un Systéme complet d'instruction et d'éducation et de leur histoire* (3 vols. Strasburg, 1843), and Carl Schmid's *Geschichte der Pædogogik* (4 vols.) The first of these gives only the outline of the subject. The second is, I believe, considered a standard work. It does not seem to me so readable as Raumer's history, but is much more complete, and comes down to quite recent times.*

For my account of the Jesuit schools and of Pestalozzi, the authorities will be found elsewhere (pp. 19 and 199). In writing about Comenius I have had much assistance from a life of him prefixed to an English translation of his *School of Infancy*, by Daniel Benham (London, 1858). For almost all the information given about Jacotot, I am indebted to Mr. Payne's papers, which I should not have ventured to extract from so freely if they had been before the public in a more permanent form.†

I am sorry I can not refer to any English works on the history of Education, except the essays of Mr. Parker and Mr. Furnivall, and *Christian Schools and Scholars*, which are mentioned above, but we have a very good treatise on the principles of education in Marcel's *Language as a Means of Mental Culture* (2 vols. London, 1853). Edgeworth's *Practical Education* seems falling into undeserved neglect, and Mr. Spencer's recent work is not universally known even by schoolmasters.

---

* [A translation by Prof. W. H. Payne of Compayre's History of Pedagogy has recently been published at $1.75. Prof. Payne is also author of "A Short History of Education," 50 cts.]

† [They are now published in his " Lectures on the Science and Art of Education," complete English edition, $1.50; Reading-Club edition, $1.00.]

If the following pages attract but few readers it will be some consolation, though rather a melancholy one, that I share the fate of my betters.

R. H. Q.

INGATESTONE, ESSEX, MAY, 1868.

CONTENTS.

I.	Schools of the Jesuits	17
II.	Roger Ascham	35
	Michael Eygnem Montaigne	42
III.	The Innovators	45
	Wolfgang Ratich	46
	John Milton	53
IV.	John Amos Comenius	56
V.	John Locke	81
VI.	Jean Jacques Rousseau	108
VII.	John Bernhard Basedow	138
VIII.	John Henry Pestalozzi	156
	Pestalozzianism	176
IX.	Joseph Jacotot	196
X.	Herbert Spencer	224
XI.	Thoughts and Suggestions	255
XII.	Moral and Religious Education	276

Appendix.—

Class Matches	288
Doctrinale Alexandri de Villa Dei	289
Lily's Grammar	290
Colet	292
Mulcaster	293
Words and Things	296
Axiomatic Truths of Methodology	301
From *Janua Linguarum*	303
Locke on Poetry	304
Dr. Wiese on English vs. German Schools	316

I.

SCHOOLS OF THE JESUITS.

SINCE the revival of learning, no body of men has played so prominent a part in education as the Jesuits. With characteristic sagacity and energy, they soon seized on education as a stepping-stone to power and influence; and with their talent for organization, they framed a system of schools which drove all important competitors from the field, and made the Jesuits the instructors of Catholic, and even, to some extent, of Protestant, Europe. Their skill in this capacity is attested by the highest authorities, by Bacon and by Descartes, the latter of whom had himself been their pupil; and it naturally met with its reward: for more than one hundred years nearly all the foremost men throughout Christendom, both among the clergy and laity, had received the Jesuit training, and for life regarded their old masters with reverence and affection.

About these Jesuit schools—once so celebrated and so powerful, and still existing in great numbers, though little remains of their original importance—there does not seem to be much information accessible to the English reader. I have, therefore, collected the following particulars about them; and refer any one who is dissatisfied with so meagre an account, to the works which I have consulted. The Jesuit schools, as I said, still exist, but they did their great work in other centuries; and I therefore prefer to speak of them as things of the past.

When the Jesuits were first formally recognized by a Bull of Paul III. in 1540, the Bull stated that the Order was formed, among other things, "especially for the purpose of instructing boys and ignorant persons in the Christian religion." But the Society well understood that secular was more in demand than religious learning; and they offered the more valued instruction that they might have the opportunity of inculcating lessons which, to the Society at least, were the more valuable. From various Popes they obtained powers for founding schools and colleges, for giving degrees, and for lecturing publicly at universities. Their foundations rapidly extended in the Romance countries, except in France, where they were long in overcoming the opposition of the regular clergy and of the University of Paris. Over the Teutonic and Slavonic countries they spread their influence first by means of national colleges at Rome, where boys of the different nations were trained as missionaries. But, in time, the Jesuits pushed their camps forward, even into the heart of the enemy's country.

The system of education to be adopted in all the Jesuit institutions was settled during the Generalship of Aquaviva. In 1584 that General appointed a School Commission, consisting of distinguished Jesuits from the various countries of Europe. These spent nearly a year in Rome, in study and consultation; and the fruit of their labors was the *Ratio atque Institutio Studiorum Societatis Jesu* [System and Code of the Studies of the Society of Jesus], which was put forth by Aquaviva and the Fourth General Assembly. By this Code the Jesuit schools have ever since been governed; but about fifty years ago it was revised with a view to modern requirements.

The Jesuits who formed the *Societas Professa*, i. e., those who had taken all the vows, had spent from fifteen to eighteen years in preparation, viz., two years as novices and one as approved scholars, during which they were engaged chiefly in religious exercises, three years in the study of philosophy and mathematics, four years of theology, and, in case of the more distinguished students, two years more in repetition and private theological study. At some point in this course, mostly after the philosophy, the students were sent, for awhile, to teach in the elementary schools.* The method of teaching was to be learnt in the training schools, called Juvenants, one of which was founded in each province.

Few, even of the most distinguished students, received dispensation from giving elementary instruction. Salmeron and Bobadilla performed this duty in Naples, Lainez in Florence, Borgia (who had been Viceroy of Catalonia) in Cordova, Canisius in Cologne.

During the time the Jesuit held his post as teacher he

---

*According to the article in K. A. Schmid's "Encyclopädie," the usual course was this—the two years' novitiate was over by the time the youth was between fifteen and seventeen. He then entered a Jesuit College as Scholasticus. Here he learnt literature and rhetoric for two years, and then philosophy (with mathematics) for three more. He then entered on his Regency, i. e., he went over the same ground as a *teacher*, for from four to six years. Then followed a period of theological study, ending with a year of trial, called the *Tertiorat*. The candidate was now admitted to Priest's Orders, and took the vows either as *professor quatuor votorum*, or as a *coadjutor*. If he was then sent back to teach, he gave only the higher instruction.

was to give himself up entirely to the work. His studies were abandoned; his religious exercises curtailed. He began generally with the lowest form, and went up the school with the same pupils, advancing a step every year, as in the system now common in Scotland. But some forms were always taught, as the highest is in Scotland, by the same master, who remained a teacher for life.

Great care was to be taken that the frequent changes in the staff of masters did not lead to alteration in the conduct of the school. Each teacher was bound to carry on the established instruction by the established methods. All his personal peculiarities and opinions were to be as much as possible suppressed. To secure this a rigid system of supervision was adopted, and reports were furnished by each officer to his immediate superior. Over all stood the General of the Order. Next came the Provincial, appointed by the General. Over the school itself was the Rector, who was appointed (for three years) by the General, though he was responsible to the Provincial, and made his reports to him. Next came the Prefect of Studies, appointed, not by the Rector, but by the Provincial. The teachers were carefully watched both by the Rector and the Prefect of Studies, and it was the duty of the latter to visit each teacher in his class at least once a fortnight, to hear him teach. The other authorities, besides the masters of classes, were usually a House Prefect, and Monitors selected from the boys, one in each form.

The school or college was to be built and maintained by gifts and bequests which the Society might receive for this purpose only. Their instruction was always given gratuitously. When sufficient funds were raised to support the officers, teachers, and at least twelve scholars, no effort was to be made to increase them; but if they fell short of this, donations were to be sought by begging from house to house. Want of money, however, was not a difficulty which the Jesuits often experienced.

The pupils in the Jesuit schools were of two kinds: 1st, those who were training for the Order, and had passed the Novitiate; 2d, the externs, who were pupils merely. When the building was not filled by the first of these (the *Scholastici*, or *Nostri*, as they are called in the Jesuit writings), other pupils were taken in to board, who had to pay simply the cost of their living, and not even this unless they could well afford it. Instruction, as I said, was gratuitous to all. "Gratis receive, gratis give," was the Society's rule, so they would neither make any charge for instruction, nor accept any gift that was burdened with conditions.

Faithful to the tradition of the Catholic Church, the Society did not estimate a man's worth simply according to his birth and outward circumstances. The Constitutions expressly laid down that poverty and mean extraction were never to be any hindrance to a pupil's admission; and Sacchini says: "Do not let any favoring of the nobility interfere with the care of meaner pupils, since the birth of all is equal in Adam, and the inheritance in Christ."

The externs who could not be received into the building were boarded in licensed houses, which were always liable to an unexpected visit from the Prefect of Studies.

The age at which pupils were admitted varied from fourteen to twenty-four.

The school was arranged in five classes (since increased to eight), of which the lowest usually had two divisions. Parallel classes were formed wherever the number of pupils was too great for five masters. The names given to the several divisions were as follows:

1. Infima [Lowest]
2. Media [Intermediate] } Classis Grammaticæ, [Grammatic Class].
3. Suprema [Highest]
4. Humanitas [Liberal], or Syntaxis [Syntactical].
5. Rhetorica [Rhetorical].

Jesuits and Protestants alike in the sixteenth and seventeenth centuries thought of no other instruction than in Latin and Greek, or rather in literature based on those languages. The subject-matter of the teaching in the Jesuit schools was to be "*præter Grammaticam, quod ad Rhetoricam, Poësim et Historiam pertinet*" [except grammatical, that which pertains to rhetoric, poetry, and history]. Reading and writing the mother tongue might not be taught without special leave from the Provincial. Latin was as much as possible to supersede all other languages, even in speaking; and nothing else might be used by the pupils in the higher forms on any day but a holiday.

Although many good school-books were written by the Jesuits, a great part of their teaching was given orally. The master was, in fact, a lecturer, who expounded sometimes a piece of a Latin or Greek author, sometimes the rules of grammar. The pupils were required to get up the substance of these lectures, and to learn the grammar-rules and parts of the classical authors by heart. The master for his part had to bestow great pains on the preparation of his lectures.

Written exercises, translations, etc., were given on every day, except Saturday; and the master had, if possible, to go over each one with its writer and his appointed rival or *æmulus.*

The method of hearing the rules, etc., committed to memory was this: Certain boys in each class, who were called Decurions, repeated their task to the master, and then in his presence heard the other boys repeat theirs. The master meanwhile corrected the written exercises.*

One of the leading peculiarities in the Jesuits' system was the pains they took to foster emulation—"*cotem ingenii puerilis, calcar industriæ,*" [the whetstone of youthful talent, the spur of industry]. For this purpose, all the boys in the lower part of the school were arranged in pairs, each pair being rivals (*æmuli*) to one another. Every boy was to be constantly on the watch, to catch his rival tripping, and was immediately to correct him. Besides this individual rivalry, every class was divided into two hostile camps, called Rome and Carthage, which had frequent pitched battles of questions on set subjects. These were the "Concertations," in which the boys sometimes had to put questions to the opposite camp, sometimes to expose erroneous

---

* In a school (not belonging to the Jesuits) where this plan was adopted, the boys, by an ingenious contrivance, managed to make it work very smoothly. The boy who was "hearing" the lesson held the book upside down in such a way that the others *read* instead of repeating by heart. The masters finally interfered with this arrangement.

answers when the questions were asked by the master.*
Emulation, indeed, was encouraged to a point where, as
it seems to me, it must have endangered the good feeling of the boys among themselves. Jouvency mentions
a practice of appointing mock defenders of any particularly bad exercise, who should make the author of it
ridiculous by their excuses; and any boy, whose work
was very discreditable, was placed on a form by himself, with a daily punishment, until he could show that
some one deserved to change places with him.

In the higher classes, a better kind of rivalry was
cultivated by means of "Academies," i. e., voluntary
associations for study, which met together, under the
superintendence of a master, to read themes, translations, etc., and to discuss passages from the classics.
The new members were elected by the old, and to be
thus elected was a much coveted distinction. In these
Academies the clever students got practice for the disputations, which formed an important part of the school
work of the higher classes.

There was a vast number of other expedients by
which the Jesuits sought to work on their pupils' *amour
propre* [self-respect], such as, on the one hand, the
weekly publication of offences *per præconem* [by the herald], and, on the other, besides prizes (which could be
won only by the externs), titles, and badges of honor,
and the like. It appears that in each class a kind of
magistracy was formed, who, as prætors, censors, etc.,

---

*Since the above was written, an account of these concertations has appeared in the Rev. R. G. Kingdon's evidence before the Schools Commission (vol. v., Answers 12,228 ff.). Mr. Kingdon, who is Prefect of Studies at Stonyhurst, mentions that the side which wins in most concertations gets an extra half-holiday.

had in some cases to try delinquents. "There are," says Jouvency, "hundreds of expedients of this sort, all tending to sharpen the boys' wits, to lighten the labor of the master, and to free him from the invidious and troublesome necessity of punishing."

The school-hours were remarkably short: two hours and a half in the morning, and the same in the afternoon, with a whole holiday a week in summer, and a half holiday in winter. The time was spent in the first form after the following manner: During the first half-hour, the master corrected the exercises of the previous day, while the Decurions heard the lesson which had been learnt by heart. Then the master heard the piece of Latin which he had explained on the previous day. With this construing was connected a great deal of parsing, conjugating, declining, etc. The teacher then explained the piece for the following day, which, in this form, was never to exceed four lines. The last half-hour of the morning was spent in explaining grammar. This was done very slowly and carefully. In the words of the *Ratio Studd.: Pluribus diebus fere singula præcepta inculcanda sunt*," [On many days hardly more than a single principle should be taught]. For the first hour of the afternoon, the master corrected exercises, and the boys learnt grammar. If there was time, the master put questions about the grammar he had explained in the morning. The second hour was taken up with more explanations of grammar, and the school closed with half an hour's concertation, or the master corrected the notes which the pupils had taken during the day. In the other forms, the work was very similar to this, except that Greek was added, and also in the higher classes a little mathematics.

It will be observed, from the above account, that almost all the strength of the Jesuit teaching was thrown into the study of the Latin language, which was to be used, not only for reading, but also in writing and speaking. But some amount of instruction in other subjects, especially in history and geography, was given in explaining, or rather lecturing on, the classical authors. Jouvency says that this lecture must consist of the following parts: 1st, the general meaning of the whole passage; 2d, the explanation of each clause, both as to the meaning and construction; 3d, any information, such as accounts of historical events, or of ancient manners and customs, which could be connected with the text; 4th, in the higher forms, applications of the rules of rhetoric and poetry; 5th, an examination of the Latinity; 6th, the inculcation of some moral lesson. This treatment of a subject he illustrates by examples. Among these is an account of a lesson for the first (i. e. lowest) class in the Fable of the Fox and the Mask; 1st, comes the argument and the explanation of words; 2d, the grammar and parsing, as *vulpes*, a substantive of the third declension, etc., like *proles*, *clades*, etc. (here the master is always to give among his examples some which the boys already know); 3d, comes the *eruditio* [information] —something about foxes, about tragedy, about the brain; and hence about other parts of the head; 4th, the Latinity, the order of the words, choice of words, synonyms, etc. Then the sentences may be parodied; other suitable substantives may be found for the adjectives, and vice versa, and every method is to be adopted of showing the boys how to *use* the words they have learnt. Lastly comes the moral.

The practical teacher will be tempted to ask, How is the attention of the class to be kept up whilst all this information is given? This the Jesuits did partly by punishing the inattentive. Every boy was subsequently required to reproduce what the teacher had said, and to show his written notes of it. But no doubt this matter of attention was found a difficulty. Jouvency tells the teachers to break off from time to time in their lectures, and to ask questions; and he adds: "*Variæ sunt artes excitandæ attentionis quas docebit usus et sua cuique industria suggeret*," [There are various expedients for arousing the attention that experience will teach and that his own diligence will suggest to any one].

For private study, besides written exercises and learning by heart, the pupils were recommended subjects to get up in their own time; and this, and also as to the length of some of the regular lessons, they were permitted to decide for themselves. Here, as everywhere, the Jesuits trusted to the sense of honor and emulation —those who did extra work were praised and rewarded. One of the maxims of this system was: "*Repetitio mater studiorum*," [Repetition is the mother of learning"]. Every lesson was connected with two repetitions—one before it began, of preceding work, and the other at the close, of the work just done. Besides this, one day a week was devoted entirely to repetition. In the three lowest classes the desire of laying a solid foundation even led to the second six months in the year being given to again going over the work of the first six months. By this means, boys of extraordinary ability could pass through these forms in eighteen months, instead of three years.

Thoroughness in work was the one thing insisted on. Sacchini says that much time should be spent in going over the more important things, which are "*veluti multorum fontes et capita*" [like the sources and central points of many things]; and that the master should prefer to teach a few things perfectly to giving indistinct impressions of many things. We should remember, however, that there were usually no pupils in the Jesuit schools under fourteen years of age. Subjects such as grammar can not, by any expenditure of time and trouble, be perfectly taught to children, because they can not perfectly understand them; so that the Jesuit thoroughness is not always attainable.

The usual duration of the course in the lower schools was six years—i. e., one year in each of the four lower classes, and two years in the highest class. Every year closed with a very formal examination. Before this examination took place, the pupils had lessons in the manner of it, so that they might come prepared, not only with a knowledge of the subjects, but also of the laws of writing for examination ("*scribendi ad examen leges*"). The examination was conducted by a commission appointed for the purpose, of which commission the Prefect of Studies was an ex-officio member. The masters of the classes, though they were present and could make remarks, were not of the examining body. For the *viva voce* [oral], the boys were ushered in, three at a time, before the solemn conclave. The results of the examination, both written and verbal, were joined with the records of the work done in the past year; and the names of those pupils who had distinguished themselves were then published in order of merit, but the poll was arranged alphabetically, or according to birthplace.

As might be expected, the Jesuits were to be very careful of the moral and religious training of their pupils. " *Quam maxime in vitæ probitate ac bonis artibus doctrinaque proficiant ad Dei gloriam,*" [That as far as possible, they may advance in integrity of character and in right conduct and in learning to the glory of God]. (*Ratio Studd.,* quoted by Schmid.) And Sacchini tells the master to remember how honorable his office is; as it has to do, not with grammar only, but also with the science and practice of a Christian and religious life: "*atque eo quidem ordine ut ipsa ingenii eruditio sit expolitio morum, et humana literatura divinæ ancilletur sapientiæ,*" [and in such a way especially that learning itself may lead to refinement of manners, and that human scholarship may become the handmaid of divine wisdom].

Each lesson was to begin with a prayer or sign of the cross. The pupils were to hear mass every morning, and were to be urged to frequent confession and receiving of the Holy Communion.

The bodily health also was to be carefully attended to. The pupils were not to study too much or too long at a time. Nothing was to be done for a space of from one to two hours after dinner. On holidays excursions were made to farms in the country.

Punishments were to be as light as possible, and the master was to shut his eyes to offences whenever he thought he might do so with safety. Grave offences were to be visited by flogging, performed by a "corrector," who was not a member of the Order. Where flogging did not have a good effect, the pupil was to be expelled.

The dry details into which I have been drawn by faithfully copying the manner of the *Ratio Studiorum* may seem to the reader to afford no answer to the question which naturally suggests itself—to what did the school-system of the Jesuits owe its enormous popularity? But in part, at least, these details do afford an answer. They show us that the Jesuits were intensely practical. They title *Ratio Studiorum* has been called a misnomer, for the book so designated hardly contains a single principle; but what it does is this—it points out a perfectly attainable goal, and carefully defines the road by which that goal is to be approached. For each class was prescribed not only the work to be done, but also the end to be kept in view. Thus method reigned throughout;—perhaps not the best method, as the object to be attained was assuredly not the highest object; but the method, such as it was, was applied with undeviating exactness. In this particular the Jesuit schools contrasted strongly with their rivals of old, as indeed with the ordinary school of the present day. The Head Master, who is to the modern English school what the General, Provincial, Rector, Prefect of Studies, and *Ratio Studiorum* combined were to a school of the Jesuits, has perhaps no standard in view up to which the boy should have been brought when his school course is completed.* The masters of forms teach just those portions of their subjects in which

---

* As the recent Commission has pointed out, the Head Master often thinks of nothing but the attainment of University honors, even when the great majority of his pupils are not going to the University.

they themselves are interested, in any way that occurs to them, with by no means uniform success; so that when two forms are examined with the same examination paper, it is no very uncommon occurrence for the lower to be found superior to the higher. It is, perhaps, to be expected that a course in which uniform method tends to a definite goal would on the whole be more successful than one in which a boy has to accustom himself by turns to half-a-dozen different methods, invented at haphazard by individual masters with different aims in view, if indeed they have any aim at all.

I have said that the object which the Jesuits proposed in their teaching was not the highest object. They did not aim at developing *all* the faculties of their pupils, but merely the receptive and reproductive faculties. When the young man had acquired a thorough mastery of the Latin language for all purposes, when he was well versed in the theological and philosophical opinions of his preceptors, when he was skillful in dispute, and could make a brilliant display from the resources of a well-stored memory, he had reached the highest point to which the Jesuit sought to lead him. Originality and independence of mind, love of truth for its own sake, the power of reflecting, and of forming correct judgments, were not merely neglected—they were suppressed in the Jesuits' system. But in what they attempted they were eminently successful, and their success went a long way toward securing their popularity.*

---

* Ranke, speaking of the success of the Jesuit schools, says: "It was found that young persons learned more under them in half a year than with others in two years. Even Protestants called back their children from distant schools, and put them under the care of the Jesuits."—*Hist. of Popes*, book v., p. 138. Kelly's Trans.

Their popularity was due, moreover, to the means employed, as well as to the result attained. The Jesuit teachers were to *lead*, not drive their pupils; to make "*disciplinam non modo tolerabilem, sed etiam amabilem,*" [discipline not only endurable but even agreeable]. Sacchini expresses himself very forcibly on this subject. "It is," says he, "the unvarying decision of wise men, whether in ancient or modern times, that the instruction of youth will always be best when it is pleasantest: whence this application of the word *ludus*, [game]. The tenderness of youth requires of us that we should not overstrain it, its innocence that we should abstain from harshness. . . . That which enters into willing ears the mind as it were runs to welcome, seizes with avidity, carefully stows away and faithfully preserves." The pupils were therefore to be encouraged in every way to take kindly to their learning. With this end in view (and no doubt other objects, also), the masters were carefully to seek the boys' affections. "When pupils love the master," says Sacchini, "they will soon love his teaching. Let him, therefore, show an interest in everything that concerns them and not merely in their studies. Let him rejoice with those that rejoice, and not disdain to weep with those that weep. After the example of the apostle let him become a little one amongst little ones, that he may make them adult in Christ, and Christ adult in them. . . Let him unite the grave kindness and authority of a father with a mother's tenderness."*

---

* Unfortunately, the Jesuit's kind manner loses its value from being due not so much to kind feeling as to some ulterior object, or to a rule of the Order. I think it is Jouvency who recommends that when a boy is absent

In order that learning might be pleasant to the pupils, it was necessary that they should not be overtasked. To avoid this the master had to study the character and capacity of each boy in his class, and to keep a book with all particulars about him, and marks from one to six indicating proficiency. Thus the master formed an estimate of what should be required, and the amount varied considerably with the pupil, though the quality of the work was always to be good.

Not only was the work not to be excessive, it was never to be of great difficulty. Even the grammar was to be made as easy and attractive as possible. "I think it a mistake," says Sacchini, "to introduce at an early stage the more thorny difficulties of grammar: . . . for when the pupils have become familiar with the easier parts, use will, by degrees, make the more difficult clear to them. His mind expanding and his judgment ripening as he grows older, the pupil will often see for himself that which he could be hardly made to see by others. Moreover, in reading an author, examples of grammatical difficulties will be more easily observed in connection with the context, and will make more impression on the mind, than if they are taught in an abstract form by themselves. Let them, then, be carefully explained whenever they occur."

In collecting these particulars about the Jesuit schools, I have considered not how this or that might be used in attacking or defending the Order, but, simply,

---

from sickness or other sufficient reason, the master should send daily to inquire after him, *because the parents will be pleased by such attention.* When the motive of the inquiry is suspected, the parents will be pleased no longer.

B

what would be of most interest to those who are engaged in education.

No other school system has been built up by the united efforts of so many astute intellects; no other system has met with so great success, or attained such wide-spread influence. It deserves, therefore, our careful consideration; and, however little we may approve that system, and wish to imitate it as a whole, it may suggest to us not a few useful reflections on our own practice; may lead us to be clearer in our aims; and to value more highly a well-organized plan of instruction—without which even humble aims will mostly prove unattainable.

II.

ASCHAM AND MONTAIGNE.

MASTERS and scholars who sigh over what seem to them the intricacies and obscurities of the "Head-masters' Primer" may find some consolation in thinking that, after all, matters might have been worse, and that their fate is enviable indeed compared with that of the students of Latin 400 years ago. Did the reader ever open the *"Doctrinale"* of Alexander de Villa Dei, which was the grammar in general use from the middle of the thirteenth to the end of the fifteenth century? If so, he is aware how great a step toward simplicity was made by our grammatical reformers, Lily, Colet, and Erasmus. Indeed, those whom we now regard as the forgers of our chains were, in their own opinion and that of their contemporaries, the champions of freedom.

I have given elsewhere a remarkable passage from Colet, in which he recommends the leaving of rules and the study of examples in good Latin authors. Wolsey also, in his directions to the masters of Ipswich School (dated 1528), proposes that the boys should be exercised in the eight parts of speech in the first form, and should begin to speak Latin and translate from English into Latin in the second. If the masters think fit, they may also let the pupils read Lily's *"Carmen Monitorum,"* or Cato's *"Distichs."* From the third upward a regular course of classical authors was to be read, and Lily's rules were to be introduced by degrees. "Although I confess such things are necessary," writes Wolsey, " yet, as far as possible, we could wish them so appointed as not to occupy the more valuable part of the day." Only in the sixth form, the highest but two, Lily's syntax was to be begun. In these schools the boys' time was wholly taken up with Latin, and the speaking of Latin was enforced even in play hours, so we see that anomalies in the Accidence as taught in the *As in præsenti* were not given till the boys had been some time using the language; and the syntax was kept until they had a good practical knowledge of the usages to which the rules referred.

These great men, however, though they showed the interest they took in the instruction of the young, and the insight they had into the art of teaching, never attempted a perfect treatise on the subject. This was done some fifty years afterward by the celebrated Roger Ascham in his "Scholemaster." If *laudari a laudatus* [praise from the praised] is any test of merit, we may assume that this book is still deserving of attention. "It contains, perhaps," says Dr. Johnson, "the best advice that was ever given for the study of languages."* And Mr. J. E. B. Mayor (no mean authority) ventures on a still stronger assertion. "This book sets forth," says he, *the only sound method of acquiring a dead language.*" Mr. George Long has also borne witness on the same side.

And yet, I believe, few teachers of the dead languages have read Ascham's book, or know the method

---
*Life of Ascham.

he proposes. I will, therefore, give an account of it, as nearly as I can in Ascham's own words.

Latin is to be taught as follows: First, let the child learn the eight parts of speech, and then the right joining together of substantives with adjectives, the noun with the verb, the relative with the antecedent. After the concords are learned, let the master take Sturm's selection of Cicero's Epistles, and read them after this manner: "first, let him teach the child, cheerfully and plainly, the cause and matter of the letter; then, let him construe it into English so oft as the child may easily carry away the understanding of it; lastly, parse it over perfectly. This done, then let the child by and by both construe and parse it over again; so that it may appear that the child doubteth in nothing that his master has taught him before. After this, the child must take a paper book, and, sitting in some place where no man shall prompt him, by himself let him translate into English his former lesson. Then showing it to his master, let the master take from him his Latin book, and pausing an hour at the least, then let the child translate his own English into Latin again in another paper book. When the child bringeth it turned into Latin, the master must compare it with Tully's book, and lay them both together, and where the child doth well, praise him, where amiss point out why Tully's use is better. Thus the child will easily acquire a knowledge of grammar, and also the ground of almost all the rules that are so busily taught by the master, and so hardly learned by the scholar in all common schools." "We do not contemn rules, but we gladly teach rules; and teach them more plainly, sensibly, and orderly, than they be commonly taught in common schools. For when the master shall compare Tully's book with the scholar's translation, let the master at the first lead and teach the scholar to join the rules of his grammar book with the examples of his present lesson, until the scholar by himself be able to fetch out of his grammar every rule for every example; and let the grammar book be ever in the scholar's hand, and also used by him as a dictionary for every present use. This is a lively and perfect way of teaching of rules; where the common way used in common schools to read the grammar alone by itself is tedious for the master, hard for the scholar, cold and uncomfortable for them both." And elsewhere Ascham says: "Yea I do wish that all rules for young scholars were shorter than they be. For, without doubt, *grammatica* itself is sooner and surer learned by examples of good authors than by the naked rules of grammarians."

"As you perceive your scholar to go better on away, first, with understanding his lesson more quickly, with parsing more readily, with translating more speedily and perfectly than he was wont; after, give him longer lessons to translate, and, withal, begin to teach him, both in nouns and verbs, what is *proprium* [the individual meaning of the word] and what is *translatum* [its meaning in a particular passage], what *synonymum* [the shades of difference between it and similar words], what *diversum* [other words of like meaning], which be *contraria* [other words of opposite meaning], and which be most notable *phrases*, in all his lectures, as—

    Proprium . . Rex sepultus est magnifice. [The king is buried magnificently.]

Translatum . .	Cum illo principe, sepulta est et gloria et salus reipublicæ. [With that chief is buried the glory and the safety of the republic.]
Synonyma . .	Ensis, gladius, laudare, prædicare.
Diversa . . .	Diligere, amare, colere, exardescere, inimicus, hostis.
Contraria . .	Acerbum et luctuosum bellum, dulcis et læta pax. [War is bitter and sorrowful, peace is sweet and joyful.]
Phrases . . .	Dare verba, abjicere obedientiam." [To deceive, to revolt.]

Every lesson is to be thus carefully analyzed, and entered under these headings in a third MS. book.

All this time, though the boy is to work over some Terence, he is to speak no Latin. Subsequently the master must translate easy pieces from Cicero into English, and the boy, without having seen the original passage, is required to put the English into Latin. His translation must then be carefully compared with the original, for "of good heed-taking springeth chiefly knowledge."

In the Second Book of the "Scholemaster," Ascham discusses the various branches of the study then common, viz: 1. Translatio linguarum [Translation of languages]; 2. Paraphrasis [Paraphrase]; 3. Metaphrasis [Metaphrase]; 4. Epitome; 5. Imitatio [Imitation]; 6. Declamatio [Declamation]. He does not lay much stress on any of these, except *translatio* and *imitatio*. Of the last he says: "All languages, both learned and mother-tongue, be gotten, and gotten only by imitation. For, as ye use to hear, so ye use to speak; if ye hear no other, ye speak not yourself; and whom ye only hear, of them ye only learn." But translation was his great instrument for all kinds of learning. "The translation," he says, "is the most common and most commendable of all other exercises for youth; most common, for all your constructions in grammar schools be nothing else but translations, but because they be not *double* translations (as I do require) they bring forth but simple and single commodity: and because also they lack the daily use of writing, which is the only thing that breedeth deep root, both in the wit for good understanding and in the memory for sure keeping of all that is learned; most commendable also, and that by the judgment of all authors which entreat of these exercises."

After quoting Pliny, he says: "You perceive how Pliny teacheth that by this exercise of double translating is learned easily, sensibly, by little and little, not only all the hard congruities of grammar, the choice of ablest words, the right pronouncing of words and sentences, comeliness of figures, and forms fit for every matter and proper for every tongue: but, that which is greater also, in marking daily and following diligently thus the footsteps of the best authors, like invention of arguments, like order in disposition, like utterance in elocution, is easily gathered up; and hereby your scholar shall be brought not only to like eloquence, but also to all true understanding and rightful judgment, both for writing and speaking."

Again he says: "For speedy attaining, I durst venture a good wager if a scholar in whom is aptness, love, diligence, and constancy, would but translate after this sort some little book in Tully (as '*De Senectute*,' with two epistles, the first '*Ad Quintum Fratrem*,' the other

'*Ad Lentulum*'), that scholar, I say, should come to a better knowledge in the Latin tongue than the most part do that spend from five to six years in tossing all the rules of grammar in common schools." After quoting the instance of Dion Prussæus, who came to great learning and utterance by reading and following only two books, the "*Phædo*" and "*Demosthenes de Falsa Legatione*," he goes on: "And a better and nearer example herein may be our most noble Queen Elizabeth, who never took yet Greek or Latin grammar in her hand after the first declining of a noun and a verb; but only by this double translating of Demosthenes and Isocrates daily, without missing, every forenoon, and likewise some part of Tully every afternoon, for the space of a year or two, hath attained to such a perfect understanding in both the tongues, and to such a ready utterance of the Latin, and that with such a judgment, as there be few now in both Universities or elsewhere in England that be in both tongues comparable with Her Majesty." Ascham's authority is indeed not conclusive on this point, as he, in praising the Queen's attainments, was vaunting his own success as a teacher; and, moreover, if he flattered her he could plead prevailing custom. But we have, I believe, abundant evidence that Elizabeth was an accomplished scholar.

Before I leave Ascham, I must make one more quotation, to which I shall more than once have occasion to refer. Speaking of the plan of double translation, he says: "Ere the scholar have construed, parsed, twice translated over by good advisement, marked out his six points by skillful judgment, he shall have necessary occasion to read over every lecture a *dozen times at the least;* which because he shall do always in order, he shall do it always with pleasure. . . . And pleasure allureth love; love hath lust to labor; labor always obtaineth his purpose."

MONTAIGNE.

Montaigne was a contemporary of Ascham, but about thirty years younger. In his essays he may be said to have founded a school of thinkers on the subject of education, of which Locke and Rousseau were afterward the great exponents. As far as regards method of teaching languages, he simply discarded grammatical teaching, and wished that all could be taught Latin as he had been, i. e., by conversation. His father had found a German tutor for him, who spoke Latin, but not French; and the child thus grew up to consider Latin his mother-tongue. At six years old he knew no more French, he tells us, than Arabic.

As I intend giving an account of Montaigne's principles in the form in which they were presented by Locke and Rousseau, I need not state them fully in this place; but a quotation or two will show how much his successors were indebted to him. He complains of common education as being too much taken up with language. "Fine speaking," says he, "is a very good and commendable quality, but not so excellent or so necessary as some would make it; and I am scandalized that our whole life should be spent in nothing else. I would first understand my own language, and that of my neighbor, with whom most of my business and conversation lies. No doubt Greek and Latin are very great ornaments, and of very great use; but we may buy them too dear." From our constant study of words the world is nothing but babble; and yet of the truly educated we must say with Cicero, "*Hanc amplissimam omnium artium bene vivendi disciplinam, vita magis quam literis persecuti sunt,*" [They have cultivated this broadest of all arts, the lesson of right living, in life rather than in literature]. He would take for his models not the Athenians, but the Spartans. "Those cudgelled their brains about words, these made it their business to inquire into things; *there* was an eternal babble of the tongue, *here* a continual exercise of the soul. And therefore it is nothing strange if, when Antipater demanded of them fifty children for hostages, they made answer that they would rather give him twice as many full grown men, so much did they value the loss of their country's education."

Ordinary teaching, again, gives only the thoughts of others, without requiring the pupil to think for himself. "We suffer ourselves to lean and rely so very strongly upon the arm of another, that by doing so we prejudice our own strength and vigor. . . . I have no taste for this relative, mendicant, and precarious understanding; for though we should become learned by other men's reading, I am sure a man can never be wise but by his own wisdom." As it is, "we only toil and labor to stuff the memory, and in the meantime leave the conscience and the understanding unfurnished and void. And, like birds who fly abroad to forage for grain bring it home in their beak without tasting it themselves, to feed their young, so our pedants go picking knowledge here and there out of several authors, and hold it at their tongue's end only to spit it out and distribute it amongst their pupils." The dancing-master might as well attempt to teach us to cut capers by our listening to his instructions without moving from our seats, as the tutor to inform our understandings without setting them to work. "Yet 'tis the custom of schoolmasters to be eternally thundering in their pupil's ears, as they were pouring into a funnel, whilst the pupil's business is only to repeat what the others said before. Now I would have a tutor to correct this error, and that at the very first: he should, according to the capacity he has to deal with, put it to the test, permitting his pupil himself to taste and relish things, and of himself to choose and discern them, sometimes opening the way to him, and sometimes making him break the ice himself; that is, I would not have the governor alone to invent and speak, but that he should also hear his pupils speak. Socrates, and since him Arcesilaus, first made their scholars speak, and then spoke to them. *Obest plerumque iis qui discere volunt auctoritas eorum qui docent,* [It is especially harmful to those who wish to learn to be under the authority of those that teach].

He also insisted on the importance of physical education. "We have not to train up a soul, nor yet a body, but a man; and we cannot divide him."

III.
THE INNOVATORS.

The Papal system was connected, in the minds of the Reformers, with scholastic subtilties, monkish Latin, and ignorance of Greek; the Reformation itself, with the revival of classical learning. Their opponents, the Jesuits, also fostered Latin as the language of the Church, and taught Greek as necessary for controversy. So, for a time, the effect of the Reformation was to confine instruction more exclusively to the classical languages. The old *Trivium* (grammar, logic, and rhetoric), and *Quadrivium* (arithmetic, geometry, music, and astronomy), had recognized, at least in name, a course of instruction in what was then the encyclopædia of knowledge. But now all the great school-masters— Ascham in England, Sturm in Germany, the Jesuits everywhere—thought of nothing but Latin and Greek. Before long, other voices besides Montaigne's were heard objecting to this bondage to foreign languages, and demanding more attention for the mother tongue and for the study of *things*.* This demand has been kept up by a series of reformers, with whom the classicists, after withstanding a siege of nearly three centuries, seem at length inclined to come to terms.

The chief demands of these reformers, or Innovators, as Raumer calls them, have been, 1st, that the study of *things* should precede, or be united with, the study of

---

* Mulcaster shows in his *Elementarie*, how soon the advantage of studying the mother-tongue and rejecting the dominion of Latin was advocated in this country.

words; 2d, that knowledge should be communicated, where possible, by appeals to the senses; 3d, that all linguistic study should begin with that of the mother-tongue; 4th, that Latin and Greek should be taught to such boys only as would be likely to complete a learned education; 5th, that physical education should be attended to in all classes of society for the sake of health, not simply with a view to gentlemanly accomplishments; 6th, that a new method of teaching should be adopted, framed " according to nature."

Their notions of method have, of course, been very various; but their systems mostly agree in these particulars.

1. They proceed from the concrete to the abstract, giving some knowledge of the thing itself before the rules which refer to it. 2. They employ the student in analyzing matter put before him, rather than in working synthetically according to precept. 3. They require the student to *teach himself*, under the superintendence of the master, rather than be taught by the master and receive anything on the master's authority. 4. They rely on the interest excited in the pupil by the acquisition of knowledge, and renounce coercion. 5. Only that which is understood may be committed to memory.

RATICH.

During the early years of the seventeenth century, there was a man traveling over Europe, to offer to Princes and Universities a wonderful discovery whereby old or young might with ease, in a very short time, learn Hebrew, Greek, Latin, or any other tongue. This, however, was but a small part of what the discoverer promised. He would also found a school, in which all arts and sciences should be rapidly learnt and advanced; he would introduce, and peacefully maintain throughout the continent, a uniform speech, a uniform government, and, more wonderful still, a uniform religion. From these modest proposals, we should naturally infer that the promiser was nothing but a quack of more than usual impudence; but the position which the name of Ratich holds in the history of education is sufficient proof that this is by no means a complete account of the matter.

Ratich was born at Wilster, in Holstein, in 1571. He was educated in the Hamburg Gymnasium, studied theology at Rostock, and being prevented, by some defect of utterance, from taking Holy Orders, he traveled, first to England, and then to Amsterdam, where he elaborated his system, and offered his secret to Prince Maurice of Orange. The Prince wished to stipulate that he should confine himself to teaching Latin; but Ratich was far too much impressed with the importance of his scheme to agree to this. So he went about from Court to Court, from University to University, to find some ruler or learned body who would agree to his terms. In 1612 he memorialized the Electoral Diet, then sitting at Frankfort; and his memorial attracted so much notice, that several Princes appointed learned men to inquire into his system. Helvicus, one of the most celebrated of these, published a Report, in which he declared strongly in favor of Ratich. "We are," says he, "in bondage to Latin. The Greeks and Saracens would never have done so much for posterity, if they had spent their youth in acquiring a foreign tongue. We must study our own language and then sciences. Ratich has discovered the art of teaching according to nature. By his method, languages will be quickly learned, so that we shall have time for science; and science will be learned even better still, as the natural system suits best with science, which is the study of nature."

Influenced by this Report, the town of Augsburg in 1614 summoned Ratich to reform their schools. Here the innovator found, to his cost, that he who leaves the high road has rough ground to travel over, and all kinds of obstacles to surmount. Even his best friends, among them Helvicus, were forced to admit that they were disappointed with the result of the experiment. They did not desert him, however, and, in 1619, Prince Lewis of Anhalt-Köthen, with Prince Ernest of Weimar, resolved that the great discovery should not be lost to the world for want of a fair trial: so Ratich was established at Köthen, and all his demands were complied with. A printing-press was set up for him, with Eastern as well as European types. A body of teachers (bound over to secrecy) came to receive his instructions, and then carried them out, under his directions, in a school of 230 boys and 200 girls, which the Prince got together for him. But everything was soon in disorder. Instead of introducing the uniform religion, he offended the Calvanistic Kötheners by his uncompromising Lutheranism. And his success was by no means such as to defy hostile criticism. His enemies soon declared the whole scheme a failure, and naturally went on to denounce its author as an impostor. The prince, exasperated by the utter break-down of his expectations, revenged himself on Ratich by throwing him into prison, and after a confinement of some months dismissed him with a public declaration that he had promised what he was unable to perform.

For more than twenty years after this, Ratich continued to trumpet his system; but in the din of the Thirty Years' War he did not receive much attention. He died in 1635.

Although Ratich's pretensions were manifestly absurd, and his binding over his pupils to secrecy makes us suspect him of being a charlatan, he really seems to have been the first to propound many of those principles which I have mentioned as the common property of the Innovators. Although he professed to teach a foreign language in six months, he gave extreme prominence to the study of the mother-tongue. The children at Köthen had to go through three classes before they began any other language. His maxims are these: 1. "Everything after the order and course of Nature." 2. "One thing at a time." 3. "One thing again and again repeated." 4. "Nothing shall be learnt by heart." In learning by by heart, he says, the attention is fixed on the words, not on the ideas; but if a thing is thoroughly grasped by the understanding, the memory retains it without further trouble. 5. "Uniformity in all things." Everything was to be taught in the same way. Grammars of different languages were to be constructed on the same plan, and were to differ only in those parts where the idioms of the languages differed. 6. "Knowledge of the thing itself must be given before that which refers

c

to the thing." "*Accidens rei priusquam rem ipsam quærere prorsus absonum et absurdum esse videtur. . . . Ne modus rei ante rem,*" [To search into the attributes of a thing before the thing itself seems utterly incongruous and absurd. . . . Let not the manner of a thing take precedence of the thing itself]. You do not give the properties of the square or circle before the pupil knows what square and circle are, says Ratich; why then, should you give rules about patronymics, e. g., before the pupil knows anything of patronymics, or, indeed, of the simple facts of the language? The use of rules is to confirm previous knowledge, and not to give knowledge. 7. "Everything by experiment and analysis." *Per inductionem et experimentum omnia.* Nothing was to be received on authority. Indeed, Ratich even adopted the motto "*Vetustas cessit, ratio vicit*" [Antiquity has yielded, reason has conquered], as if the opposite to *ratio* was *vetustas*. 8. "Everything without coercion." The human understanding, he says, is so formed that it best retains what it finds pleasure in receiving.* The rod should be used to correct offences against morals only. Ratich laid great stress on the maintenance of a good feeling between the teacher and the taught, and, lest this should be endangered by necessary discipline, he would hand over the care of discipline to a separate officer, called the Scholarch.

When we examine Ratich's method of teaching, we shall find that here, too, he deserves to be considered the Coryphæus of the Innovators. The teacher of the

---

* The reader will find that the unanimity of the writers on education in advocating this principle is almost as great as that of the schoolmasters in neglecting it.

lowest class at Köthen had to talk with the children, and to take pains with their pronunciation. When they knew their letters, the teacher read the book of Genesis through to them, each chapter twice over, requiring the children to follow with eye and finger. Then the teacher began the chapter again, and read about four lines only, which the children read after him. When the book had been worked over in this way, the children were required to read it through without assistance. Reading once secured, the teacher proceeded to grammar. He explained, say, what a substantive was, and then showed instances in Genesis, and next required the children to point out others. In this way grammar was verified throughout from Genesis, and the pupils were exercised in declining and conjugating words taken from the book.

When they advanced to the study of Latin, they were given a *translation* of a play of Terence, and worked over it several times before they were shown the Latin. The master then translated the play to them, each half-hour's work twice over. At the next reading, the master translated the first half hour, and the boys translated the same piece the second. Having thus got through the play, they began again, and only the boys translated. After this there was a course of grammar, which was applied to the Terence, as the grammar of the mother-tongue had been to Genesis. Finally, the pupils were put through a course of exercises, in which they had to turn into Latin sentences imitated from the Terence, and differing from the original only in the number or person used.

Raumer gives other particulars, and quotes largely

from the almost unreadable account of Kromayer, one of Ratich's followers, in order that we may have, as he says, a notion of the tediousness of the method. No doubt any one who has followed me hitherto, will consider that this point has been brought out already with sufficient distinctness.

When we compare Ratich's method with that of Ascham, we find that they have much in common. Ratich began the study of a language with one book, which he worked over with the pupil a great many times. Ascham did the same. Each lecture, he says, would, according to his plan, be gone over a dozen times at the least. Both construed to the pupil, instead of requiring him to make out the sense for himself. Both taught grammar, not independently, but in connection with the model book. So far as the two methods differed, I have no hesitation in pronouncing Ascham's the better. It gave the pupil more to do, and contained the very important element, *writing*. By this means there was a chance of the interest of the pupil surviving the constant repetition; but Ratich's pupils must have been bored to death. His plan of making them familiar with the translation first, was subsequently advocated by Comenius, and may have advantages, but in effect the pupil would be tired of the play before he began to translate it. Then Ratich's plan of going through and through seems very inferior to that of thoroughly mastering one lesson before going on to the next. I should say that whatever merit there was in Ratich's plan, lay in its insisting on complete knowledge of a single book, and that this knowledge would be much better attained by Ascham's practice of double translation.

JOHN MILTON.

In the middle of the seventeenth century there was in England a schoolmaster, and author of a Latin "Accidence," who was perhaps the most notable man who ever kept a school or published a school-book. This was John Milton. His notions of education have been briefly recorded by him in his Tract to Hartlib,* and have been read by many of us, not, I fancy, without a feeling of disappointment. His proposals, indeed, like everything connected with him, are of heroic mould. The reader (especially if he is a schoolmaster) gasps for breath at the mere enumeration of the subjects to be learned and the books to be read. In natural philosophy "they (the scholars) may proceed leisurely from the history of meteors, minerals, plants, and living creatures, as far as anatomy." In law, "they are to dive into the grounds of law and legal justice, delivered first, and with best warrant, by Moses, and, as far as human prudence can be trusted, in those extolled remains of Grecian lawgivers, Lycurgus, Solon, Zaleucus, Charondas, and thence to all the Roman edicts and tables with their Justinian, and so down to Saxon and common laws of England and the

---

*[Reprinted in this country as No. 7 of the School-Room Classics, price 15 cts. Not all authorities agree with this estimate of Milton's "Tractate." Oscar Browning in the article on Education in the *Encyclopædia Britannica* says: " For more important in the literature of this subject than the treatise of Locke is the *Tractate on Education* by Milton. . . The important truth enunciated is quite in the spirit of Comenius that the learning of things and words are to go hand in hand. . . . The whole treatise is full of wisdom, and should be studied again and again."]

Statutes." "To set them right and firm in the knowledge of virtue and hatred of vice, their young and pliant affections are to be led through all the moral works of Plato, Xenophon, Cicero, Plutarch, and those Locrian remnants." "At some set hour they are to learn Hebrew," with the Chaldee and Syrian dialects, and "they may have easily learned at any odd hour the Italian tongue!" "This," says Milton (and here at least he carries the reader with him), "is not a bow for every man to shoot in, that calls himself a teacher."

But though Milton flew so high, we shall find, if we examine his proposals, that he took the same direction as the other Innovators. (1) He denounced, as they did, "the asinine feast of sow-thistles and brambles, to which we now haul and drag our choicest and hopefullest wits, as all the food and entertainment of their tenderest and most docilable age." In the schools he complains that nothing but grammar was taught, at the universities nothing but logic and metaphysics. He would turn from these verbal toils to the study of things. Language was not to be studied for itself, but merely as an instrument conveying to us things useful to be known. Latin and Greek must therefore be acquired by a method that will take little time. This method he does not describe at length, but his words seem to refer to some such plan as that of Ascham or Ratich. "Whereas," he says, "if after some preparatory grounds of speech by their certain forms got into memory, they were led to the praxis thereof *in some chosen short book lessoned thoroughly to them*, they might then forthwith proceed to learn the substance of good things and arts in due order, which would bring the whole language quickly into their power." (2) The young were to be led on "by the infinite desire of a happy nurture; for the hill of knowledge, laborious indeed at the first ascent, else is so smooth, so green, so full of goodly prospect and melodious sounds on every side, that the harp of Orpheus was not more charming." "Arithmetic and the elements of geometry might be learnt even playing, as the old manner was." (3) So averse was Milton to a merely bookish training, that he would procure for his pupils "the helpful experience of hunters, fowlers, fishermen, shepherds, gardeners, and apothecaries; and in other sciences, architects, engineers mariners and anatomists." The boys were both to hear and be taught music—a commencement of æsthetic culture. (4) A thorough physical training was to be provided by warlike exercises, both on horse and foot, and by wrestling, "wherein Englishmen are wont to excel."*

We see, then, that the great authority of Milton may be claimed by the Innovators, and a protest against a purely literary education comes with tremendous force from the student who sacrificed his sight to his reading, the accomplished scholar whose Latin works were known throughout Europe, and the author of "Paradise Lost."

---
* I have been assisted here by Professor Seeley's remarks in his article on Milton's political opinions, *Macmillan's Magazine*, February, 1868.

IV.

JOHN AMOS COMENIUS.

John Amos Comenius, the son of a miller, who belonged to the Moravian Brethren, was born at the Moravian village of Comna, in 1592. Of his early life we know nothing but what he himself tells us in the following passage: "Losing both my parents while I was yet a child, I began, through the neglect of my guardians, but at sixteen years of age, to taste of the Latin tongue. Yet, by the goodness of God, that taste bred such a thirst in me that I ceased not from that time by all means and endeavors, to labor for the repairing of my lost years; and now not only for myself, but for the good of others also. For I could not but pity others also in this respect, especially in my own nation, which is too slothful and careless in matter of learning. Thereupon, I was continually full of thoughts for the finding out of some means whereby more might be inflamed with the love of learning, and whereby learning itself might be made more compendious, both in matter of the charge and cost, and of the labor belonging thereto, that so the youth might be brought by a more easy method unto some notable proficiency in learning."* With these thoughts in head, he pursued his studies in several Ger-

---

* Preface to the *Prodromus*.

man towns, especially at Herborn in Nassau. Here he saw the Report on Ratich's method, published in 1612 for the Universities of Jena and Giessen; and we find him shortly afterward writing his first book,* "*Grammaticæ facilioris Præcepta*," which was published at Prague in 1616. On his return to Moravia, he was appointed to the Brethren's school at Prerau, but (to use his own words) "being shortly after, at the age of twenty-four, called to the service of the Church, because that divine function challenged all my endeavors, these scholastic cares were laid aside." His pastoral charge was at Fulneck, the headquarters of the Brethren. As such, it soon felt the effects of the Battle of Prague, being in the following year (1621) taken and plundered by the Spaniards. On this occasion, Comenius lost almost everything he possessed. The year after his wife died, and then his only child. In 1624, all Protestant ministers were banished, and, in 1627, a new decree extended the banishment to Protestants of every description. Comenius bore up against wave after wave of calamity with Christian courage and resignation, and his writings at this period were of great value to his fellow-sufferers.

For a time he found a hiding-place in the family of a Bohemian nobleman, Baron Sadowsky, at Sloupna, in the Bohemian mountains, and in this retirement his attention was again directed to the science of teaching. The Baron had engaged Stadius, one of the proscribed, to educate his three sons, and, at Stadius' request, Comenius wrote "some canons of a better method," for his use. We find him, too, endeavoring to enrich the liter-

---

* [For bibliography of Comenius, see Payne's "Short History of Education."]

ature of his mother-tongue, making a metrical translation of the Psalms of David, and even writing imitations of Virgil, Ovid, and Cato's *Distichs.*

In 1627, however, the persecution waxed so hot that Comenius, with most of the Brethren, had to flee their country, never to return. On crossing the border, Comenius and the exiles who accompanied him knelt down and prayed that God would not suffer his truth to fail out of their native land.

Many of the banished, and Comenius among them, settled at the Polish town of Leszno, or, as the Germans call it, Lissa, near the Silesian frontier. Here there was an old established school of the Brethren, in which Comenius found employment. Once more engaged in education, he earnestly set about improving the traditional methods. As he himself says,* "Being, by God's permission, banished my country, with divers others, and forced, for sustenance, to apply myself to the instruction of youth, I gave my mind to the perusal of divers authors, and lighted upon many which in this age have made a beginning in reforming the method of studies, as Ratichius, Helvicus, Rhenius, Ritterus, Glaumius, Cæcilius, and who indeed should have had the first place, Joannes Valentinus Andræ, a man of a nimble and clear brain; as also Campanella and the Lord Verulam, those famous restorers of philosophy;—by reading of whom I was raised in good hope that at last those so many various sparks would conspire into a flame; yet observing here and there some defects and gaps as it were, I could not contain myself from attempting something that might rest upon an immovable foundation,

---

* Preface to the *Prodromus.*

and which, if it could be once found out, should not be subject to any ruin. Therefore, after many workings and tossings of my thoughts, by reducing everything to the immovable laws of nature, I lighted upon my *Didactica Magna*, which shows the art of readily and solidly teaching all men all things."

This work did not immediately see the light, but in 1631, Comenius published a book which made him and the little Polish town where he lived, known throughout Europe and beyond it. This was the *Janua Linguarum Reserata*, or "Gate of Tongues unlocked." Writing about it many years afterward he says that he never could have imagined that that little work, fitted only for children (*puerile istud opusculum*), would have been received with applause by all the learned world. Letters of congratulation came to him from every quarter; and the work was translated not only into Greek, Bohemian, Polish, Swedish, Belgian, English, French, Spanish, Italian, Hungarian, but also into Turkish, Arabic, Persian, and even "Mogolic, which is familiar in the East Indies." (Dedication of *Schola Ludus* in Vol. I. of collected works.)*

Incited by the applause of the learned, Comenius now planned a scheme of universal knowledge, to impart which a series of works would have to be written, far exceeding what the resources and industry of one man, however great a scholar, could produce. He therefore

---

* Bayle, speaking of the *Janua* in his article on Comenius (Dict. *sub. v.*), says: "Quand Coménius n' aurait publié que ce livre là, il se serait immortalisé," [Had Comenius published no other book than this he would have immortalized himself]. He published a more celebrated book than this (viz., *Orbis Pictus*), and yet his "immortality" seems already of the feeblest.

looked about for a patron to supply money for his support, and that of his assistants, whilst these works were in progress. "The vastness of the labors I contemplate," he writes to a Polish nobleman, "demands that I should have a wealthy patron, whether we look at their extent, or at the necessity of securing assistants, or at the expenses generally."

At Leszno there seemed no prospect of his obtaining the aid he required; but his fame now procured him invitations from distant countries. First he received a call to improve the schools of Sweden. After declining this, he was induced by his English friends to undertake a journey to London, where Parliament had shown its interest in the matter of education, and had employed Hartlib, an enthusiastic admirer of Comenius, to attempt some reforms. Hartlib procured an order summoning Comenius, who gives the following account of his journey:—

"When seriously proposing to abandon the thorny studies of Didactics, and pass on to the pleasing studies of philosophical truth, I find myself again among the same thorns. . . . After the *Pansophiæ Prodromus* had been published and dispersed through various kingdoms of Europe, many of the learned approved of the object and plan of the work, but despaired of its ever being accomplished by one man alone, and therefore advised that a college of learned men should be instituted to carry it into effect. Mr. S. Hartlib, who had forwarded the publication of the *Pansophiæ Prodromus* in England, labored earnestly in this matter, and endeavored, by every possible means, to bring together for this purpose a number of men of intellectual activity.

And at length, having found one or two, he invited me also, with many very strong entreaties. As my friends consented to my departure, I proceeded to London, and arrived there on the day of the autumnal equinox, 1641, and I then learned that I had been called thither by an order of Parliament. But in consequence of the King's having gone to Scotland, the Parliament had been dismissed for three months, and consequently I had to winter in London, my friends in the meantime examining the 'Apparatus Philosophicus,' small though it was at that time. . . . At length Parliament having assembled, and my presence being known, I was commanded to wait until after some important business having been transacted, a Commission should be issued to certain wise and learned men, from amongst themselves, to hear me, and be informed of my plan. As an earnest, moreover, of their intentions, they communicated to me their purpose to assign to us a college with revenues, whence some men of learning and industry, selected from any nation, might be honorably sustained, either for a certain number of years, or in perpetuity. The Savoy in London, and beyond London, Winchester, and again near the city, Chelsea, were severally mentioned, and inventories of the latter, and of its revenues, were communicated to me. So that nothing seemed more certain than that the design of the great Verulam to open a Universal College of all nations, devoted solely to the advancement of the sciences was now in the way of being carried into effect. But a rumor that Ireland was in a state of commotion, and that more than 200,000 of the English there had been slaughtered in one night, the sudden departure of the King from London, and the clear indications that a most cruel war was on the point of breaking out, threw all these plans into confusion, and compelled me and my friends to hasten our return."

While Comenius was in England, where he stayed till August, 1642, he received an invitation to France. This invitation, which he did not accept, came perhaps through his correspondent Mersenne, a man of great learning, who is said to have been highly esteemed and often consulted by Descartes. It is characteristic of the state of opinion in such matters in those days, that Mersenne tells Comenius of a certain Le Maire, by whose method a boy of six years old, might, with nine months' instructions, acquire a perfect knowledge of three languages. Mersenne also had dreams of a universal alphabet, and even of a universal language.

Comenius' hopes of assistance in England being at an end, he thought of returning to Leszno, but a letter now reached him from a rich Dutch merchant, Lewis de Geer, who offered him a home and means for carrying out his plans. This Lewis de Geer, "The Grand Almoner of Europe," as Comenius called him, displayed a princely munificence in the assistance he gave the exiled Protesants. At this time he was living at Nordcoping in Sweden. Comenius having now found such a patron as he was seeking, set out from England and joined him there.

Soon after the arrival of Comenius in Sweden, the great Oxenstiern sent him to Stockholm, and with John Skyte, the Chancellor of Upsal University, examined him in several interviews about his system. "From my early youth," said Oxenstiern, "I observed something forced and incoherent in the method of instruction commonly used, but could not discover where the impediment lay. At length being sent by my King, of glorious memory, as a legate to Germany, I held conferences there on the subject with various learned men, and when I was informed that Ratich had attempted an amendment of the method, I could not rest till I had had a personal interview with him; when, instead of favoring me with a conference, he presented me with a large quarto volume. I went through the task imposed upon me, and then perceived that he had succeeded in discovering the diseases of the schools, but the remedies he suggested seemed very insufficient. Your remedies rest upon a surer foundation." Comenius said it was his wish to get beyond the teaching of boys to a great philosophical, or rather "pansophical" work. But both Oxenstiern and Skyte urged him to confine himself, for the present, to a task less ambitious, but more practically useful. "My counsel," said Oxenstiern, "is that you first satisfy the wants of the schools by rendering a knowledge of the Latin language of easier acquisition, and thereby preparing the path of a readier approach toward those more sublime studies. As De Geer gave the same advice, Comenius felt himself constrained to follow it, so he agreed to settle at Elbing in Prussia, and there write a work on teaching, in which the principles of the "*Didactica Magna*" should be worked out with especial reference to teaching languages. Notwithstanding the remonstrances of his English friends, to which Comenius would gladly have listened, he was kept by Oxenstiern and De Geer strictly to his agreement, and thus, much against his will, he was held fast for eight years in what he calls the "miry entanglements of logomachy."

Elbing, where, after a journey to Leszno to fetch his family (for he had married again), Comenius now settled, is in West Prussia, 36 miles southeast of Dantzic. From 1577 to 1660, an English trading company was settled here with which the family of Hartlib is said in one account to have been connected. This perhaps is one reason why Comenius chose this town for his residence. But Hartlib, instead of assisting with money, seems at this time to have needed assistance, for in October, 1642, Comenius writes to De Geer that he fears Fundanius and Hartlib are suffering from want, and that he intends for them 200*l*. promised by the London booksellers: he suggests that De Geer shall give them 30*l*. each meanwhile.

The relation between Comenius and his patron naturally proved a difficult one. The Dutchman thought that as he supported Comenius, and contributed something more for the assistants, he might expect of Comenius that he would devote all his time to the scholastic treatise he had undertaken. Comenius, however, was a man of immense energy and of widely extended sympathies and connections. He was a "bishop" of the religious body to which he belonged, and in this capacity he engaged in controversy, and attended some religious conferences. Then, again, pupils were pressed upon him, and as money to pay five writers whom he kept at work was always running short, he did not decline them. De Geer complained of this, and supplies were not furnished with wonted regularity. In 1647 Comenius writes to Hartlib that he is almost overwhelmed with cares, and sick to death of writing begging-letters. Yet in this year he found means to publish a book "On the Causes of this (i. e., the Thirty Years') War," in which the Roman Catholics are attacked with great bitterness—a bitterness for which the position of the writer affords too good an excuse.

The year 1648 brought with it the downfall of all Comenius' hopes of returning to his native land. The Peace of Westphalia was concluded without any provision being made for the restoration of the exiles. But though thus doomed to pass the remaining years of his life in banishment, Comenius, in this year, seemed to have found an escape from all his pecuniary difficulties. The senior bishop, the head of the Moravian Brethren, died, and Comenius was chosen to succeed him. In consequence of this, Comenius returned to Leszno, where due provision was made for him by the Brethren. Before he left Elbing, however, the fruit of his residence there, "*Methodus Linguarum Novissima*" [Newest Language Method], had been submitted to a commission of learned Swedes, and approved by them. The MS. went with him to Leszno, where it was published.

As head of the Moravian Church, there now devolved upon Comenius the care of all the exiles, and his widespread reputation enabled him to get situations for many of them in all Protestant countries. Indeed, he was now so much connected with the science of education, that even his post at Leszno did not prevent his receiving and accepting a call to reform the schools at Transylvania. A model school was formed at Saros-Patak, in which Comenius labored from 1650 till 1654. At this time he wrote his most celebrated book, which is indeed only an abridgement of his "Janua" with the important addition of pictures, and sent it to Nürnberg, where it appeared three years later (1657). This was the famous "*Orbis Pictus*" [The world in Pictures].

Full of trouble as Comenius' life had hitherto been, its greatest calamity was still before him. After he was again settled at Leszno, Poland was invaded by the Swedes, on which occasion the sympathies of the Brethren were with their fellow-Protestants, and Comenius was imprudent enough to write a congratulatory address to the Swedish King. A peace followed, by the terms of which, several towns, and Leszno among them, were made over to Sweden, but when the King withdrew, the Poles took up arms again, and Leszno, the headquarters of the Protestants, the town in which the chief of the Moravian Brethren had written his address welcoming the enemy, was taken and plundered.

Comenius and his family escaped, but his house was marked for special violence, and nothing was preserved. His sole remaining possessions were the clothes in which he and his family traveled. All his books and manuscripts were burnt, among them his valued work on Pansophia, and a Latin-Bohemian and Bohemian-Latin Dictionary, giving words, phrases, idioms, adages and aphorisms—a book on which he had been laboring for forty years. "This loss," he writes, "I shall cease to lament only when I cease to breathe." After wandering for some time about Germany, and being prostrated by fever at Hamburg, he at length came to Amsterdam, where Lawrence De Geer, the son of his deceased patron, gave him an asylum. Here were spent the remaining years of his life in ease and dignity. Compassion for his misfortunes was united with veneration for his learning and piety. He earned a sufficient income by giving instruction in the families of the wealthy, and by the liberality of De Geer he was enabled to publish a fine folio edition of all his writings on Education (1657). His political works, however, were to the last a source of trouble to him. His hostility to the Pope and the House of Hapsburg made him the dupe of certain " prophets " whose soothsayings he published as " *Lux in Tenebris* " [Light in Darkness]. One of these prophets, who had announced that the Turk was to take Vienna, was executed at Pressburg, and the " *Lux in Tenebris* " at the same time burnt by the hangman. Before the news of this disgrace reached Amsterdam, Comenius was no more. He died in the year 1671, at the advanced age of eighty, and with him terminated the office of Chief Bishop among the Moravian Brethren.

Before Comenius, no one had brought the mind of a philosopher to bear practically on the subject of education. Montaigne, Bacon, Milton, had advanced principles, leaving others to see to their application. A few able schoolmasters, as Ascham and Ratich, had investigated new methods, but had made success in teaching the test to which they appealed, rather than any abstract principle. Comenius was at once a philosopher who had learnt of Bacon, and a schoolmaster who had earned his livelihood by teaching the rudiments. Dissatisfied with the state of education as he found it, he sought for a better system by an examination of the laws of Nature. Whatever is thus established, we must allow to be on an immovable foundation, and, as Comenius himself says, "not liable to any ruin;" but looking back on the fruit of Comenius' labors, we find that much which he thought thus based, was not so in reality—that he often believed he was appealing to Nature, when in truth he was merely using fanciful illustrations from her. But whatever mistakes he and others may have made in consulting the oracle, it is no proof of wisdom to attempt, as "practical men" often do, to use these mistakes in disparagement of the oracle itself; and because some have gone wrong when they thought they were following Nature, to treat every appeal to her with contempt. It will hardly be disputed, when broadly stated, that there are laws of Nature which must be obeyed in dealing with the mind, as with the body. No doubt these laws are not so easily established in the first case as in the second, but whoever in any way assists or even tries to assist in the discovery, deserves our gratitude, and greatly are we indebted to him who first boldly set about the task, and devoted to it years of patient labor.

Every one who has studied Comenius' voluminous writings is agreed that the "*Didactica Magna,*" though one of his earlier works, contains, in the best form, the principles he afterward endeavored to work out in the "*Janua,*" "*Orbis Pictus,*" and "*Novissima Methodus.*" A short account of this book will give some notion of what Comenius did for education.

We live, says Comenius, a threefold life—a vegetative, an animal, and an intellectual or spiritual. Of these, the first is perfect in the womb, the last in heaven. He is happy who comes with healthy body into the world, much more he who goes with healthy spirit out of it. According to the heavenly idea, man (1) should know all things; (2) should be master of all things, and of himself; (3) should refer everything to God. So that within us Nature has implanted the seeds of (1) learning, (2) virtue, and (3) piety. To bring these to maturity is the object of education. All men require education, and God has made children unfit for other employments that they may have leisure to learn.

But schools have failed, and instead of keeping to the true object of education, and teaching the foundations, relations, and intentions of all the most important things, they have neglected even the mother-tongue, and confined the teaching to Latin; and yet that has been so badly taught, and so much time has been wasted over grammar rules and dictionaries, that from ten to twenty years are spent in acquiring as much knowledge of Latin as is speedily acquired of any modern tongue.

The cause of this want of success is that the system does not follow nature. Everything natural goes smoothly and easily. There must, therefore, be no pressure. Learning should come to children as swimming to fish, flying to birds, running to animals. As Aristotle says, the desire of knowledge is implanted in man: and the mind grows as the body does—by taking proper nourishment, not by being stretched on the rack.

If we would ascertain how teaching and learning are to have good results, we must look to the known processes of Nature and Art. A man sows seed, and it comes up he knows not how, but in sowing it he must attend to the requirements of Nature. Let us then look to Nature to find out how instruction is to be sown in young minds. We find that Nature waits for the fit time. Then, too, she has prepared the material before she gives it form. In our teaching we constantly run counter to these principles of hers. We give instruction before the young minds are ready to receive it. We give the form before the material. Words are taught before the things to which they refer. When a foreign tongue is to be taught, we commonly give the form, i. e., the grammatical rules, before we give the material, i. e., the language, to which the rules apply. We should begin with an author, or properly prepared translation-book, and abstract rules should never come before the examples.

Again, Nature begins each of her works with its inmost part. Moreover, the crude form comes first, then the elaboration of the parts. The architect, acting on this principle, first makes a rough plan or model, and then by degrees designs the details; last of all he attends to the ornamentation. In teaching, then, let the inmost part, i. e., the understanding of the subject, come first; then let the thing understood be used to exercise the memory, the speech, and the hands; and let every language, science, and art be taught first in its rudimentary outline; then more completely with example and rules; finally, with exceptions and anomalies. Instead of this, some teachers are foolish enough to require beginners to get up all the anomalies in Latin Grammar, and the dialects in Greek.

Again, as nature does nothing *per saltum* [at a leap], nor halts when she has begun, the whole course of studies should be arranged in strict order, so that the earlier studies prepare the way for the latter. Every year, every month, every day and hour even, should have its task marked out beforehand, and the plan should be rigidly carried out. Much loss is occasioned by absence of boys from school, and by changes in the instruction. Iron that might be wrought with one heating should not be allowed to get cold, and be heated over and over again.

Nature protects her work from injurious influences, so boys should be kept from injurious companionships and books.

In a chapter devoted to the principles of easy teaching, Comenius lays down, among rules similar to the foregoing, that children will learn if they are taught only what they have a desire to learn, with due regard to their age and the method of instruction, and especially when everything is first taught by means of the senses. On this point Comenius laid great stress, and he was, I believe, the first who did so. Education should proceed, he said, in the following order: first, educate the senses, then the memory, then the intellect; last of all the critical faculty. This is the order of Nature. The child first perceives through the senses. *Nihil est in intellectu quod non prius in sensu* [There is nothing in the mind that was not first in the senses]. These perceptions are stored in the memory, and called up by the imagination. By comparing one with another, the understanding forms general ideas, and at length the judgment decides between the false and the true. By keeping to this order, Comenius believed it would be possible to make learning entirely pleasant to the pupils, however young. Here Comenius agreed with the Jesuits, and in part he would use the same means to make the road to learning agreeable. Like them, he would have short school-hours, and would make great use of praise and blame; but he did not depend, as they did, almost exclusively on emulation. He would have the desire of learning fostered in every possible way—by parents, by teachers, by school buildings and apparatus, by the subjects themselves, by the method of teaching them, and lastly, by the public authorities. (1) The parents must praise learning and learned men, must show children beautiful books, etc., must treat the teachers with great respect. (2) The teacher must be kind and fatherly, he must distribute praise and reward, and must always, where it is possible, give the children something to look at. (3) The school buildings must be light, airy, and cheerful, and well furnished with apparatus, as pictures, maps, models, collections of specimens. (4) The subjects taught must not be too hard for the learner's comprehension, and the more entertaining parts of them must be especially dwelt upon. (5) The method must be natural, and everything that is not essential to the subject or is beyond the pupil must be omitted. Fables and allegories should be introduced, and enigmas given for the pupils to guess. (7) The authorities must appoint public examinations and reward merit.

Nature helps herself in various ways, so the pupils should have every assistance given them. It should especially be made clear what the pupils are to learn, and how they should learn it.

The pupils should be punished for offences against morals only. If they do not learn the fault is with the teacher.

One of Comenius' most distinctive principles was, that the knowledge of things should be communicated *together with the knowledge of words.* This, together with his desire of submitting everything to the pupil's senses, would have introduced a great change in the course of instruction, which was then, as it has for the most part continued, purely literary. We should learn, says Comenius, as much as possible, not from books, but from the great book of Nature, from heaven and earth, from oaks and beeches.

When languages are to be learnt, he would have them taught separately. Till the pupil is from eight to ten years old, he should be instructed only in the mother-tongue, and about things. Then other languages can be acquired in about a year each; Latin (which is to be studied more thoroughly) in about two years. Every language must be learnt by use rather than by rules; i. e., it must be learnt by hearing, reading, and re-reading, transcribing, attempting imitations in writing, and verbally, and by using the language in conversation. Rules assist and confirm practice, but they must come after, not before it. The first exercises in a language should take for their subject something of which the sense is already known, so that the mind may be fixed on the words and their connections.* The Catechism and Bible History may be used for this purpose.

Considering the classical authors not suited to boys' understanding, and not fit for the education of Christians, Comenius proposed writing a set of Latin manuals for the different stages between childhood and manhood: these were to be called, "*Vestibulum,*" [Threshhold], "*Janua,*" [Gate], "*Palatium,*" [Palace], "*Thesau-*

---

* Comenius here follows Ratich, who, as I have mentioned above (p. —), required beginners to study the translation *before the original.*

rus," [Treasure House]. The "Vestibulum" and "Janua" were really carried out.

In Comenius' scheme there were to be four kinds of schools for a perfect educational course: 1st, the mother's breast for infancy; 2d, the public vernacular school for children, to which all should be sent from six years old till twelve; 3d, the Latin school or Gymnasium; 4th, residence at a University and traveling, to complete the course.

As the *Ludus literarius seu schola vernacula*, [Elementary school or vernacular instruction] was a very distinctive feature in Comenius' plan, it may be worth while to give his programme of studies. In this school the children should learn—1st, to read and write the mother-tongue *well*, both with writing and printing letters; 2d, to compose grammatically; 3d, to cipher; 4th, to measure and weigh; 5th, to sing, at first popular airs, then from music; 6th, to say by heart sacred psalms and hymns; 7th, Catecism, Bible History and texts; 8th, moral rules, with examples; 9th, economy and politics, as far as they could be understood; 10th, general history of the world; 11th, figure of the earth and motion of stars, etc., physics and geography, especially of native land; 12th, general knowledge of arts and handicrafts.

Each school was to be divided into six classes, corresponding to the six years the pupil should spend in it. The hours of work were to be, in school, two hours in the morning and two in the afternoon, with nearly the same amount of private study. In the morning the mind and memory were to be exercised, in the afternoon the hands and voice. Each class was to have its proper lesson-book written expressly for it, so as to contain everything that class had to learn. When a lesson was to be got by heart from the book, the teacher was first to read it to the class, explain it, and re-read it; the boys then to read it aloud by turns till one of them offered to repeat it without book; the others were to do the same as soon as they were able, till all had repeated it. This lesson was then to be worked over again as a writing lesson, etc. In the higher forms of the vernacular school a modern language was to be taught and duly practised.

From this specimen of the "*Didactica Magna*" the reader will see the kind of reforms at which Comenius aimed. Before his time the Jesuits alone had had a complete educational course planned out, and had pursued a uniform method in carrying this plan through. They, too, already were distinguished for their endeavors to make learning pleasant to their pupils, to lead, not to drive them. But Comenius, advancing so far with the Jesuits, entirely differed trom them as to the subjects to be taught. The Jesuits' was as purely a literary training as that in our public schools. Comenius was among the first who laid stress on the teaching about *things*, and called in the senses to do their part in the work of early education. Thus he was the forerunner of Pestalozzi, and of the champions of science as Tyndall and H. Spencer among ourselves.

It was not his principles, however, that first attracted the notice of Comenius' contemporaries, but his book, "*Janua Linguarum Reserata*," in which, with very imperfect success he endeavored to carry out those principles.

For the idea of the work Comenius was beholden to a Jesuit, as he candidly confesses. It seems that one

Batty, a Jesuit of Irish birth, engaged in the Jesuit college of Salamanca, had endeavored to construct a "Noah's Ark for words;" i. e., a work treating shortly of all kinds of subjects, in such a way as to introduce in a natural connection every word in the Latin language.* "The idea," says Comenius, "was much better than the execution. Nevertheless, inasmuch as they (the Jesuits) were the prime inventors, we thankfully acknowledge it, nor will we upbraid them with those errors they have committed." † The plan commended itself to Comenius on various grounds. First, he had a notion of giving an outline of all knowledge before anything was taught in detail. Next, he could by such a book connect the teaching about simple things with instruction in the Latin words which applied to them. And thirdly, he hoped by this means to give such a complete Latin vocabulary as to render the use of Latin easy for all requirements of modern society. He accordingly wrote a short account of things in general, which he put in the form of a dialogue, and this he published in Latin and German at Leszno about 1531. The success of this work, as we have already seen, was prodigious. No doubt the spirit which animated Bacon was largely diffused among educated men in all countries, and they hailed the appearance of a book which called the youth from the study of old philosophical ideas to observe the facts around them.

The countrymen of Bacon were not backward in adopting the new work, as the following, from the title-

---

* This book attracted some notice in England. An edition with English instead of Spanish, was published in London about 1515.

† Preface to Anchoran's translation of *Janua*.

page of a volume in the British Museum, will show: "The Gate of Tongues Unlocked and Opened; or else, a Seminary or Seed-plot of all Tongues and Sciences. That is, a short way of teaching and thoroughly learning, within a year and a half at the furthest, the Latin, English, French, and any other tongue, with the ground and foundation of arts and sciences, comprised under a hundred titles and 1058 periods. In Latin first, and now, as a token of thankfulness, brought to light in Latin, English, and French, in the behalf of the most illustrious Prince Charles, and of British, French, and Irish youth. The 4th edition much enlarged, by the labor and industry of John Anchoran, Licentiate in Divinity, London. Printed by Edward Griffin for Michael Sparke, dwelling at the Blew Bible in Green Arbor, 1639."

In the preface to this volume we have the complaint which has reproduced itself in various forms up to the present time, that the "youth was delayed with grammar precepts infinitely tedious, perplexed, obscure, and (for the most part) unprofitable, and that for many years." From this barren region the pupil was to escape to become acquainted with things. "Come on," says the teacher in the opening dialogue; "let us go forth into the open air. There you shall view whatsoever God produced from the beginning, and doth yet affect by nature. Afterward we will go into towns, shops, schools, where you shall see how men do both apply those Divine works to their uses, and also instruct themselves in arts, manners, tongues. Then we will enter into houses, courts, and palaces of princes, to see in what manner communities of men are governed. At last we will visit temples, where you shall observe how diversely mortals seek to worship their Creator and to be spiritually united unto Him, and how He by His Almightiness disposeth all things." (This is from the 1656 edition, by "W. D.")

The book is still amusing, but only from the quaint manner in which the mode of life two hundred years ago is described.

But though parts of the book may on first reading have gratified the youth of the seventeenth century, a great deal of it gave scanty information about difficult subjects, such as physiology, geometry, logic, rhetoric, and that, too, in the driest and dullest way. Moreover, Comenius boasts that no important word occurs twice; so that the book to attain the end of giving a perfect stock of Latin words, would have to be read and re-read till it was almost known by heart; and however amusing boys might find an account of their toys written in Latin the first time of reading, the interest would somewhat wear away by the fifth or sixth time. We can not then feel much surprised on reading this "general verdict," written some thirty years later, touching those earlier works of Comenius: "They are of singular use, and very advantageous to those of more discretion (especially to such as have already got a smattering in Latin), to help their memories to retain what they have scatteringly gotten here and there, and to furnish them with many words which perhaps they had not formerly read or so well observed; but to young children, as those that are ignorant altogether of most things and words, they prove rather a mere toil and burden than a delight and furtherance."*

---

* Hoole's preface to his translation of *Orbis Pictus*.

The "*Janua*" would, therefore, have had but a short-lived popularity with teachers, and a still shorter with learners, if Comenius had not carried out his principle of appealing to the senses, and called in the artist. The result was the "*Orbis Pictus*," a book which proved a favorite with young and old, and maintained its ground in many a school for more than a century. The "*Orbis*" was, in substance, the same as the "*Janua*," though abbreviated; but it had this distinctive feature, that each subject was illustrated by a small engraving, in which everything named in the letter-press below was marked with a number, and its name was found connected with the same number in the text. I am sorry I can not give a specimen of this celebrated book with its quaint pictures. The artist, of course, was wanting in the technical skill which is now commonly displayed even in very cheap publications, but this renders his delineations none the less entertaining. As a picture of the life and manners of the seventeenth century, the work has great historical interest, which will, I hope, secure for it another English edition; especially as the last (that of 1777, reprinted in America in 1812), which is now occasionally to be met with, is far inferior to those of an earlier date.

In the beginning of the tract to Hartlib, Milton would seem to deny that he had learned anything from Comenius. Whether this is his meaning or not, he gives expression in the tract to the principle of which Comenius was the great exponent. "Because one's understanding can not, in this body, found itself but on sensible things, nor arrive so clearly to the knowledge of God and things invisible as by orderly conning over the visible and inferior creature, the same method is necessarily to be followed in all discreet teaching." This conviction, which bore fruit in the Baconian philosophy, was systematically brought to bear by Comenius on the instruction of youth.

[The best life of Comenius is by Prof. S. S. Laurie, of which an American edition has been published at $1.00. Much matter of interest is also given in Prof. Payne's "Short History of Education," 50 cts. Copies of the *Janua* and of the *Orbis Pictus* are usually to be found in the collection of Pedagogical Books for sale by C. W. Bardeen, Syracuse, N. Y.]

V.

LOCKE.

AMONG the writers on education and inventors of new methods, there are only two Englishmen who have a European celebrity—Locke and Hamilton. The latter of these did, in fact, little more than carry out a suggestion of the former, so that almost all the influence which England has had on the theory of education must be attributed to Locke alone. Locke's authority on this subject has indeed been due chiefly to his fame as a philosopher. His "Thoughts on Education," had they proceeded from an unknown author, would probably have never gained him a reputation even in his native country; and yet, when we read them as the work of the great philosopher, we feel that they are not unworthy of him. He was no enthusiast, conscious of a mission to renovate the human race by some grand educational discovery; but as a man of calm good sense, who found himself encharged with the bringing up of a young nobleman, he examined the ordinary education of the day, and when it proved unsatisfactory, he set about such alterations as seemed expedient. His thoughts were written for the advice of a friend, and, as we may infer from the title, are not intended as a complete treatise. The book, however, has placed its author in the first rank of those innovators whose innovations, after a struggle of two hundred years, have not been adopted, and yet seem now more than ever likely to make their way.

Locke's thoughts were concerned exclusively with the training of a young gentleman, at a time when gentlemen were a caste having little in common with "the abhorred rascality." The education of those of inferior station might be of interest and importance to individuals, but the nation was chiefly concerned with the bringing up of its gentlemen. "That most to be taken care of," he writes, "is the gentleman's calling; for if those of that rank are by their education once set right, they will quickly bring all the rest into order."

Locke would have the education of a gentleman intrusted to a tutor. His own experience had made him no friend to grammar-schools, and while he admits the inconveniences of home education, he makes light of them in comparison with the dangers of a system in which the influence of schoolmates is greater than that of schoolmasters. Locke's argument is this: It is the business of the master to train the pupils in virtue and good manners, much more than to communicate learning. This function, however, must of necessity be neglected in schools. "Not that I blame the schoolmaster in this, or think it to be laid to his charge. The difference is great between two or three pupils in the same house and three or fourscore boys lodged up and down; for let the master's industry and skill be never so great, it is impossible that he should have fifty or a hundred scholars under his eye any longer than they are in the school together; nor can it be expected that he should instruct them successfully in anything but their books; the forming of their minds and manners requiring a constant attention and particular application to every single boy, which is impossible in a numerous flock, and would be wholly in vain (could he have time to study and correct every one's particular defects and wrong inclinations), when the lad was to be left to himself, or the prevailing infection of his fellows the greatest part of the four-and-twenty hours." Again he says, "Till you can find a school wherein it is possible for the master to look after the manners of his scholars, and can show as great effects of his care of forming their minds to virtue and their carriage to good-breeding, as of forming their tongues to the learned languages, you must confess that you have a strange value for words when preferring the languages of the ancient Greeks and Romans to that which made them such brave men, you think it worth while to hazard your son's innocence for a little Greek and Latin. For as for that boldness and spirit which lads get among their playfellows at school, it has ordinarily such a mixture of rudeness and ill-turned confidence that those misbecoming and disingenuous ways of shifting in the world must be unlearned, and all tincture washed out again to make way for better principles and such manners as make a trustworthy man. He that considers how diametrically opposite the skill of living well and managing as a man should do his affairs in the world is to that malapertness, trickery, or violence learnt amongst schoolboys, will think the faults of a privater education infinitely to be preferred to such improvements, and will take care to preserve his child's innocence and modesty at home, as being more of kin and more in the way of those qualities which make a useful and able man."

If we consider how far Locke is undoubtedly right in these remarks, we shall agree with him at least in two things: 1st, that virtue and good manners are more valuable than school learning, or, indeed, any learning; 2d, that the influence of the masters over the boys' characters in a large school (and I may add, in a small school also), is less than the influence of the boys on one another. Moreover, those who know much of schoolboys will probably admit that their average morality is not high. Though not without strong generous impulses, the ordinary schoolboy-character is marked by selfishness—not a premeditated, calculating selfishness, but one which arises from the absence of high motives, and from a tacit understanding among boys that the rule is, "Every one for himself." High motives are no doubt uncommon in adult age, and the same rule is sometimes acted on then also, but custom requires us, except in the case of very near relations, to treat one another with outward respect and consideration—in other words, to behave unselfishly in social intercourse, and no such custom is established among schoolboys. They are, therefore, as a rule unmannerly in their behavior to one another. Vices, moreover, though not so prevalent as bad manners, are well known in all schools. Lying is often found, especially among young boys; bad language, and worse, among younger and elder alike. The natural deduction would seem to be that large schools are the worst possible places in which to train boys to virtue and good manners.

This deduction, however, is very far from the truth. The direct influence of the private tutor is, I believe, *less*, and the indirect influence of the masters of a school *more*, than Locke and those who side with him imagine. Indeed, the influence of a really great head-master over the whole school is immense, as was proved by Dr. Arnold. Then, again, the system and the traditions of a great school are very powerful, and almost compel a boy to aim at the established standard of excellence, whereas the boy at home has no such standard before him, and the boy at the small school may possibly have one which is worse than none at all.* As far as our character depends on others, it is formed mainly by our companions at every age. Men have not enough in common with boys to be their *companions*, even when they are never out of their company. The character of boys must, therefore, be formed chiefly by *boys*, and where they associate together in large numbers and are allowed as much freedom as is consistent with discipline,

---

* "At nine or ten the masculine energies of the character are beginning to develop themselves; or, if not, no discipline will better aid in their development than the bracing intercourse of a great English classical school. Even the selfish are *there* forced into accommodating themselves to a public standard of generosity, and the effeminate into conforming to a rule of manliness. I was myself at two public schools, and I think with gratitude of the benefits which I reaped from both; as also I think with gratitude of that guardian in whose quiet household I learned Latin so effectually. But the small private schools of which I had opportunities for gathering some brief experience—schools containing from thirty to forty boys, were models of ignoble manners, as regarded part of the Juniors, and of favoritsm as regarded the masters. Nowhere is the sublimity of public justice so broadly exemplified as in an English public school on the old Edward VI. or Elizabeth foundation. There is not in the universe such an Areopagus of fair play and abhorrence of all crooked ways as an English mob, or one of the time-honored English 'foundation' schools." (De Quincey's Autobiographic Sketches, Works, i. 150.) Of late years, the age at which boys are mostly sent to the great public schools has advanced from ten or eleven to thirteen or fourteen. I think this a gain where boys can be kept at home, but very much the reverse when they are sent as boarders to private schools. What we stand urgently in need of is good day schools for the younger boys of all classes.

the healthy feeling of "open-airiness,"* the common sense of most, and the love of right which is found ultimately both in boys and men, prove most powerful in checking flagrant wrong-doing and forming a type of character which has many good points in it.

But whichever side may seem to have the best of the argument, our public schools may fairly meet their assailants by an appeal to results. We know, indeed, that parents, as a rule, are too careless about the learning their boys acquire at Eaton and Harrow, and that many leave these schools with little Latin, less Greek, and no book knowledge besides; but parents are not yet indifferent about the morals and manners of their children, and if it were found that the generality of public school-men were less virtuous and less gentlemanly than the generality of those who had been educated elsewhere, our public schools could hardly enjoy their present popularity.

Locke had himself acquired great influence over his pupil, a delicate youth, who, under Locke's care, became a strong man. By this the philosopher was led to exaggerate the effects of formal education so much, that he ascribes it to nine parts out of ten in every man. I believe this estimate to be quite erroneous. Nature seems to have placed a fairly healthy state, both of body and mind, as it were *in stable equilibrium*. There are certain things necessary for the existence of the body—food, air, exercise. But when a sufficient amount of these is once secured, the quantity and quality may vary con-

---

* I borrow the phrase from Miss Davies, who, in her excellent little book on "The Higher Education of Women," advocates the starting of schools for girls on the model of our public schools.

siderably, without making any important difference. Moreover, the healthy body has, to some extent, the power of resisting noxious influences. If we were as liable to injuries as anxious mothers suppose, we should have to give almost all our time and attention to the care of our health, and even then could hardly hope to preserve it. The same, probably, is true of the mind, though not to so great a degree.

These facts are fully recognized by the majority of mankind, who look to them for a justification of *laissez faire* [let alone]. But writers on education, on dietetics, and the like, in their great zeal against *laissez faire*, generally run in into the opposite extreme, and talk as if narrow indeed were the way that leads to health, and as if only the few who implicitly followed their directions could ever find it.

If I agreed with Locke, that nine parts out of ten in the pupil were due to the master, I should also agree that the master of a school could not bestow proper attention on all the boys.

As Locke had studied medicine, and had been prevented from undertaking the cure of other people's maladies only by his own, he naturally attached great importance to physical education, and begins his work with it. He was a champion of the hardening system, which has, no doubt, as Mr. H. Spencer puts it, hardened many children out of the world. Scanty clothing, thin boots with holes to admit wet, hard fare, and irregular meals, are now condemned by all our best authorities. In other particulars, where he seems more happy, Locke's suggestions have become established customs. We have got to believe in the use of cold water, though we should not think to appease the fears of mothers by quoting the example of Seneca. But there are two or three points in Locke's very practical directions which are still worth special attention. He urges that all clothes should be loose, and speaks as emphatically as every doctor has spoken since against the madness of "strait-lacing." He rejoices that mothers can not attempt any improvements in their children's shapes before birth; otherwise, says he, we should have no perfect children born. Do we not seem to hear the voice of Rousseau?

Another point on which he is very emphatic is, that action of the bowels should be secured daily at the same hour by the force of habit.

The following quotation would have been thought folly only a few years ago. Now, it has a chance of a fair hearing. "Have a great care of tampering that way (i. e., with apothecaries' medicines), lest, instead of preventing, you draw on diseases. Nor even upon every little indisposition is physic to be given, or the physician called to children, especially if he be a busy man that will presently fill their windows with gallipots and their stomachs with drugs. It is safer to leave them wholly to Nature than to put them into the hands of one forward to tamper, or that thinks children are to be cured in ordinary distempers by anything but diet, or by a method very little distant from it; it seeming suitable both to my reason and experience, that the tender constitutions of children should have as little done to them as possible, and as the absolute necessity of the case requires." Among many practical suggestions which he gives in this part of the book, the following shows that his hardening discipline did not proceed from want of sympathy with the little ones. "Let children be very carefully aroused in the morning with the voice only, and let them have nothing but kind treatment before they are wide awake."*

Locke's own summing up of his recommendations concerning the body and health is: "Plenty of open air, exercise and sleep, plain diet, no wine or strong drink, and very little or no physic; not too warm and strait clothes, especially the head and feet kept cold, and the feet often used to cold water, and exposed to wet."

"As the strength of the body lies chiefly in being able to endure hardships, so also does that of the mind, and the great principle and foundation of all virtue and worth is placed in this—that a man is able to deny himself his own desires, cross his own inclinations, and purely follow what reason directs as best, though the appetite leans the other way."

Again, he says, "He that has not mastery over his inclinations, he that knows not how to resist the importunity of present pleasure or pain, for the sake of what reason tells him is fit to be done, wants the true principle of virtue and industry, and is in danger of never being good for anything. This temper then, therefore, so contrary to unguided Nature, is to be got betimes; and this habit, as the true foundation of future ability and happiness, is to be wrought into the mind, as early as may be, even from the first dawnings of any knowledge or apprehension in children, and so to be confirmed in them, by all the care and ways imaginable, by those who

---

* Locke is, however, only copying from Montaigne, who tells us that, in his childhood, his father had him awakened by *music*.

have the oversight of their education." Here the philosopher seems to ground all virtue on *Reason*. Less intellectual people might be inclined to seek the ground of most virtue in the affections.

"The practice of self-denial," says Locke, "is to be got and improved by custom—made easy and familiar by an early practice. The practice should be begun *from their very cradles*. Whenever the children craved what was not fit for them to have, they should not be permitted it because they were little and desired it. Nay, whatever they were importunate for, they should be sure, for that very reason, to be denied. The younger they are, the less, I think, are their unruly and disorderly appetites to be complied with; and the less reason they have of their own, the more are they to be under the absolute power and restraint of those in whose hands they are. From which, I confess, it will follow, that none but discreet people should be about them.

"Be sure to establish the authority of a father as soon as the child is capable of submission, and can understand in whose power he is. If you would have him stand in awe of you, imprint it in his *infancy*, and as he approaches more to a man admit him nearer to your familiarity, so shall you have him your obedient subject (as is fit) whilst he is a child, and your affectionate friend when he is a man." This passage advises a complete inversion of the ordinary mode, which is to fondle children when young, and "to keep them in their proper place" by a more distant behavior, and by the more rigorous exercise of authority, as they grow up. But is not the treatment which estranges the son from the father wrong in both cases? The difference of age puts only too great a gulf between them already. To make either the child or young man stand in awe of his father is not exactly the way to bridge this gulf over. This can only be done by the father's endeavoring to enter into the feelings of the son, and seeking his sympathy in return. As for establishing the parental authority, a consistent firmness will do this without the aid of "the power derived from fear and awe."

But, whilst advising that whatsoever rigor is necesary should be "the more used the younger children are," Locke is very strong against great severity. The children must be taught self-denial; but on the other side, "if the mind be curbed or humbled too much in children, if their spirits be debased and humbled much by too strict a hand over them, they lose all their vigor and industry, and are in a worse state than (in the other extreme). For extravagant young fellows that have liveliness and spirit come sometimes to be set right, and so make able and great men; but dejected minds, timorous and tame, and low spirits are hardly ever to be raised, and very seldom attain to anything." Slavish discipline makes slavish temper, and so leads to hypocrisy; and where it is most successful, it breaks the mind, and then you have a low-spirited, moped creature, who however with his unnatural sobriety he may please silly people, who commend tame, inactive children because they make no noise, nor give them any trouble, yet, at last, will probably prove as uncomfortable a thing to his friends, as he will be all his life a useless thing to himself and others." "To avoid the danger that is on either hand, is the great art; and he that has found a way how to keep up a child's spirit easy, active, and free, and yet at the same time to restrain him from many things he has a mind to, and to draw him to things that are uneasy to him; he, I say, that knows how to reconcile these seeming contradictions, has, in my opinion, got the true secret of education."

No corporal punishment, Locke tells us, is useful where the shame of suffering for having done amiss does not work more than the pain; otherwise, we merely teach boys to act from the worst motives of all—regard to bodily pleasure or pain. The tutor must be sparing in his correction, for it is his business to create a liking for learning, and "children come to hate things which were at first acceptable to them, when they find themselves whipped and chid and teazed about them. . . Offensive circumstances ordinarily infect innocent things which they are joined with, and the very sight of a cup wherein any one uses to take nauseous physic turns his stomach so that nothing will relish well out of it, though the cup be never so clean and well-shaped, and of the richest materials." From this, Locke would almost seem to agree with Comenius, that no punishment should be connected with learning. The notion may appear utopian, but if boys could once be interested in their work it would not be found so.*

In passing, I may observe that teachers of a kindly

---

* Since I wrote the above, a remark from a schoolboy of more than average industry (or, perhaps I ought to say, of less than average laziness) has rather shaken me in this opinion: "Somehow I can't get up work for Mr. —— : *we never get anything if we don't.*" Both boys and grown people are apt to shrink from exertion where there is no *must* in the case, even though the exertion be not in itself distasteful to them. I doubt, therefore, if a wise master would entirely give up compulsion, though he would never apply it to young children, or trust to it *exclusively* in the case of older pupils.

disposition are sometimes guilty of great cruelty, from neglecting the truth Locke dwells upon with such emphasis, viz., that the mind will not act during any depression of the animal spirits. A boy fails to say his task, and he is kept in till he does: or he can not be made to understand some simple matter, and the teacher's patience gets exhausted, when he has explained the thing again and again, and then can get no answer, or only an utterly absurd answer to the easiest question about it. Perhaps the boy is not a stupid boy, so the master accuses him of sullen inattention. The truth is, that the boy is frightened or dejected, and his mind no longer works at the command of the will. As Locke says, "It is impossible children should learn anything whilst their thoughts are possessed and disturbed with any passion, especially fear, which makes the strongest impression on their yet tender and weak spirits. Keep the mind in an easy, calm temper, when you would have it receive your instructions, or any increase of knowledge. It is as impossible to draw fair and regular characters on a trembling mind, as on a shaking paper." We all know, from our own experience, that when the mind is disturbed, or jaded, it no longer obeys the will, and yet in school-work we always consider the lads' mental power a constant quantity. Miss Davies well says: "Probably, if the truth were known, it would be found that injustice and unkindness are comparatively seldom caused by harshness of disposition. They are the result of an incapacity for imagining ourselves to be somebody else" ("Higher Education of Women," p. 137). This I take to be especially true of the unkindness of schoolmasters.

Rewards and punishments are largely employed in Locke's mode of education; but they are to be the rewards and punishments of the *mind*—esteem and disgrace. The sense of honor should be carefully cultivated. Whatever commendation the child deserved should be bestowed openly; the blame should be in private. Flogging is to be reserved for stubbornness and obstinate disobedience. Locke concludes his advice on discipline by saying, that if the right course be taken with children, there will be not so much need of the application of the common rewards and punishments as usage has established. Children should not be too much checked. "The gamesome humor, which is wisely adapted by nature to their age and temper, should rather be encouraged to keep up their spirits and to improve their strength and health, than curbed and restrained; and the chief art is to make all that they have to do, sport and play too."

Locke's observations about manners and affectation have merely an historic interest. The dancing-master has a higher *role* allotted him than he plays in our present education. Locke writes: "Since nothing appears to me to give children so much becoming confidence and behavior, and so to raise them to the conversation of those above their age, as *dancing*, I think they should be taught to dance as soon as they are capable of learning it. For though this consists only in outward gracefulness of motion, yet, I know not how, it gives children manly thoughts and carriage more than anything. But, otherwise," he adds, "I would not have little children much tormented about punctilios, or niceties of breeding." Good company will teach them good manners. "Children (nay, and men too) do most by example. We are all a sort of cameleons, that still take a tincture from things near us; nor is it to be wondered at in children, who better understand what they see than what they hear."

When speaking of company, Locke points out the harm done by clownish or vicious servants. To avoid this, the children must be kept as much as possible *in the company of their parents;* and by being allowed all proper freedom, must be led to take pleasure in it.

Although I would go much further than most school-masters in endeavoring to make the pupil's intellectual exertions *pleasurable* to him, I can not go all the way with Locke. His directions, though impracticable in a school, might, perhaps, be carried on by a private tutor—with, I should say, by no means satisfactory results. One employment Locke seems to think is, in itself, as pleasurable as another; so, if nothing which has to be learnt is made a burden, or imposed a task, the pupil will like work just as well as play. "Let a child be but ordered to whip his top at a certain time every day, whether he has, or has not, a mind to it; let this be but required of him as a duty wherein he must spend so many hours morning and afternoon, and see whether he will not be soon weary of any play at this rate." The tutor should, therefore, be on the watch for "*seasons of aptitude and inclination,*" and so "make learning as much a recreation to their play, as their play is recreation to their learning." Locke gives, however, two cautions, which might be found rather to clog the wheels of the chariot—first, the child is not to be allowed to grow idle; and secondly, the mind must be taught mastery over itself, "which will be an advantage of more consequence than Latin or logic, or most of those things children are usually required to learn." His scheme is no doubt an admirable one, if it can be carried out with these qualifications.

As we have seen, Locke was opposed to any harshness about lessons, though much seems to have been used in schools of that period. "Why," asks Locke, "does the learning of Latin and Greek need the rod, when French and Italian need it not? Children learn to dance and fence without whipping; nay, arithmetic, drawing, etc., they apply themselves well enough to without beating; which would make me suspect that there is something strange, unnatural, and disagreeable to that age, in the things required in grammar-schools, or in the methods used there, that children can not be brought to without the severity of the lash, and hardly with that too; or else it is a mistake that those tongues could not be taught them without beating."

Instead of this harshness, Locke would use *reasoning* with children. "This," says he, "they understand as early as they do language; and, if I misobserve not, they love to be treated as rational creatures sooner than is imagined. It is a pride should be cherished in them, and as much as can be made an instrument to turn them by."

In the necessary qualifications of the tutor, the first and principal, according to Locke, are breeding and knowledge of the world. "Courage, in an ill-bred man, has the air, and escapes not the opinion, of brutality. Learning becomes pedantry; wit, buffoonery; plainness, rusticity; good-nature, fawning; and there can not be a good quality in him which want of breeding will not warp and disfigure to his disadvantage. By means of the tutor's knowledge of the world, Locke hoped to protect the pupil against the dangers which beset "an old boy, at his first appearance, with all the gravity of his ivy bush about him;" but he who is to steer a vessel over a difficult course, will hardly fit himself for the task by taking lessons even of the most skillful pilot, *on shore*.

Locke's account of the work of a tutor gives so much insight into his notion of education generally, that it seems worth quoting at length:—

"The great work of a governor is to fashion the carriage and form the mind, to settle in his pupil good habits and the principles of virtue and wisdom, to give him, by little and little, of mankind, and work him into a love and imitation of what is excellent and praiseworthy; and, in the prosecution of it, to give him vigor, activity, and industry. The studies which he sets himself upon are but, as it were, the exercises of his faculties and employment of his time; to keep him from sauntering and idleness; to teach him application, and accustom him to take pains, and to give him some little taste of what his own industry must perfect. For who expects that under a tutor, a young gentleman should be an accomplished orator or logician? go to the bottom of metaphysics, natural philosophy, or mathematics? or be a master in history or chronology? Though something of each of these is to be taught him; but it is only to open the door that he may look in and, as it were, begin an acquaintance, but not to dwell there; and a governor would be much blamed that should keep his pupil too long, and lead him too far in most of them. But of good breeding, knowledge of the world, virtue, industry, and a love of reputation he can not have too much; and if he have these he will not long want what he needs or desires of the other. And since it can not be hoped that he should have time and strength to learn all things, most pains should be taken about that which is most necessary, and that principally looked after which will be of most and frequentest use to him in the world."

It is curious to observe how little store Locke sets by learning. Indeed, it would seem that in those days school-learning was even more estranged from the business of life than it has been since. "A great part of the learning now in fashion in the schools of Europe," says Locke, "and that goes ordinarily into the round of education, a gentleman may, in good measure, be unfurnished with, without any great disparagement to himself, or prejudice to his affairs." Again he says, "We learn not to live, but to dispute, and our education fits us rather for the university than for the world. But it is no wonder, if those who make the fashion suit it to *what they have, and not to what their pupils want.*" This last remark is not without its application in our time.

When we come to Locke's directions about teaching we find him carrying out his notion of combining amusement with instruction. "Children should not have anything like work or serious laid on them; neither their minds nor bodies will bear it. It injures their healths; and their being forced and tied down to their books in an age at enmity with all such restraints has, I doubt not, been the reason why a great many have hated books and learning all their lives after. It is like a surfeit, that leaves an aversion behind that cannot be removed." I know a person of great quality (more yet to be honored for his learning and virtue than for his rank and high place), who by pasting on the six vowels (for in our language 'y' is one) on the six sides of a die, and the remaining 18 consonants on the sides of three other dice, has made this a play for his children, that he shall win, who, at one cast, throws most words on these four dice, whereby his eldest son, yet in coats, has *played* himself *into spelling* with great eagerness, and without once having been chid for it, or forced to it."

When the child has acquired reading, he should have some amusing book, such as Æsop and Reynard the Fox. Pictures of animals, with the names printed below them should be shown him from the time he knows his letters. He is to be encouraged to give an account of his reading. "Children," says Locke, "are commonly not taught to make any use of their reading, and so get to look upon books as "fashionable amusements or impertinent troubles, good for nothing."

For religious instruction, the child should learn some easy Catechism, and should read some portions of Scripture, but should not be allowed to read the whole Bible.

When he begins to learn writing, he must be perfect in holding his pen, before paper is put before him: "for not only children, but anybody else that would do anything well, should never be put upon too much of it at once, or be set to perfect themselves in two parts of an action at the same time, if they can possibly be separated." The child should then be given paper, on which is red-ink writing, in large hand. This writing he is to go over with black ink.

He is next to learn drawing, "a thing very useful to a gentleman on several occasions;" but in this, as in all other things not absolutely necessary, the rule holds good, "Nihil invita Minerva," [Nought unless Minerva wills].

He should now learn French. "People are accustomed to the right way of teaching that language, which is by talking it unto children in constant conversation, and not by grammatical rules. The Latin tongue might easily be taught in the same way."

"Latin," says Locke, "I look upon as absolutely necessary to a gentleman." But he ridicules the folly of sending boys to grammar-schools, when they are intended for trade. "Yet, if you ask the parents why they do this, they think it as strange a question as if you should ask them why they go to church. Custom stands for reason; and has, to those who take it for reason, so consecrated the method, that it is almost religiously observed by them, and they stick to it as if their children had scarce an orthodox education unless they learn Lily's Grammar."

But, though Latin should be taught to gentlemen, this should be done by conversation, and thus time might be gained for "several sciences: such as are a good part of geography, astronomy, chronology, anatomy, besides some parts of history, and all other parts of knowledge of things that fall under the senses, and require little more than memory: for there, if we would take the true way, our knowledge should begin, and in those things should be laid the foundations; and not in the abstract notions of logic and metaphysics, which are fitter to amuse than inform the understanding in its first setting out toward knowledge." Again he says, " The learning of Latin being nothing but the learning of words, a very unpleasant business to both young and old, join as much other real knowledge* with it as you can, beginning still with that which lies most obvious to the senses; such as is the knowledge of minerals, plants, and animals; and particularly timber and fruit trees, their parts, and ways of propagation, wherein a great deal may be taught the child which will not be useless to the man: but more especially, geography, astronomy, and anatomy." He would also introduce some geometry.

But Locke was not blind to the difficulty that few teachers would be found capable of talking Latin. He would, therefore, have the mother make a beginning by getting a Latin Testament with the quantities marked, and reading it with her children. He also suggests the use of interlinear translations. "Take," says he, "some easy and pleasant book, such as Æsop's Fables, and write the English translation (made as literal as can be) in one line, and the Latin words which answer each of them, just over it in another. These let the child read every day, over and over again, till he perfectly understands the Latin, and then go on to another fable, till he be also perfect in that, not omitting what he is already perfect in, but sometimes re-

---

* Real knowledge is here knowledge of *things*, as distinguished from all other knowledge. Our loss of this meaning of the word *real* shows how small has been the influence of the Innovators in this country. Both the word and the party have been more successful in Germany.

viewing that, to keep it in his memory. And when he comes to write, let these be set him for copies, which, with the exercise of his hand, will also advance him in Latin. This being a more imperfect way than by talking Latin unto him, the formation of the verbs first, and afterward the declension of the nouns and pronouns perfectly learned by heart, may facilitate his acquaintance with the genius and manner of the Latin tongue, which varies the signification of the verbs and nouns not, as the modern languages do, by particles prefixed, but by changing the last syllables. More than this of grammar I think he need not have till he can read himself 'Sanctii Minerva,' with Scioppius and Perizonius' notes." It is no objection to his plan, he says, that children will learn merely by rote. Languages must be learned by rote, and used without any thought of grammar: "if grammar ought to be taught at any time, it must be to one that can speak the language already: how else can he be taught the grammar of it?" "Grammar is, in fact, an introduction to rhetoric."* "I grant the grammar of a language is sometimes very carefully to be studied; but it is only to be studied by a grown man, when he applies himself to the understanding of any language critically, which is seldom the business of any but professed scholars." "This, I think, will be agreed to, that if a gentleman be to study any

---

* Much confusion has arisen, as Bishop Dupanloup has observed, from the double use of the word *grammar*; first, for the science of language, and second, for the mere statement of the facts of a language. Those who teach what is called "Latin Grammar" to children may argue that they only teach them, in order and connection, facts which they would otherwise have to pick up at random. See also M. Arnold: *Schools, etc.*, p. 88.

language, it ought to be that of his own country, that he may understand the language which he has constant use of, with the utmost accuracy." And yet "young gentlemen are forced to learn the grammars of foreign and dead languages, and are never once told of the grammar of their own tongue; they do not so much as know that there is any such thing, much less is it made their business to be instructed in it. Nor is their own language ever proposed to them as worthy their care and cultivating, though they have daily use of it, and are not seldom, in the future course of their lives, judged of by their handsome or awkward way of expressing themselves in it. Whereas the languages whose grammars they have been so much employed in, are such as probably they shall scarce ever speak or write; or if, upon occasion, this should happen, they should be excused for the mistakes and faults they make in it. Would not a Chinese, who took notice of this way of breeding, be apt to imagine that all our young gentlemen were designed to be teachers and professors of the dead languages of foreign countries, and not to be men of business in their own?"

Locke grants that in some sciences where their reasons are to be exercised, difficulties may be proposed, on purpose to excite industry, and accustom the mind to employ its own strength and sagacity in solving them. "But yet," he continues, "I guess this is not to be done to children whilst very young, nor at their entrance upon any sort of knowledge. Then everything of itself is difficult, and the great use and skill of a teacher is to make all as easy as he can."

Locke inveighs strongly against the ordinary practice

of writing themes on such subjects as *"omnia vincit amor,"* [Love conquers all things], or *" Non licet in bello bis peccare,"* [In war one has no chance to blunder twice]. "Here the poor lad who wants knowledge of those things he is to speak of, which is to be had only from time and observation, must set his invention on the rack to say something where he knows nothing, which is a sort of Egyptian tyranny, to bid them make bricks who have not yet any of the materials." Verse-making found equally little favor in his eyes.

He denounces also the practice of making boys say large portions of authors by heart, to strengthen the memory. He thinks that "the learning pages of Latin by heart no more fits the memory for retention of anything else than the graving of one sentence in lead makes it the more capable of retaining any other characters. If such a sort of exercise of the memory were to give it strength, and improve our parts, players, of all other people, must needs have the best memories, and be the best company.* " What the mind is intent upon and careful of, that it remembers best; to which, if method and order be joined, all is done, I think, that can be for the help of a weak memory; and he that will take any other way to do it, especially that of charging it with a train of other people's words, which he that learns cares not for, will, I guess, scarce find the profit answer half the time and pains employed in it." Boys, however, should learn by heart passages which are valuable in themselves, and these they should give an account

---

* From the little I have seen of gentlemen of this profession, I am by no means disposed to consider this, as Locke does apparently, a *reductio ad absurdum*, [proof of the opposite view from the absurdity of this inference].

of, and repeat again and again, that they may always remember them, and may also be taught to reflect on what they learn.

As an exercise in English, "there should be proposed to young gentlemen rational and useful questions suited to their age and capacities, and on subjects not wholly unknown to them, nor out of their way. Such as these, when they are ripe for exercises of this nature, they should *extempore* [without preparation], or after a little meditation upon the spot, speak to, without penning of anything." Even at an earlier age children should often tell a story of anything they know, such as a fable from Æsop ("the only book almost that I know fit for children"), and at first the teacher is to correct only the most remarkable fault they are guilty of in their way of putting it together. They must also write narratives, and, when more advanced, letters. "They must also read those things that are well writ in English, to perfect their style in the purity of our language; for since it is English that an English gentleman will have constant use of, that is the language he should chiefly cultivate, and wherein most care should be taken to polish and perfect his style."

On another point he was at variance with the custom of his day. "If the use and end of right reasoning," he says, "be to have right notions and a right judgment of things, to distinguish between truth and falsehood, right and wrong, and to act accordingly, be sure not to let your son be bred up in the art and formality of disputing, either practicing it himself or admiring it in others." Of logic and rhetoric he also speaks very disparagingly.

To the studies already mentioned, viz., geography, chronology, history, astronomy, anatomy, Locke would add the principles of civil law and the laws of England.

"Natural philosophy, as a speculative science," writes Locke, "I imagine we have none; and perhaps I may think I have reason to say we never shall be able to make a science of it. The works of nature are contrived by a Wisdom and operate by ways too far surpassing our faculties to discover, or capacities to conceive, for us ever to be able to reduce them to a science." He allows, however, that the incomparable Mr. Newton has shown how far mathematics, applied to some parts of Nature, may, upon principles that matter of fact justifies, carry us in the knowledge of some, as I may call them, particular provinces of the incomprehensible universe."

Greek does not enter into Locke's curriculum. Latin and French, "as the world now goes," are required of a gentleman, but Greek only of a professed scholar. If the pupil has a mind to carry his studies further for himself, he can do so; but, as it is, "how many are there of a hundred, even amongst scholars themselves, who retain the Greek they carried from school; or ever improve it to a familiar, ready, and perfect understanding of Greek authors?" The tutor must remember "that his business is not so much to teach the pupil all that is knowable, as to raise in him a love and esteem of knowledge, and to put him in the right way of knowing and improving himself when he has a mind to it."

In the matter of accomplishments, Locke is rather hard upon music, "which leads into jovial company," and painting, which is a sedentary, and therefore not a healthy occupation. Wrestling he prefers to fencing. "Riding the great horse" (whatever that may mean) should not be made a business of.

By all means let a gentleman learn at least one manual trade, especially such as can be practiced in the open air. This will make his leisure pleasant to him, and will keep him from useless and dangerous pastimes.

From the last part of education—travel—Locke thinks more harm is commonly derived than good: not that travel is bad in itself, but the time usually chosen, viz., from sixteen to twenty-one, is the worst time of all.

This short review of the "Thoughts on Education," shows us that Locke's aim was to give a boy a robust mind in a robust body. His body was to endure hardness, his reason was to teach him self denial. But this result was to be brought about by leading, not driving him. He was to be trained, not for the University, but for the world. Good principles, good manners, and discretion were to be cared for first of all; intelligence and intellectual activity next, and actual knowledge last of all. His spirits were to be kept up by kind treatment, and learning was never to be made a drudgery. With regard to the subjects of instruction, those branches of knowledge which concern things were to take precedence of those which consist of abstract ideas. The prevalent drill in the grammar of the classical languages was to be abandoned. The mother-tongue was to be carefully studied, and other languages acquired either by conversation, or by the use of translations. In everything, the part the pupil was to play in life was steadily to be kept in view; and the ideal which Locke proposed was not the finished scholar, but the finished gentleman.

VI.

ROUSSEAU'S "EMILE."

In education, as in politics, no school of thinkers has succeeded, or can succeed, in engrossing all truth to itself. No party, no individual even, can take up a central position between the Conservatives and Radicals, and judging everything on its own merits, try to preserve that only which is worth preserving, and to destroy just that which is worth destroying. Nor do we find that judicial minds often exercise the greatest influence in these matters. The only force which can overcome the *vis inertiæ* [power of inertion] of use and wont is enthusiasm; and this, springing from the discovery of new truths and hatred of old abuses, can hardly exist with due respect for truth that has become commonplace, and usage which is easily confounded with corruptions that disfigure it. So advances are made somewhat after this manner: the reformer, urged on by his enthusiasm, attacks use and wont with more spirit than discretion, Those who are wedded to things as they are, try to draw attention from the weak points of their system, to the mistakes or extravagances of the reformer. In the end, both sides are benefited by the encounter, and when their successors carry on the contest, they differ as much from those whose causes they espouse as from each other.

In this way we have already made great progress. Compare, for instance, our present teaching of grammar with the ancient method; and our short and broken school-time with the old plan of keeping boys in for five consecutive hours twice a day. Our Conservatives and Reformers are not so much at variance as their predecessors. To convince ourselves of this we have only to consider the state of parties in the second half of the last century. On the one side we find the schoolmasters who turned out the courtiers of Louis XV.; on the other, the most extravagant, the most eloquent, the most reckless of innovators—J. J. Rousseau.

Rousseau has told us that he resolved on having fixed principles by the time he was forty years old. Among the principles of which he accordingly laid in a stock, were these: 1st, Man, as he might be, is perfectly good; 2d, Man, as he is, is utterly bad. To maintain these opinions, Rousseau undertook to show, not only the rotten state of the existing society, which he did with notable success, but also the proper method of rearing children so as to make them all that they ought to be—an attempt at construction which was far more difficult and hazardous than his phillipics.

This was the origin of the "Emile," perhaps the most influential book ever written on the subject of education. The school to which Rousseau belonged may be said, indeed, to have been founded by Montaigne, and to have met with a champion, though not a very enthusiastic champion, in Locke. But it was reserved for Rousseau to give this theory of education its complete development, and to expound it in the clearest and most eloquent language. In the form in which Rousseau left it, the theory greatly influenced Basedow and Pestalozzi, and still influences many educational reformers who differ from Rousseau as much as our schoolmasters differ from those of Louis XV.

Of course as man was corrupted by ordinary education, the ideal education must differ from it in every respect. "Take the road directly opposite to that which is in use, and you will almost always do right." This was the fundamental maxim. So thorough a radical was Rousseau, that he scorned the idea of half-measures. "I had rather follow the established practice entirely," says he, "than adopt a good one by halves."

In the society of that time everything was artificial; Rousseau therefore demanded a return to Nature. Parents should do their duty in rearing their own offspring. "Where there is no mother, there can be no child." The father should find time to bring up the child whom the mother has suckled. No duty can be more important than this. But although Rousseau seems conscious that family life is the natural state, he makes his model child an orphan, and hands him over to a governor, to be brought up in the country without companions.

This governor is to devote himself, for some years, entirely to imparting to his pupil these difficult arts — the art of being ignorant and of losing time. Till he is twelve years old, Emile is to have no direct instruction whatever. "At that age he shall not know what a book is," says Rousseau; though elsewhere we are told that he will learn to read of his own accord by the time he is ten, if no attempt is made to teach him. He is to be under no restraint, and is to do nothing but what he sees to be useful.

Freedom from restraint is, however, to be apparent, not real. As in ordinary education the child employs all its faculties in duping the master, so in education "according to Nature," the master is to devote himself to duping the child. "Let him always be his own master in appearance, and do you take care to be so in reality. There is no subjection so complete as that which preserves the appearance of liberty; it is by this means even the will is led captive."

"The most critical interval of human nature is that between the hour of our birth and twelve years of age. This is the time, wherein vice and error take root without our being possessed of any instrument to destroy them."

Throughout this season, the governor is to be at work inculcating the art of being ignorant and losing time. "This first part of education ought to be purely negative. It consists neither in teaching virtue nor truth, but in guarding the heart from vice and the mind from error. If you could do nothing and let nothing be done; if you could bring up your pupil healthy and robust to the age of twelve years, without his being able to distinguish his right hand from his left, the eyes of his understanding would be open to reason at your first lesson; void both of habit and prejudice, he would have nothing in him to operate against your endeavors; soon under your instruction he would become the wisest of men. Thus, by setting out with doing nothing, you would produce a prodigy of education."

"Exercise his body, his senses, faculties, powers, but keep his mind inactive as long as possible. Distrust all the sentiments he acquires, previous to the judgment which should enable him to scrutinize them. Prevent or restrain all foreign impressions; and in order to hinder the rise of evil, be not in too great a hurry to instill good; for it is only such when the mind is enlightened by reason. Look upon every delay as an advantage: it is gaining a great deal to advance without losing anything. Let childhood ripen in children. In short, whatever lesson becomes necessary for them to take care not to give them to-day, if it may be deferred without danger till to-morrow."

" Do not, then, alarm yourself much about this apparent idleness. What would you say of the man, who, in order to make the most of life, should determine never to go to sleep? You would say, The man is mad: he is not enjoying the time; he is depriving himself of it: to avoid sleep he is hurrying toward death. Consider, then, that it is the same here, and that childhood is the sleep of reason."

Such is the groundwork of Rousseau's educational scheme. His ideal boy, of twelve years old, is to be a thoroughly well-developed animal, with every bodily sense trained to its highest perfection. "His ideas," says Rousseau, "are confined, but clear; he knows nothing by rote, but a great deal by experience. If he reads less well than another child in our books, he reads better in the book of nature. His understanding does not lie in his tongue, but in his brain; he has less memory than judgment; he can speak only one language, but then he understands what he says; and although he may not talk of things so well as others, he will do them much better. He knows nothing at all of custom, fashion, or habit; what he did yesterday has no influence on what he is to do to-day; he follows no formula, is influenced by no authority or example, but acts and speaks just as it suits him. Do not, then, expect from him set discourses or studied manners, but always the faithful expression of his ideas, and the conduct which springs naturally from his inclinations." Furthermore, this model child looks upon all men as equal, and will ask assistance from a king as readily as from a foot-boy. He does not understand what a command is, but will readily do anything for another person, in order to place that person under an obligation, and so increase his own rights. He knows also no distinction between work and play. As a climax to this list of wonders, I may add that his imagination has remained inactive, and he only sees what is true in reality.

The reader will probably have concluded, by this time, that no child can possibly be so educated as to resemble Emile, and, perhaps, further, that no wise father would so educate his son if it were possible. A child who does not understand what a command is, and who can be induced to do anything for another only by the prospect of laying that person under an obligation; who has no habits, and is guided merely by his inclinations—such a child as this is, fortunately, nothing but a dream of Rousseau's.

But fantastical as Rousseau often is, the reader of his "Emile" is struck again and again, not more by the charm of his language than by his insight into child-nature, and the wisdom of his remarks upon it.

The "Emile" is a large work, and the latter part is interesting rather from a literary and philosophical point of view, than as it is connected with education.

I purpose, therefore, confining my attention to the earlier portion of the book, and giving some of the passages, of which a great deal since said and written on education has been a comparatively insipid decoction.

"All things are good, as their Creator made them, but everything degenerates in the hands of man." These are the first words of the "Emile," and the key-note of Rousseau's philosophy.

"We are born weak, we have need of strength; we are born destitute of everything, we have need of assistance; we are born stupid, we have need of understanding. All that we are not possessed of at our birth, and which we require when grown up, is bestowed on us by education.

"This education we receive from nature, from men, or from things. The internal development of our organs and faculties is the education of nature; the use we are taught to make of that development is the education given us by men; and in the acquisitions made by our own experience on the objects that surround us, consists our education from things." "Since the concurrence of these three kinds of education is necessary to their perfection, it is by that one which is entirely independent of us, we must regulate the two others."

Now "to live is not merely to breathe; it is to act, it is to make use of our organs, our senses, our faculties, and of all of those parts of ourselves which give us the feeling of our existence. The man who has lived most, is not he who has counted the greatest number of years, but he who has most thoroughly felt life."

The aim of education, then, must be complete living. But ordinary education (and here for a moment I am expressing my own conviction, and not simply reporting Rousseau), instead of seeking to develop the life of the child, sacrifices childhood to the acquirement of knowledge, or rather the semblance of knowledge, which it is thought will prove useful to the youth, or the man. Rousseau's great merit lies in his having exposed this fundamental error. He says, very truly, "People do not understand childhood. With the false notions we have of it, the further we go the more we blunder. The wisest apply themselves to what it is important to *men* to know, without considering what *children* are in a condition to learn. They are always seeking the *man* in the *child,* without reflecting what he is before he can be a man. This is the study to which I have applied myself most; so that, should my practical scheme be found useless and chimerical, my observation will always turn to account. I may possibly have taken a very bad view of what ought to be done, but I conceive I have taken a good one of the subject to be wrought upon. Begin then by studying your pupils better; for most assuredly you do not at present understand them. So if you read my book with that view, I do not think it will be useless to you." "Nature requires children to be children before they are men. If we will pervert this order, we shall produce forward fruits, having neither ripeness nor taste, and sure soon to become rotten; we shall have young professors and old children. Childhood has its manner of seeing, perceiving, and thinking, peculiar to itself; nothing is more absurd than our being anxious to substitute our own in its stead." "We never know how to put ourselves in the place of children; we do not enter into their ideas, we lend them our own: and following always our own train of thought, we fill their heads, even while we are discussing incontestible truths, with extravagance and error." "I wish some judicious hand would give us a treatise on the art of studying children; an art of the greatest importance to understand, though fathers and preceptors know not as yet even the elements of it."

The governor, then, must be able to sympathize with his pupil, and, on this account, Rousseau requires that he should be *young*. "The governor of a child should be young, even as young as possible, consistent with his having obtained necessary discretion and sagacity. I would have him be himself a child, that he might become the companion of his pupil, and gain his confidence by partaking of his amusements. There are not things enough in common between childhood and manhood, to form a solid attachment at so great a distance. Children sometimes caress old men, but they never love them." *

The governor's functions are threefold: 1st, that of keeping off hurtful influences—no light task in Rousseau's eyes, as he regarded almost every influence from the child's fellow-creatures as hurtful; 2d that of developing the bodily powers, especially the senses; 3d, that of communicating the one science for children—moral behavior. In all these, even in the last, he must be gov-

---

* Here, and in some other instances, I have selected as characteristic of their author, opinions which I believe to be totally erroneous. The distance between the child and the man is no doubt very great (so great, indeed, that the distance between the young man and the old bears no appreciable ratio to it); but this does not preclude the most intense affection of the young toward grown persons of any age, as our individual experience has probably convinced us. Perhaps the old have more in common with children than those have who are in the full vigor of manhood.

ernor rather than preceptor, for it is less his province to instruct than to conduct. He must not lay down precepts, but teach his pupil to discover them. "I preach a difficult art," says Rousseau, "the art of guiding without precepts, and of doing everything by doing nothing."

The most distinctive characteristic of childhood is vitality. "In the heart of the old man the failing energies concentrate themselves: in that of the child, they overflow and spread outward; he is conscious of life enough to animate all that surrounds him. Whether he makes or mars, it is all one to him: he is satisfied with having changed the state of things; and every change is an action. This vitality is to be allowed free scope. Swaddling-clothes are to be removed from infants; the restraints of school and book-learning from children. Their love of action is to be freely indulged.*

The nearest approach to teaching which Rousseau permitted, was that which became afterward, in the hands of Pestalozzi, the system of object-lessons. "As soon as a child begins to distinguish objects, a proper choice should be made in those which are presented to him." He must learn to feel heat and cold, the hardness, softness, and weight of bodies; to judge of their magnitude, figure, and other sensible qualities, by look-

* Lord Stanley, than whom no man can be more "practical," follows Rousseau in this particular. "People are beginning to find out, what, if they would use their own observation more, and not follow one another like sheep, they would have found out long ago, that it is doing positive harm to a young child, mental and bodily harm, to keep it learning, or pretending to learn, the greater part of the day. Nature says to a child, 'Run about,' the schoolmaster says, 'Sit still;' and as the schoolmaster can punish on the spot, and Nature only long afterward, he is obeyed, and health and brain suffer."—Speech reported in the "*Evening Mail*," December 9, 1864.

ing, touching, hearing, and particularly by comparing the sight with the touch, and judging, by means of the eye, of the sensation acquired by the fingers." These exercises should be continued through childhood. "A child has neither the strength nor the judgment of a man; but he is capable of feeling and hearing as well, or at least nearly so. His palate also is as sensible, though less delicate: and he distinguishes odors as well, though not with the same nicety. Of all our faculties, the senses are perfected the first: these, therefore, are the first we should cultivate; they are, nevertheless, the only ones that are usually forgotten, or the most neglected." "Observe a cat, the first time she comes into a room; she looks and smells about; she is not easy a moment: she distrusts everything till everything is examined and known. In the same manner does a child examine into everything, when he begins to walk about, and enters, if I may so say, the apartment of the world. All the difference is, that the sight, which is common to both the child and the cat, is in the first assisted by the feeling of the hands, and in the latter by the exquisite scent which nature has bestowed on it. It is the right or wrong cultivation of this inquisitive disposition that makes children either stupid or expert; sprightly or dull, sensible or foolish. The primary impulses of man urge him to compare his forces with those of the objects about him, and to discover the sensible qualities of such objects as far as they relate to him; his first study is a sort of experimental philosophy relative to self-preservation, from which it is the custom to divert him by speculative studies before he has found his place on this earth. During the time that his supple and delicate organs can adjust themselves to the bodies on which they should act, while his senses are as yet exempt from illusions, this is the time to exercise both the one and the other in their proper functions; this is the time to learn the sensuous relations which things have with us. As everything that enters the human understanding is introduced by the senses; the first reason in man is a sensitive reason; and this serves as the basis of his intellectual reason. Our first instructors in philosophy are our feet, hands, and eyes. Substituting books for all this is not teaching us to reason, but teaching us to use the reasoning of others; it is teaching us to believe a great deal, and never to *know* anything." "To exercise any art, we must begin by procuring the necessary implements; and to employ those implements to any good purpose, they should be made sufficiently solid for their intended use. To learn to think, therefore, we should exercise our limbs and our organs, which are the instruments of our intelligence; and in order to make the best use of those instruments, it is necessary that the body furnishing them should be robust and hearty. Thus, so far is a sound understanding from being independent of the body, that it is owing to a good constitution that the operations of the mind are effected with facility and certainty." "To exercise the senses is not merely to make use of them; it is to learn rightly to judge by them; to learn, if I may so express myself, to perceive; for we know how to touch, to see, to hear, only as we have learned. Some exercises are purely natural and mechanical, and serve to make the body strong and robust, without taking the least hold on the judgment: such are those of swimming, running, leaping, whipping a top, throwing stones, etc. All these are very well: but have we only arms and legs? Have we not also eyes and ears; and are not these organs necessary to the expert use of the former? Exercise, therefore, not only the strength, but also all the senses that direct it; make the best possible use of each, and let the impressions of one confirm those of another. Measure, reckon, weigh, compare."

According to the present system, "The lessons which school-boys learn of each other in playing about their bounds, are a hundred times more useful to them than all those which the master teaches in the school."

He also suggests experiments in the dark, which will both train the senses and get over the child's dread of darkness. "*Ab assuetis non fit passio,*" [Passion does not arise from things accustomed].

Emile, living in the country and being much in the open air, will acquire a distinct and emphatic way of speaking. He will also avoid a fruitful source of bad pronunciation among the children of the rich, viz., saying lessons by heart. These lessons the children gabble when they are learning them, and afterward, in their efforts to remember the words, they drawl, and give all kinds of false emphasis. Declamation is to be shunned as *acting*. If Emile does not understand anything, he will be too wise to pretend to understand it.

Rousseau seems perhaps inconsistent, in not excluding music and drawing from his curriculum of ignorance: but as a musician, he naturally relaxed toward the former;[*] and drawing he would have his pupil culti-

---

[*] The followers of the Tonic Sol-Fa system have in Rousseau a strong ally in attacking the method which makes Do the tonic of the natural key only.

vate, not for the sake of the art itself, but only to give him a good eye and supple hand. He should, in all cases, draw from the objects themselves, "my intention being, not so much that he should know how to imitate the objects, as to become fully acquainted with them."

The instruction given to ordinary school-boys, was of course an abomination in the eyes of Rousseau. "All the studies imposed on these poor unfortunates tend to such objects as are entirely foreign to their minds. Judge, then, of the attention they are likely to bestow on them." The pedagogues, who make a great parade of the instructions they give their scholars, are paid to talk in a different strain: one may see plainly, however, by their conduct, that they are exactly of my opinion: for, after all, what is it they teach them? Words, still words, and nothing but words. Among the various sciences they pretend to teach, they take particular care not to fall upon those which are really useful; because there would be the sciences of things, and in them they would never succeed; but they fix on such as appear to be understood when their terms are once gotten by rote, viz., geography, chronology, heraldry, the languages, etc., all studies so foreign to the purposes of man, and particularly to those of a child, that it is a wonder if ever he may have occasion for them as long as he lives. "In any study whatever, unless we possess the ideas of the things represented, the signs representing them are of no use or consequence. A child is, nevertheless, always confined to these signs, without our being capable of making him comprehend any of the things which they represent." What is the world to a child? It is a globe of pasteboard.* "As no science consists in the knowledge of words, so there is no study proper for children. As they have no certain ideas, so they have no real memory; for I do not call that so which is retentive only of mere sensations What signifies imprinting on their minds a catalogue of signs which to them represent nothing? Is it to be feared that, in acquiring the knowledge of things, they will not acquire also that of signs? Why, then, shall we put them to the unnecessary trouble of learning them twice? And yet what dangerous prejudices do we not begin to instill, by making them take for knowledge, words which to them are without meaning? In the very first unintelligible sentence with which a child sits down satisfied, in the very first thing he takes upon trust, or learns from others without being himself convinced of its utility, he loses part of his understanding; and he may figure long in the eyes of fools before he will be able to repair so considerable a loss. No; if nature has given to the child's brain that pliability which renders it fit to receive all impressons, it is not with a view that we should imprint thereon the names of kings, dates, terms of heraldry, of astronomy, of geography, and all those words, meaningless at his age, and useless at any age, with which we weary his sad and sterile childhood; but that all the ideas which he can conceive, and which are useful to him, all those which relate to his happiness, and will one day make his duty plain to him, may trace

---

*Rousseau, like his pupil Basedow, would avoid the use even of representations, where possible. "It ought to be laid down as a general rule, never to substitute the shadow unless where it is impossible to exhibit the substance; for the representation engrossing the attention of the child, generally makes him forget the object represented."

themselves there in characters never to be effaced, and may assist him in conducting himself through life in a manner appropriate to his nature and his faculties."
"That kind of memory which is possessed by children, may be fully employed without setting them to study books. Everything they see, or hear, appears striking, and they commit it to memory. A child keeps in his mind a register of the actions and conversation of those who are about him; every scene he is engaged in is a book from which he insensibly enriches his memory, treasuring up his store till time shall ripen his judgment and turn it to profit. In the choice of these scenes and objects, in the care of presenting those constantly to his view which he ought to be familiar with, and in hiding from him such as are improper, consists the true art of cultivating this primary faculty of a child. By such means, also, it is, that we should endeavor to form that magazine of knowledge which should serve for his education in youth, and to regulate his conduct afterward. This method, it is true, is not productive of little prodigies of learning, nor does it tend to the glorification of the governess or preceptor: but it is the way to form robust and judicious men, persons sound in body and mind, who, without being admired while children, know how to make themselves respected when grown up."

As for reading and writing, if you can induce a *desire* for them, the child will be sure to learn them. "I am almost certain that Emile will know perfectly well how to read and write before he is ten years old, because I give myself very little trouble whether he learn it or not before he is fifteen; but I had much rather he should never learn to read at all, than to acquire that knowledge at the expense of everything that would render it useful to him; and of what service will the power of reading be to him when he has renounced its use forever?"

The following passage is perhaps familiar to Mr. Lowe: "If, proceeding on the plan I have begun to delineate, you follow rules directly contrary to those which are generally received; if, instead of transporting your pupil's mind to what is remote—if, instead of making his thoughts wander unceasingly in other places, in other climates, in other centuries, to the ends of the earth, and to the very heavens, you apply yourself to keeping him always at home and attentive to that which comes in immediate contact with him, you will then find him capable of perception, of memory, and even of reason: this is the order of nature. In proportion as the sensitive becomes an active being, he acquires a discernment proportional to his bodily powers; when he possesses more of the latter, also, than are necessary for his preservation, it is with that redundancy, and not before, that he displays those speculative faculties which are adapted to the employment of such abilities to other purposes. Are you desirous, therefore, to cultivate the understanding of your pupil? cultivate those abilities on which it depends. Keep him in constant exercise of body; bring him up robust and healthy, in order to make him reasonable and wise; let him work, let him run about, let him make a noise, in a word, let him be always active and in motion; let him be once a man in vigor, and he will soon be a man in understanding."

Let us now examine what provision was made, in

Rousseau's system, for teaching the one science for children, that of moral behavior (*des devoirs de l'homme*). His notions of this science were by no means those to which we are accustomed. As a believer in the goodness of human nature, he traced all folly, vanity, and vice to ordinary education, and he would therefore depart as widely as possible from the usual course. "Examine the rules of the common method of education," he writes, "and you will find them all wrong, particularly those which relate to virtue and manners."

A simple alteration of method, however, would not suffice. Rousseau went further than this. He discarded all received notions of goodness, and set up one of his own in their stead. "The only lesson of morality proper for children, and the most important to persons of all ages, is never to do an injury to any one. Even the positive precept of doing good, if not made subordinate to this, is dangerous, false, and contradictory. Who is there that does not do good? All the world does good, the wicked man as well as others: he makes one person happy at the expense of making a hundred miserable; hence arise all our calamities. The most sublime virtues are negative; they are also the most difficult to put in practice, because they are attended with no ostentation, and are even above the pleasure, so sweet to the heart of man, of sending away others satisfied with our benevolence. O how much good must that man necessarily do his fellow-creatures, if such a man there be, who never did any of them harm! What intrepidity of soul, what constancy of mind are necessary here! It is not, however, by reasoning on this maxim, but by endeavoring to put it in practice, that all its difficulty is to be discovered." "The precept of never doing another harm, implies that of having as little to do as possible with human society; for in the social state the good of one man necessarily becomes the evil of another. This relation is essential to the thing itself, and can not be changed. We may inquire, on this principle, which is best, man in a state of society or in a state of solitude?" "A certain noble author has said, none but a wicked man might exist alone: for my part, I say, none but a good man might exist alone."

This passage fully explains Rousseau's enthusiasm for Robinson Crusoe, for he must have regarded him as the best and most beneficent of mortals. "Happy are the people among whom goodness requires no self-denial, and men may be just without virtue." And the fortunate solitary had one-half of goodness ready made for him. "That which renders man essentially good, is to have few wants, and seldom to compare himself with others; that which renders him essentially wicked, is to have many wants, and to be frequently governed by opinion." Rousseau, however, did not vaunt the merits of negation with absolute consistency. Elsewhere he says, "He who wants nothing will love nothing, and I can not conceive that he who loves nothing can be happy."

As Rousseau found the root of all evil in the action of man upon man, he sought to dissever his child of nature as much as possible from his fellow creatures, and to assimilate him to Robinson Crusoe. Anything like rule and obedience was abomination to Rousseau, and he confounds the wise rule of superior intelligence with the tyranny of mere caprice. He writes: "We always either do that which is pleasing to the child, or exact of him what pleases ourselves: either submitting to his humors or obliging him to submit to ours. There is no medium, he must either give orders or receive them. Hence the first ideas it acquires are those of absolute rule and servitude." The great panacea for all evils was, then, "liberty," by which Rousseau understood independence. "He only performs the actions of his own will, who stands in no need of the assistance of others to put his designs in execution: and hence it follows that the greatest of all blessings is not authority, but liberty. A man, truly free, wills only that which he can do, and does only that which pleases him. This is my fundamental maxim. It need only be applied to childhood, and all the rules of education will naturally flow from it."

"Whosoever does what he will is happy, provided he is capable of doing it himself; this is the case with man in a state of nature."

But a very obvious difficulty suggests itself. A child is necessarily the most dependent creature in the world. How, then, can he be brought up in what Rousseau calls liberty? Rousseau sees the difficulty, and all that he can say is, that as real liberty is impossible for a child, you must give him sham liberty instead. "Let him always be his own master in appearance, and do you take care to be so in reality. There is no subjection so complete as that which preserves the appearance of liberty; it is by this means even the will itself is led captive. The poor child, who knows nothing, who is capable of nothing, is surely sufficiently at your mercy. Don't you dispose, with regard to him, of everything about him? Are not you capable of affecting him just as you please? His employment, his sports, his pleasures, his pains, are they not all in your power, without his knowing it? Assuredly, he ought not to be compelled to do anything contrary to his inclinations; but then he ought not to be inclined to do anything contrary to yours: he ought not to take a step which you had not foreseen; nor open his lips to speak without your knowing what he is about to say. When you have once brought him under such regulations, you may indulge him freely in all those corporal exercises which his age requires, without running the hazard of blunting his intellects. You will then see, that instead of employing all his subtle arts to shake off a burdensome and disagreeable tyranny, he will be busied only in making the best use of everything about him. It is in this case you will have reason to be surprised at the subtility of his invention, and the ingenuity with which he makes everything that is in his power contribute to his gratification, without being obliged to prepossession or opinion. In thus leaving him at liberty to follow his own will, you will not augment his caprice. By being accustomed only to do that which is proper for his state and condition he will soon do nothing but what he ought; and though he should be in continual motion of body, yet, while he is employed only in the pursuit of his present and apparent interest, you will find his reasoning faculties display themselves better, and in a manner more peculiar to himself, than if he was engaged in studies of pure speculation."

After this astonishing passage, the reader will probably consider Rousseau's opinions of moral behavior mere matters of curiosity. Yet some of his advice is well worth considering.

Although children should be made happy, they should by no means be shielded from every possible hurt. "The first thing we ought to learn, and that which it is of the greatest consequence for us to know, is to suffer. It seems as if children were formed little and feeble to learn this important lesson without danger." "Excessive severity, as well as excessive indulgence, should be equally avoided. If you leave children to suffer, you expose their health, endanger their lives, and make them actually miserable; on the other hand, if you are too anxious to prevent their being sensible of any kind of pain and inconvenience, you only pave their way to feel much greater; you enervate their constitutions, make them tender and effeminate; in a word, you remove them out of their situation as human beings, into which they must hereafter return in spite of all your solicitude."

His advice on firmness is also good. "When the child desires what is necessary, you ought to know and immediately comply with its request: but to be induced to do anything by its tears, is to encourage it to cry; it is to teach it to doubt your good-will, and to think you are influenced more by importunity than benevolence. Beware of this, for if your child once comes to imagine you are not of a good disposition, he will soon be of a bad one; if he once thinks you complain, he will soon grow obstinate. You should comply with his request immediately if you do not intend to refuse it. Mortify him not with frequent denials, but never revoke a refusal once made him." Caprice, whether of the governor or of the child, is carefully to be shunned.

"There is an innate sense of right and wrong implanted in the human heart." In proof of this, he gives an anecdote of an infant who almost screamed to death on receiving a blow from the nurse. "I am very certain," he says, "had a burning coal fallen by accident on the hand of the child, it would have been less agitated than by this slight blow, given with a manifest intention to hurt it."

For punishments he gives a hint which has been worked out by Mr. H. Spencer. "Oppose to his indiscreet desires only physical obstacles, or *the inconveniences naturally arising from the actions themselves;* these he will remember on a future occasion."

Even in the matter of liberty, about which no one disagrees more heartily with Rousseau than I do, we may, I think, learn a lesson from him. "Emile acts from his own thoughts, and not from the dictation of others." "If your head always directs your pupil's hands, his own head will become useless to him." There is a great truth in this. While differing so far from Rousseau, that I should require the most implicit obedience from boys, I feel that we must give them a certain amount of independent action and freedom from restraint, as a means of education. In many of our private schools, a boy is hardly called upon to exercise his will all day long. He rises in the morning when he must; at meals, he eats till he is obliged to stop; he is taken out for exercise like a horse; he has all his indoor work prescribed for him, both as to time and quantity. "You accustom him to being always conducted, to being always a mere machine in the hands of others." As Montaigne quotes from Seneca, "*nunquam tutelæ suæ fiunt*" [they never become their own guardians]. Thus a boy grows up without having any occasion to think or act for himself. He is therefore without self-reliance. So much care is taken to prevent his doing wrong, that he gets to think only of checks from without. He is therefore incapable of self-restraint. Our public schools give more "liberty," and turn out better *men*.

We will now suppose the child to have reached the age of twelve, a proficient in ignorance. His education must, at this period, alter entirely. The age for learning has arrived. "Give me a child of twelve years of age who knows nothing at all, and at fifteen I will return him to you as learned as any that you may have instructed earlier; with this difference, that the knowledge of yours will be only in his memory, and that of mine will be in his judgment." "To what use is it proper a child should put that redundancy of abilities, of which he is at present possessed, and which will fail him at another age? He should employ it on those things which may be of utility in time to come. He should throw, if I may so express myself, the superfluity of his present being into the future. The robust child should provide for the subsistence of the feeble man; not in laying up his treasure in coffers whence thieve may steal, nor by intrusting it to the hands of others; but by keeping it in his own. To appropriate his acquisitions to himself he will secure them in the strength and dexterity of his own arms, and in the capacity of his own head. This, therefore, is the time for employment, for instruction, for study. Observe, also, that I have not arbitrarily fixed on this period for that purpose: nature itself plainly points it out to us.

The education of Emile was to be, to use the language of the present day, scientific, not literary. Rousseau professed a hatred of books, which he said kept the student so long engaged upon the thoughts of other people as to have no time to make a store of his own. "The abuse of reading is destructive to knowledge. Imagining ourselves to know everything we read, we conceive it unneccessary to learn it by other means. Too much reading, however, serves only to make us presumptuous blockheads. Of all the ages in which literature has flourished, reading was never so universal as in the present, nor were men in general ever so ignorant."

Even science was to be studied, not so much with a view to knowledge, as to intellectual vigor. "You will remember it is my constant maxim, not to teach the boy a multiplicity of things, but to prevent his acquiring any but clear and precise ideas. His knowing nothing does not much concern me, provided he does not deceive himself."

Again he says: "Emile has but little knowledge; but what he has is truly his own; he knows nothing by halves. Among the few things he knows, and knows *well*, the most important is, that there are many things which he is now ignorant of, and which he may one day know; that there are many more which some men know and he never will; and that there is an infinity of others which neither he nor anybody else will ever know. He possesses a universal capacity, not in point of actual knowledge, but in the faculty of acquiring it; an open, intelligent genius, adapted to everything, and, as Montaigne says, if not instructed, capable of receiving instruction. It is sufficient for me that he knows how to discover the utility of his actions, and the reason for his opinions. Once again, I say, my object is not to furnish his mind with knowledge, but to teach him the method of acquiring it when he has occasion for it; to instruct him how to hold it in estimation, and to inspire him, above all, with a love for truth. By this method, indeed, we make no great advances; but then we never take a useless step, nor are are we obliged to turn back again."

The method of learning, therefore, was to be chosen with the view of bringing out the pupil's powers: and the subjects of instruction were to be sufficiently varied to give the pupil a notion of the connection between various branches of knowledge, and to ascertain the direction in which his taste and talent would lead him.

The first thing to be aimed at is exciting a desire for knowledge. "Direct the attention of your pupil to the phenomena of nature, and you will soon awaken his curiosity; but to keep that curiosity alive, you must be in no haste to satisfy it. Put questions to him adapted to his capacity, and leave him to resolve them. He is not to know anything because you have told it to him, but because he has himself comprehended it: he should not learn, but discover science. If ever you substitute authority in the place of argument, he will reason no longer; he will be ever afterward bandied like a shuttlecock between the opinions of others." Curiosity, when aroused, should be fostered by suspense, when the tutor must, above all things, avoid what Mr. Wilson, of Rugby, has lately called "didactic teaching." I do not at all admire explanatory discourses," says Rousseau; "young people give little attention to them, and never retain them in memory. The things themselves are the best explanations. I can never enough repeat it, that we make words of too much consequence; with our prating modes of education we make nothing but praters."

The grand thing to be educed, was *self-teaching.* "Obliged to learn of himself, the pupil makes use of his own reason, and not of that of others; for to give no influence to opinion, no weight should be given to authority; and it is certain that our errors arise less from ourselves than from others. From this continual exercise of the understanding will result a vigor of mind, like that which we give the body by labor and fatigue. Another advantage is, that we advance only in proportion to our strength. The mind, like the body, carries that only which it can carry. But when the understanding appropriates everything before it commits it to the memory, whatever it afterward draws from thence is properly its own; whereas, in overcharging the mind without the knowledge of the understanding, we expose ourselves to the inconvenience of never drawing out anything which belongs to us."

Again he writes: "We acquire, without doubt, notions more clear and certain of things we thus learn of ourselves, than of those we are taught by others. Another advantage also resulting from this method is, that we do not accustom ourselves to a servile submission to the authority of others; but, by exercising our reason, grow every day more ingenious in the discovery of the relations of things, in connecting our ideas and in the contrivance of machines; whereas, by adopting those which are put into our hands, our invention grows dull and indifferent, as the man who never dresses himself, but is served in everything by his servants, and drawn about everywhere by his horses, loses by degrees the activity and use of his limbs. Boileau boasted that he had taught Racine to rhyme with difficulty. Among the many admirable methods taken to abridge the study of the sciences, we are in great want of one to make us learn them with *effort*."

Following in the steps of Locke, Rousseau required his model pupil to learn a trade. But this was not to be acquired as a mere amusement. First, Rousseau required it to secure the self-dependence of his pupil, and secondly, to improve his head, as well as his hands. "If, instead of keeping a boy poring over books, I employ him in a workshop, his hands will be busied to the improvement of his understanding; he will become a philosopher, while he thinks himself only an artisan."

I hope the quotations I have now given, will suffice to convey to the reader some of Rousseau's main ideas on the subject of education. The "Emile" was once a popular book in this country. In David Williams' Lectures (dated 1789) was read, "Rousseau is in full possession of public attention. . . . To be heard on the subject of education it is expedient to direct our observations to his works." But now the case is different. In the words of Mr. Herman Merivale, "Rousseau was dethroned with the fall of his extravagant child the Republic." Perhaps we have been less influenced by both father and child than any nation of Europe; and if so, we owe this to our horror of extravagance. The English intellect is eminently decorous,* and Rousseau's disregard for

---

* How is it that we have so many of us taken to making observations on the English mind, as if we were as external to it as the Japanese jugglers? Do we owe this to Matthew Arnold?

"appearances," or rather his evident purpose of making an impression by defying "appearances" and saying just the opposite of what is expected, simply distresses it. Hence the "Emile" has long ceased to be read in this country, and the only English translation I have met with was published in the last century, and has not been reprinted.* So Rousseau now works upon us only through his disciples, especially Pestalozzi; but the reader will see from the passages I have selected, that we have often listened to Rousseau unawares.

The truths of the "Emile" will survive the fantastic forms which are there forced upon them. Of these truths, one of the most important, to my mind, is the distinction drawn between childhood and youth. I do not, of course, insist with Rousseau, that a child should be taught nothing till the day on which he is twelve years old, and then that instruction should begin all at once. There is no hard and fast line that can be drawn between the two stages of development: the change from one to the other is gradual, and in point of time differs greatly with the individual. But as I have elsewhere said, I believe the difference between the child and the youth to be greater than the difference between the youth and the man; and I believe further, that this is far too much overlooked in our ordinary education.

---

*The above quotations are from this translation, but in correcting the proofs, I have discovered that it will not stand the test of being brought into such close contact with the French. I have altered it in many places, and am by no means satisfied with what I have left.

[A translation of the selections from the first three books by Jules Steig, published in Paris, 1880, has been made, and may be had for $1.00. The full translation referred to in the text is found in two, in three, and in four volumes, and commands from $5.00 to $10.00.]

Rousseau, by drawing attention to the sleep of reason and to the activity and vigor of the senses in childhood, became one of the most important educational reformers, and a benefactor of mankind.*

---

* This teaching of Rousseau's seems especially deserving of our consideration now that it has been proposed to elect boys of thirteen to Christ's Hospital, and to scholarships in other schools, by competitive examination. Whatever advantages may have resulted from such competition in the case of older pupils, we can not fairly assume that the system ought to be extended to children. Examinations can not test the proper development of children, or mark out the cleverest. Indeed, what they would really decide for us would be, not which were the cleverest children, but which had been entrusted to the cleverest "crammers." Thus the master would be stimulated to "ply the memory and load the brain" for their livelihood; and a race of precocious children terminating their intellectual career at the point where it ought to begin, would convince us of the wisdom of Rousseau, and drive us back to the neglected arts of being ignorant and losing time. See Mr. Arnold's vigorous protest against examinations of children, *Schools and Universities of the Continent*, chap. v., pp. 60, 61.

VII.

BASEDOW AND THE PHILANTHROPIN.

One of the most famous movements ever made in educational reform was started in the last century by John Bernard Basedow. Basedow was born at Hamburg in 1723, the son of a wigmaker. His early years were not spent in the ordinary happiness of childhood. His mother he describes as melancholy, almost to madness, and his father was severe almost to brutality. It was the father's intention to bring up his son to his own business, but the lad ran away, and engaged himself as servant to a gentleman in Holstein. The master soon perceived what had never occurred to the father, viz., that the youth had very extraordinary abilities. Sent home with a letter from his master pointing out this notable discovery, Basedow was allowed to renounce the paternal calling, and to go to the Hamburg Grammar school (*Gymnasium*), where he was under Reimarus, the author of the "Wolfenbüttel Fragment." In due course his friends managed to send him to the University of Leipzig to prepare himself for the least expensive of the learned professions—the clerical. Basedow, however, was not a man to follow the beaten tracks. After an irregular life he left the university too unorthodox to think of being ordained, and in 1749 became private tutor to the children of Herr von Quaalen, in Holstein.

In this situation his talent for inventing new methods of teaching first showed itself. He knew how to adapt himself to the capacity of the children, and he taught them much by conversation, and in the way of play, connecting his instruction with surrounding objects in the house, garden, or fields. Through Quaalen's influence, he next obtained a professorship at Soroe, in Denmark, where he lectured for eight years; but his unorthodox writings raised a storm of opposition, and the Government finally removed him to the Gymnasium at Altona. Here he still continued his efforts to change the prevailing opinion in religious matters, and so great a stir was made by the publication of his "*Philalethia,*" and his "Methodical Instruction in both Natural and Biblical Religion," that he and his family were refused the Communion at Altona, and his books were excluded, under a heavy penalty, from Lübeck.

About this time Basedow, incited by Rousseau's "*Emile,*" turned his attention to a fresh field of activity, in which he was to make as many friends as in theology he had found enemies. A very general dissatisfaction was then felt with the condition of the schools. Physical education was not attempted in them. The mother-tongue was neglected. Instruction in Latin and Greek, which was the only instruction given, was carried on in a mechanical way, without any thought of improvement. The education of the poor and of the middle classes received but little attention. "Youth," says Raumer, "was in those days, for most children, a sadly harassed period. Instruction was hard and heartlessly severe. Grammar was caned into the memory; so were portions of Scripture and poetry. A common school punishment was to learn by heart Psalm cxix. School-rooms were dismally dark. No one conceived it possible that the young could find pleasure in any kind of work, or that they had eyes for aught besides reading and writing. The pernicious age of Louis XIV. had inflicted on the poor children of the upper classes, hair curled by the barber and messed with powder and pomade, braided coats, knee breeches, silk stockings, and a dagger by the side—for active, lively children a perfect torture" (*Geschichte der Pædagogik*, ii. 297). Kant gave expression to a very wide-spread feeling when he said that what was wanting in education was no longer a reform but a revolution.

Here, then, was a good scope offered for innovators, and Basedow was a prince of innovators.

Having succeeded in interesting the Danish minister, Bernsdorf, in his plans, he was permitted to devote himself entirely to a work on the subject of education whilst retaining his income from the Altona Gymnasium. The result was, his "Address to the Philanthropists and Men of Property, on Schools and Studies, and their influence on the Public Weal," in which he announces the plan of his "Elementary."* In this address he calls upon princes, governments, town-councils, dignitaries of the Church, freemasons' lodges, etc., if they loved their fellow-creatures, to come to his assistance in bringing out his book. Nor did he call in vain. When the "Elementary" at length appeared (in 1774), he had to acknowledge contributions from the emperor Joseph II., from Catherine II. of Russia, from Christian VII. of

---

* I avail myself of the old substantival use of the word *elementary* to express its German equivalent *Elementarbuch*.

Denmark, from the Grand Prince Paul, and many other celebrities, the total sum received being over 2000*l*.

While Basedow was traveling about to get subscriptions, he spent some time in Frankfort, and thence made an excursion to Ems with two distinguished companions, one of them Lavater, and the other a young man of five-and-twenty, already celebrated as the author of "*Gœtz von Berlichingen*," and the "Sorrows of Werther." Of Basedow's personal peculiarities at this time, Gœthe has left us an amusing description in the "*Wahrheit und Dichtung*"; but we must accept the portrait with caution: the sketch was thrown in as an artistic contrast with that of Lavater, and no doubt exaggerates those features in which the antithesis could be brought out with best effect.

"One could not see," writes Gœthe, "a more marked contrast than between Lavater and Basedow. As the lines of Lavater's countenance were free and open to the beholder, so were Basedow's contracted, and as it were drawn inward. Lavater's eye clear and benign, under a very wide eyelid; Basedow's on the other hand, deep in his head, small, black, sharp, gleaming out from under shaggy eyebrows, whilst Lavater's frontal bone seemed bounded by two arches of the softest brown hair. Basedow's impetuous rough voice, his rapid and sharp utterances, a certain derisive laugh, an abrupt changing of the topic of conversation, and whatever else distinguished him, all were opposed to the peculiarities and the behavior by which Lavater had been making us overfastidious."

Gœthe approved of Basedow's desire to make all instruction lively and natural, and thought that his system would promote mental activity and give the young a fresher view of the world: but he finds fault with the "Elementary," and prefers the "*Orbis Pictus*" of Comenius, in which subjects are presented in their natural connection. Basedow himself, says Gœthe, was not a man either to edify or to lead other people. Although the object of his journey was to interest the public in his philanthropic enterprise, and to open not only hearts but purses, and he was able to speak eloquently and convincingly on the subject of education, he spoilt everything by his tirades against prevalent religious belief, especially on the subject of the Trinity.

Gœthe found in Basedow's society an opportunity of "exercising, if not enlightening," his mind, so he bore with his personal peculiarities, though apparently with great difficulty. Basedow seems to have delighted in worrying his associates. "He would never see any one quiet but he provoked him with mocking irony, in a hoarse voice, or put him to confusion by an unexpected question, and laughed bitterly when he had gained his end; yet he was pleased when the object of his jests was quick enough to collect himself, and answer in the same strain." So far Gœthe was his match, but he was nearly routed by Basedow's use of bad tobacco, and of some tinder still worse with which he was constantly lighting his pipe and poisoning the air insufferably. He soon discovered Gœthe's dislike to this preparation of his, so he took a malicious pleasure in using it and dilating upon its merits.

Here is an odd account of their intercourse. During their stay at Ems, Gœthe went a great deal into fashionable society. "To make up for these dissipations," he writes, "I always passed a part of the night with Basedow. He never went to bed, but dictated without cessation. Occasionally he cast himself on the couch and slumbered, while his amanuensis sat quietly, pen in hand, ready to continue his work when the half-awakened author should once more give free course to his thoughts. All this took place in a close confined chamber, filled with the fumes of tobacco and the odious tinder. As often as I was disengaged from a dance I hastened up to Basedow, who was ready at once to speak and dispute on any question; and when after a time I hurried again to the ball-room, before I had closed the door behind me he would resume the thread of his essay as composedly as if he had been engaged with nothing else."

It was through a friend of Gœthe's, Behrisch, whose acquaintance we make in the "*Wahrheit und Dichtung*," that Basedow became connected with Prince Leopold of Dessau. Behrisch was tutor to the Prince's son, and by him the Prince was so interested in Basedow's plans that he determined to found an Institute in which they should be realized. Basedow was therefore called to Dessau, and under his direction was opened the famous Philanthropin. Then for the first, and probably for the last time, a school was started in which use and wont were entirely set aside, and everything done on "improved principles." Such a bold enterprise attracted the attention of all interested in education, far and near: but it would seem that few parents considered their own children *vilia corpora* [cheap material] on whom experiments might be made for the public good. When, in May, 1776, a number of schoolmasters and others collected from different parts of Germany, and even from beyond

Germany, to be present by Basedow's invitation at an examination of the children, they found only thirteen pupils in the Philanthropin, including Basedow's own son and daughter.

Before we investigate how Basedow's principles were embodied in the Philanthropin, let us see the form in which he had already announced them. The great work from which all children were to be taught was the "Elementary." As a companion to this was published the "Book of Method" (*Methoden-buch*) for parents and teachers. The "Elementary" is a work in which a great deal of information about things in general is given in the form of dialogue, interspersed with tales and easy poetry. Except in bulk, it does not seem to me to differ very materially from many of the reading books which, in late years, have been published in this country. It had the advantage, however, of being accompanied by a set of engravings to which the text referred, though they were too large to be bound up with it. The root-ideas of Basedow put forth in his "Book of Method," and other writings, are those of Rousseau. For example, "You should attend to nature in your children far more than to art. The elegant manners and usages of the world are for the most part unnatural (*Unnatur*). These come of themselves in later years. Treat children like children, that they may remain the longer uncorrupted. A boy whose acutest faculties are his senses, and who has no perception of anything abstract, must first of all be made acquainted with the world as it presents itself to the senses. Let this be shown him in nature itself, or where this is impossible, in faithful drawings or models. Thereby can he, even in play, learn how the various objects are to be named. Comenius alone has pointed out the right road in this matter. By all means reduce the wretched exercises of the memory." Elsewhere he gives instances of the sort of things to which this method should be applied. 1st. Man. Here he would use pictures of foreigners and wild men; also a skeleton, a hand in spirits, and other objects still more appropriate to a surgical museum. 2d. Animals. Only such animals are to be depicted as it is useful to know about, because there is much that ought to be known, and a good method of instruction must shorten rather than increase the hours of study. Articles of commerce made from the animals may also be exhibited. 3d. Trees and plants. Only the most important are to be selected. Of these the seeds also must be shown, and cubes formed of the different woods. Gardeners' and farmers' implements are to be explained. 4th. Minerals and chemical substances. 5th. Mathematical instruments for weighing and measuring; also the air-pump, siphon, and the like. The form and motion of the earth are to be explained with globes and maps. 6th. Trades. The use of various tools is to be taught. 7th. History. This is to be illustrated by engravings of historical events. 8th. Commerce. Samples of commodities may be produced. 9th. The younger children should be shown pictures of familiar objects about the house and its surroundings.

We see from this list that Basedow contemplated giving his educational course the charm of variety. Indeed, with that candor in acknowledging mistakes which partly makes amends for the effrontery too common in the trumpetings of his own performances, past, present, and to come, he confesses that when he began the "Elementary" he had exaggerated notions of the amount boys were capable of learning, and that he had subsequently very much contracted his proposed curriculum. And even the "Revolution," which was to introduce so much new learning into the schools, could not afford entirely to neglect the old. However pleased parents might be with the novel acquirements of their children, they were not likely to be satisfied without the usual knowledge of Latin, and still less would they tolerate the neglect of French, which, in German polite society of the eighteenth century, was the recognized substitute for the vulgar tongue. These, then, must be taught. But the old methods might be abandoned, if not the old subjects. Basedow proposed to teach both French and Latin by *conversation.* Let a cabinet of models, or something of the kind, be shown the children; let them learn the names of the different objects in Latin or French; then let questions be asked in those languages, and the right answers at first put into the children's mouths. When they have in this way acquired some knowledge of the language, they may apply it to the translating of an easy book. Basedow does not claim originality for the conversational method. He appeals to the success with which it had been already used in teaching French. "Are the French governesses," he asks, "who without vocabularies and grammars, first by conversation, then by reading, teach their language very successfully and very rapidly in schools of from thirty to forty children, better teachers than most masters in our Latin schools?"

On the subject of religion the instruction was to be quite as original as in matters of less importance. The teachers were to give an impartial account of all religions, and nothing but "natural religion" was to be inculcated.

The key-note of the whole system was to be—*everything according to nature.* The natural desires and inclinations of the children were to be educated and directed aright, but in no case to be suppressed.

These, then, were the principles and the methods which, as Basedow believed, were to revolutionize education through the success of the Philanthropin. Basedow himself, as we might infer from Gœthe's description of him, was by no means a model director for the model Institution, but he was fortunate in his assistants. Of these he had three at the time of the public examination, of whom Wolke is said to have been the ablest.

A lively description of the examination was afterward published by Herr Schummel of Magdeburg, under the title of "Fred's Journey to Dessau." It purports to be written by a boy of twelve years old, and to describe what took place without attempting criticism. A few extracts will give a notion of the instruction carried on in the Philanthropin.

"I have just come from a visit with my father to the Philanthropin, where I saw Herr Basedow, Herr Wolke, Herr Simon, Herr Schweighæuser, and the little Philanthropinists. I am delighted with all that I have seen, and hardly know where to begin my description of it. There are two large white houses, and near them a field with trees. A pupil—not one of the regular scholars, but of those they call Famulants (a poorer class, who were servitors)—received us at the door, and asked if we wished to see Herr Basedow. We said 'Yes,' and he took us into the other house, where we found Herr Basedow in a dressing-gown, writing at a desk. We came at an inconvenient time, and Herr Basedow said he was very busy. He was very friendly, however, and promised to visit us in the evening. We went into the other house, and inquired for Herr Wolke." By him we were taken to the scholars. "They have," says Fred, "their hair cut very short, and no wig-maker is employed. Their throats are quite open, and their shirt-collar falls back over their coats." Further on he describes the examination. "The little ones have gone through the oddest performances. They play at 'word-of-command.' Eight or ten stand in line like soldiers, and Herr Wolke is officer. He gives the word in Latin, and they must do whatever he says. For instance, when he says *Claudite oculos*, they all shut their eyes; when he says *Circumspicite*, they look about them; *Imitamini sartorem* [Imitate the tailor], they all sew like tailors; *Imitamini sutorem* [Imitate the cobbler], they draw the waxed thread like the cobblers. Herr Wolke gave a thousand different commands in the drollest fashion. Another game 'the hiding game,' I will also teach you. Some one writes a name, and hides it from the children—the name of some part of the body, or of a plant, or animal, or metal—and the children guess what it is. Whoever guesses right gets an apple or a piece of cake. One of the visitors wrote *Intestina* [The intestines], and told the children it was a part of the body. Then the guessing began. One guessed *caput* [head], another *nasus* [nose], another *os* [mouth], another *manus* [hand], *pes* [foot], *digiti* [fingers], *pectus* [breast], and so forth, for a long time; but one of them hit it at last. Next, Herr Wolke wrote the name of a beast, a quadruped. Then came the guesses: *leo* [lion], *ursus* [bear], *camelus* [camel], *elephas* [elephant], and so on, till one guessed right—it was *mus* [mouse]. Then a town was written, and they guessed Lisbon, Madrid, Paris, London, till a child won with St. Petersburg. They have another game which is this: Herr Wolke gave the command in Latin, and they imitated the noises of different animals, and made us laugh till we were tired. They roared like lions, crowed like cocks, mewed like cats, just as they were bid."

The subject that was next handled had also the effect of making the strangers laugh, till a severe reproof from Herr Wolke restored their gravity. A picture was brought, in which was represented a sad-looking woman, whose person indicated the approaching arrival of another subject for education. From one part of the picture it also appeared that the prospective mother, with a prodigality of forethought, had got ready clothing for both a boy and a girl. After a warning from Herr Wolke, that this was a most serious and important subject, the children were questioned on the topics the picture suggested. They were further taught the debt of gratitude they owed to their mothers, and the German fiction about the stork dismissed with due contempt.

Next came the examination in arithmetic. Here there seems to have been nothing remarkable, except that all the rules were worked *viva voce* [aloud]. From the arithmetic Herr Wolke went on to an "Attempt at various small drawings." He asked the children what he should draw. Some one answered *leonem*. He then pretended he was drawing a lion, but put a beak to it; whereupon the children shouted *Non est leo—leones non* *habent rostrum,* [It isn't a lion—lions have no beak]! He went on to other subjects, as the children directed him, sometimes going wrong that the children might put him right.* In the next exercise dice were introduced, and the children threw to see who should give an account of an engraving. The engravings represented workmen at their different trades, and the child had to explain the process, the tools, etc. A lesson on plowing and harrowing was given in French, and another, on Alexander's expedition to India, in Latin. Four of the pupils translated passages from Curtius and from Castellion's Bible, which were read to them. "These children," said the teacher, "knew not a word of Latin a year ago." "The listeners were well pleased with the Latin," writes Fred, "except two or three, whom I heard grumbling that this was all child's play, and that if Cicero, Livy, and Horace were introduced, it would soon be seen what was the value of Philanthropinist Latin." After the examination two comedies were acted by the children, one in French, the other in German.

Most of the strangers seem to have left Dessau with a favorable impression of the Philanthropin. They were especially struck with the brightness and animation of the children.

How far did the Philanthropin really deserve their good opinion? The conclusion to which we are driven by Fred's narrative is, that Basedow carried to excess his principle—"treat children as children, that they may

---

* As an amusing specimen of the taste of the time, I may mention, that when in drawing a house Herr Wolke put the door not quite in the middle, the children insisted on having another door to correspond *propter symmetriam* [for the sake of symmetry].

remain the longer uncorrupted;" and that the Philanthropin was, in fact, nothing but a good infant-school. Surely none of the thirteen children who were the subjects of Basedow's experiments could have been more than ten years old. But if we consider Basedow's system to have been intended for *children*, say between the ages of six and ten, we must allow that it possessed great merits. At the very beginning of a boy's learning, it has always been too much the custom to make him hate the sight of a book, and escape at every opportunity from school-work, by giving him difficult tasks, and neglecting his acutest faculties. "Children love motion and noise," says Basedow: "here is a hint from nature." Yet the youngest children in most schools are expected to keep quiet and to sit at their books for as many hours as the youths of seventeen or eighteen. Their vivacity is repressed with the cane. Their delight in exercising their hands and eyes and ears is taken no notice of; and they are required to keep their attention fixed on subjects often beyond their comprehension, and almost always beyond the range of their interests. Every one who has had experience in teaching boys knows how hard it is to get them to throw themselves heartily into any task whatever; and probably this difficulty arises in many cases, from the habits of inattention and of shirking school-work which the boys have acquired almost necessarily from the dreariness of their earliest lessons. Basedow determined to change all this; and in the Philanthropin no doubt he succeeded. We have already seen some of the expedients by which he sought to render school-work pleasurable. He appealed, wherever it was possible, to the children's senses; and these, especially the sight, were trained with great care by exercises, such as drawing, shooting at a mark, etc. One of these exercises, intended to give quick perception, bears a curious likeness to what has since been practiced in a very different educational system. A picture, with a somewhat varied subject, was exhibited for a short time and removed. The boys had then, either verbally or on paper, to give an account of it, naming the different objects in proper order. Houdin, if I rightly remember, tells us that the young thieves of Paris are required by their masters to make a mental inventory of the contents of a shop window, which they see only as they walk rapidly by. Other exercises of the Philanthropin connected the pupils with more honorable callings. They became acquainted with both skilled and unskilled manual labor. Every boy was taught a handicraft, such as carpentering and turning, and was put to such tasks as threshing corn. Basedow's division of the twenty-four hours was the following: Eight hours for sleep, eight for food and amusement, and, for the children of the rich, six hours of school-work, and two of manual labor. In the case of the children of the poor, he would have the division of the last eight hours inverted, and would give for school-work two, and for manual labor six. The development of the body was specially cared for in the Philanthropin. Gymnastics were now first introduced into modern schools; and the boys were taken long expeditions on foot—the commencement, I believe, of a practice now common throughout Germany.

As I have already said, Basedow proved a very unfit person to be at the head of the model Institution.

Many of his friends agreed with Herder, that he was not fit to have calves intrusted to him, much less children. He soon resigned his post; and was succeeded by Campe, who had been one of the visitors at the public examination. Campe did not remain long at the Philanthropin; but left it to set up a school, on like principles, at Hamburg. His fame now rests on his writings for the young, one of which—"Robinson Crusoe the Younger"—is still a general favorite.

Other distinguished men became connected with the Philanthropin—among them Salzman, and Matthison the poet—and the number of pupils rose to over fifty; gathered, we are told, from all parts of Europe between Riga and Lisbon. But this number is by no means a fair measure of the interest, nay, enthusiasm which the experiment excited. We find Pastor Oberlin raising money on his wife's ear-rings to send a donation. We find the philosopher Kant prophesying that quite another race of men would grow up, now that education, according to Nature, had been introduced.

These hopes were disappointed. Kant confesses as much in the following passage in his treatise "On Pedagogy:"

"One fancies, indeed, that experiments in education would not be necessary; and that we might judge by the understanding whether any plan would turn out well or ill. But this is a great mistake. Experience shows that often in our experiments we get quite opposite results from what we had anticipated. We see, too, that since experiments are necessary, it is not in the power of one generation to form a complete plan of education. The only experimental school which, to some extent, made a beginning in clearing the road, was the Institute at Dessau. This praise at least must be allowed it, notwithstanding the many faults which could be brought up against it—faults which are sure to show themselves when we come to the results of our experiments, and which merely prove that fresh experiments are necessary. It was the only school in which the teachers had liberty to work according to their own methods and schemes, and where they were in free communication both among themselves and with all learned men throughout Germany."

We observe here, that Kant speaks of the Philanthropin as a thing of the past. It was finally closed in 1793. But even from Kant we learn that the experiment had been by no means a useless one. The conservatives, of course, did not neglect to point out that young Philanthropinists, when they left school, were not in all respects the superiors of their fellow-creatures. But, although no one could pretend that the Philanthropin had effected a tithe of what Basedow promised, and the "friends of humanity" throughout Europe expected, it had introduced many new ideas, which in time had their influence, even in the schools of the opposite party. Moreover, teachers who had been connected with the Philanthropin, founded schools on similar principles in different parts of Germany and Switzerland, some of which long outlived the parent institution. Their doctrines, too, made converts among other masters, the most celebrated of whom was Meierotto of Berlin.

Little remains to be said of Basedow. He lived chiefly at Dessau, earning his subsistence by private tuition, and giving great offense by his irregularities, especially by drinking. In 1790, when visiting Magdeburg, he died, after a short illness, in his sixty-seventh year. His last words were, "I wish my body to be dissected for the good of my fellow-creatures."

VIII.

PESTALOZZI.

John Henry Pestalozzi, the most celebrated of educational reformers, was born at Zurich, in 1746. At six years old he lost his father, who, leaving his family in needy circumstances, implored his servant, "the faithful Bäbeli, never to desert his wife and children. Bäbeli kept sacredly the promise she gave to the dying man, and she had an equal share with the mother in bringing up the great educator.

With no companions of his own age, Pestalozzi became so completely a mother's child, that, as he himself tells us, he grew up a stranger to the world he lived in. This lonely childhood had its influence in making him, what he remained through life, a man of excitable feelings and lively imagination, which so entirely had the mastery over him as to prevent anything like due circumspection and forethought.*

From his grandfather, a country clergyman, with whom he often stayed, he received another important influence, strong religious impressions.

---

*This will be best understood from the following anecdote. When, in after years, he was in great pecuniary distress, and his family were without the necessaries of life, he went to a friend's house and borrowed a sum of money. On his way home, he fell in with a peasant who was lamenting the loss of a cow. Carried away as usual by his feelings, Pestalozzi gave the man all the money he had borrowed, and ran away to escape his thanks.

When at length he was sent to a day-school, he proved the awkwardest and most helpless of the scholars, and nevertheless showed signs of rare abilities. Among his playmates he was exposed to a good deal of ridicule, and was dubbed by them Harry Oddity of Foolborough, but his good nature and obliging disposition gained him many friends. No doubt his friends profited from his willingness to do anything for them. We find that when, on the shock of an earthquake, teachers and scholars alike rushed out of the school-house, Harry Oddity was the boy sent back to fetch out caps and books. In school-work, he says that though one of the best boys in the school, he often made mistakes which even the worst boys were not guilty of. He could understand the sense of what he was taught, and content with this, he neglected the form and the exercises necessary to give him a practical acquaintance with the subject.

As he grew up, the unpractical side of his character was more and more strongly developed. To use his own words, " Unfortunately, the tone of public instruction in my native town at this period was in a high degree calculated to foster this visionary fancy of taking an active interest in, and believing oneself capable of, the practice of things in which one had by no means sufficient exercise. While we were yet boys, we fancied that by a superficial school-acquaintance with the great civil life of Greece and Rome, we could eminently prepare ourselves for the little civil life in one of the Swiss cantons. By the writings of Rousseau this tendency was increased —a tendency which was calculated neither to preserve what was good in the old institutions, nor to introduce anything substantially better."

Lavater, when a young man of twenty, formed a league which was joined by Pestalozzi, a lad of fifteen. This league brought a public charge of injustice against Grebel, the governor of the Canton, and against Brunner, the mayor of Zurich. They also declared themselves against unworthy ministers of religion. "The hate of wrong and love of right," were, with Pestalozzi, not as we so often find them, mere juvenile enthusiasms, but they remained with him for life. The oppression of the peasants moved him to a strong antagonism against the aristocracy, and when he was no longer young, he spoke of them as men on stilts, who must descend among the people before they could secure a natural and firm position. He also satirizes them in some of his fables, as, e. g., that of the "Fishes and the Pikes." "The fishes in a pond brought an accusation against the pikes who were making great ravages among them. The judge, an old pike, said that their complaint was well founded, and that the defendants, to make amends, should allow two ordinary fish every year to become pikes."

His desire to be the champion of the ill-used peasantry, determined him in the choice of a profession, and he took to the study of the law. He had been intended for a clergyman, and, according to one account, had actually preached a trial sermon, which was a failure: with his usual inaccuracy, he even went wrong in repeating the Lord's prayer.

Whilst a law student, he lost his most intimate friend, Bluntschli, who died of consumption. Bluntschli showed that he thoroughly understood Pestalozzi's character by his parting advice to him: "I die," said he, "and when you are left to yourself, you must not plunge into any career which, from your good natured and confiding dispositition, might become dangerous to you. Seek for a quiet, tranquil career; and unless you have at your side a man who will faithfully assist you with a calm, dispassionate knowledge of men and things, by no means embark in any extensive undertaking the failure of which would in any way be perilous to you."

Soon after this, Pestalozzi, from over-study, or rather perhaps from over-speculation—for he employed himself rather in forming theories of what should be than in acquiring a practical acquantance with the law as it was—became dangerously ill. The doctor advised him to go into the country, and, influenced not more by this advice than by Rousseau's doctrine of the natural state, Pestalozzi renounced the study of books, burnt his MSS., and went to learn farming.

In his new employment he found himself with a friend of progress. "I had come to him," says Pestalozzi, "a political visionary, though with many profound and correct attainments, views, and anticipations in political matters. I went away from him just as great an agricultural visionary, though with many enlarged and correct ideas and intentions with regard to agriculture."

A rich Zurich firm was persuaded by Pestalozzi that the cultivation of madder would succeed on some poor land which was to be sold near the village of Birr at a very small price. With money advanced by them, he bought the land, built a house, which he called *Neuhof* (New Farm), and set to work. This was in 1767, when he was only just of age. He was of course, in love, and the lady belonged to a rich family. The following letter, which he addressed to her, has a double interest;

it gives us an insight into the noble character, as well as the weaknesses, of the writer, and is, moreover, one of the most singular love-letters in existence.

After telling her that he felt it his duty to limit his visits to her, as he had not the slightest ability to conceal his feelings, he proposed a correspondence, in which " we shall make our undisguised thoughts known to each other with all the freedom of oral conversation. Yes," he continues, " I will open myself fully and freely to you; I will even now, with the greatest candor, let you look as deep into my heart as I am myself able to penetrate; I will show you my views in the light of my present and future condition, as clearly as I see them myself. Dearest Schultheiss, those of my faults which appear to me most important in relation to the situation in which I may be placed in after-life are, improvidence, incautiousness, and a want of presence of mind to meet unexpected changes in my prospects. I know not how far these failings may be diminished by my efforts to counteract them by calm judgment and experience. At present, I have them still in such a degree that I dare not conceal them from the maiden I love; they are faults, my dear, which deserve your fullest consideration. I have other faults, arising from my irritability and sensitiveness, which oftentimes will not submit to my judgment. I very frequently allow myself to run into excesses in praising and blaming, in my liking and disliking; I cleave so strongly to many things which I possess that the force with which I feel myself attached to them often exceeds the bounds of reason. Whenever my country or my friend is unhappy, I am myself unhappy. Direct your attention to this weakness. There will be times when the cheerfulness and tranquillity of my soul will suffer under it. If even it does not hinder me in the discharge of my duties, yet I shall scarcely ever be great enough to fulfill them in such adverse circumstances with the cheerfulness and tranquillity of a wise man who is ever true to himself. Of my great, and indeed very reprehensible, negligence in all matters of etiquette, and generally in all matters which are not in themselves of importance, I need not speak; any one may see them at first sight of me. I also owe you the open confession, my dear, that I shall always consider my duties toward my beloved partner subordinate to my duties toward my country; and that, although I shall be the tenderest husband, nevertheless I shall hold myself bound to be inexorable to the tears of my wife if she should ever attempt to restrain me by them from the direct performance of my duties as a citizen, whatever this must lead to. My wife shall be the confidante of my heart, the partner of all my most secret counsels. A great and honest simplicity shall reign in my house. And one thing more. My life will not pass without important and very critical undertakings. I shall not forget the precepts of Menalk, and my first resolutions to devote myself wholly to my country. I shall never, from fear of man, refrain from speaking when I see that the good of my country calls upon me to speak. My whole heart is my country's; I will risk all to alleviate the need and misery of my fellow-countrymen. What consequences may the undertakings to which I feel myself urged on draw after them! how unequal to them am I! and how imperative is my duty to show you the possi-

J

bility of the great dangers which they may bring upon me!

"My dear, my beloved friend, I have now spoken candidly of my character and my aspirations. Reflect upon everything. If the traits which it was my duty to mention diminish your respect for me, you will still esteem my sincerity, and you will not think less highly of me, that I did not take advantage of your want of acquaintance with my character for the attainment of my inmost wishes."

The young lady addressed was worthy of the letter and of its writer. In 1769, two years after Pestalozzi had established himself at Neuhof, the marriage took place—an unequal match, as it then seemed, the bride having money and personal attractions, and the bridegroom being notably deficient in both respects. Their married life extended over fifty years, and during that period the forebodings of the letter were amply realized. Pestalozzi sacrificed the comfort and worldly prospects of his family equally with his own to the public good, and yet we may well believe that Madame Pestalozzi never repented of her choice.

The new married couple were soon in difficulties. The Zurich firm, not satisfied with the rumors which reached them of the management of the madder plantation, sent two competent judges to examine into the state of affairs, and so unfavorable was their report, that the firm preferred getting back what money they could to leaving it any longer in Pestalozzi's hands "The cause of the failure of my undertaking," says Pestalozzi, "lay essentially and exclusively in myself, and in my pronounced incapacity for every kind of undertaking which requires practical ability." By means of his wife's property, however, he was enabled to go on with his farming.

Pestalozzi now resolved on an experiment such as Bluntschli had warned him against, and such as he himself must have had in his mind when he wrote his love-letter. Some years before this, he had had his attention drawn to the subject of education by the publication of Rousseau's "*Emile*." Feeling deeply the degradation of the surrounding peasantry, he looked for some means of raising them out of it, and it seemed to him, that the most hopeful way was to begin with the young, and to train them to capacity and intelligence. He therefore, in 1775, started a poor school. He soon had fifty children sent him, whom he housed, boarded, and clothed, without payment from the parents. The children were to work for their maintenance, during the summer in the fields, and in the winter at spinning, and other handicrafts. Pestalozzi himself was the schoolmaster, Neuhof was the schoolhouse.

In this new enterprise Pestalozzi was still more unsuccessful than he had been in growing the madder. He was very badly treated both by parents and children, the latter often running away directly they got new clothes; and his industrial experiments were so carried on that they were a source of expense rather than profit. He says himself, that, contrary to his own principles, which should have led him to begin at the beginning and lay a good foundation in teaching, he put the children to work that was too difficult for them, wanted them to spin fine thread before their hands got steadiness and skill by exercise on the coarser kind, and to manufacture muslin before they could turn out well-made cotton goods. "Before I was aware of it," he adds, "I was deeply involved in debt, and the greater part of my dear wife's property and expectations had, as it were, in an instant gone up in smoke."

We have now come to the most gloomy period in Pestalozzi's history, a period of eighteen years, and those the best years in a man's life, which Pestalozzi spent in great distress, from poverty without, and doubt and despondency within. When he got into difficulties, his friends, he tells us, loved him without hope: "in the whole surrounding district it was everywhere said that I was a lost man, that nothing more could be done for me." "In his only too elegant country-house," we are told, "he often wanted money, bread, fuel, to protect himself against hunger and cold." "Eighteen years! —what a time for a soul like his to wait! History passes lightly over such a period. Ten, twenty, thirty years— it makes but a cipher difference if nothing great happens in them. But with what agony must he have seen day after day, year after year gliding by, who in his fervent soul longed to labor for the good of mankind and yet looked in vain for the opportunity!" (Palmer.)

In after years he thus wrote of this gloomy period: "Deep dissatisfaction was gnawing my heart. Eternal truth and eternal rectitude were converted by my passion to airy castles. With a hardened mind, I clung stubbornly to mere sounds, which had lost within me the basis of truth. Thus I degraded myself every day more and more with the worship of commonplace and the trumpetings of those quackeries, wherewith these modern times pretend to better the condition of mankind." Again, he says, "My head was gray, yet I was still a child. With a heart in which all the foundations of life were shaken, I still pursued, in those stormy times, my favorite object, but my way was one of prejudice, of passion, and of error."

But these years were not spent in idleness. Having no other means of influence, and indeed no other employment, he took to writing, and his experience as a teacher stood him in good stead as an author. In 1780 appeared, though not as a separate publication, the "Evening Hour of a Hermit." To this series of aphorisms Pestalozzi appealed many years afterward to prove that he had always held the same views which he subsequently tried to carry out in practice."*

We hardly know how to reconcile the calm faith which is shown in the "Evening Hour" with what Pestalozzi has told us of his frame of mind at this period, and with the fact that he joined a French revolutionary society— the Illuminati—and became their leader in Switzerland. He did not, however, continue long with them; and there is no difficulty in reconciling the "Evening Hour" with all that we know of Pestalozzi in later life.

In 1781 appeared the book on which Pestalozzi's fame as an author mainly rests—"Leonard and Gertrude"— a work extorted from him, as he says, by sympathy with the sufferings of the people. In this simple tale—which "flowed from his pen, he knew not how, and developed itself of its own accord"—we have an admirable picture of village life in Switzerland. No wonder that the

---

* [For translated extracts, see Barnard's *Journal of Education*, vi. 169.]

Berne Agricultural Society sent the author a gold medal, with a letter of thanks; and that the book excited vast interest, both in its native country and throughout Germany. It is only strange that "Leonard and Gertrude" has not become a favorite, by means of translations, in other countries. There was, indeed, an English translation, in two volumes, published more than fifty years ago; but this forerunner of the tales of Gotthelf is now hardly known in this country, even by name.* In the works of a great artist, we see natural objects represented with perfect fidelity, and yet with a life breathed into them by genius which is wanting, or at least is not visible to common eyes, in the originals. Just so do we find Swiss peasant life depicted by Pestalozzi. The delineation is evidently true to nature; and, at the same time, shows Nature as she reveals herself to genius. But for this work something more than genius was necessary, viz., sympathy and love. In the preface to the first edition, he says, "In that which I here relate, and which I have, for the most part, seen and heard myself in the course of an active life, I have taken care not once to add my own opinion to what I saw and heard the people themselves saying, feeling, believing, judging, and attempting." In a later edition (1800) he says, "I desired nothing then, and I desire nothing else now, as the object of my life, but the welfare of the people, whom I love, and whom I feel to be miserable as few

---

*[A translation of the original book was published in Barnard's *Journal of Education*, vii. 521-648. This was about one-fourth of the whole work as subsequently enlarged. The rest of this volume of the *Journal* is given to other extracts from Pestalozzi's works, and to remarks upon his teaching. An abridged translation of *Leonard and Gertrude* was published in Boston in 1885.]

feel them to be miserable, because I have with them borne their sufferings as few have borne them."

Pestalozzi's friends now came to the conclusion that he had found his vocation at last, and that it was novel-writing; but, throughout Europe he met with many more discriminating readers.

During his residence at Neuhof where he continued to drag on a weary and depressed existence till he had been there, altogether, thirty years, he published several works, none of which had the success of "Leonard and Gertrude." In 1782 appeared "Christopher and Alice,"* and in 1795 some fables, which he called "Figures to my A B C Book." But the work which gave its author most trouble to compose, on which, he says, he labored for three long years with incredible toil, and which when it did appear, was doomed to the most complete neglect, was his "Researches into the Course of Nature in the Development of the Human Race."

The consequences of the French Revolution called Pestalozzi from his philosophical speculations. French troops poured into Switzerland. Everything was remodeled after the French pattern. The government was placed in the hands of five Directors, according to the phase which the supreme power had then (1798) taken in the model country. Pestalozzi avowed himself the champion of the new order of things, and his pen was at once employed by the Directors. These men had not, however, the discernment of Lavater, who once told Madame Pestalozzi, "I would consult your husband in everything connected with the condition of the people,

---

[* Translated extracts are given in Barnard's *Journal of Education*, vii. 665.]

though I would never intrust him with a farthing of money." By the Directors, Pestalozzi was not consulted at all. "I wished for nothing," he said, "but that the sources of the savage and degraded state of the people might be stopped, and the evils flowing from them arrested. The *Novi Homines* [new men] of Helvetia, whose wishes went further, and who had no knowledge of the condition of the people, found, of course, that I was not the man for them. They took every straw for a mast, by which they might sail the Republic to a safe shore; but me, me alone, they took for a straw not fit for a fly to cling to. They did me good, however—more good than any men have ever done me—they restored me to myself." It was thought that he had espoused their cause to secure for himself some Government appointment, and the Directors asked him what he would be. His answer was, "I will be a schoolmaster"—an answer which probably confirmed his friends in the opinion they had before expressed, that he would end his days either in the poor-house or the mad-house.

Among the directors was LeGrand, who entered into Pestalozzi's views, and at once placed at his disposal the means of opening a school in Aargau: but events occurred which led him to another sphere of labor, and caused him to undertake a much more difficult task. The Catholic and democratic canton of Unterwalden did not accept the changes which the French introduced. It was consequently invaded by a French army, many of the inhabitants were killed, and Stanz, the capital, was pillaged and burnt. These strong measures of their allies were in secret disapproved of by the Swiss Directors, who were, therefore, anxious to do what they could to relieve the sufferings of their fellow-countrymen. Le Grand proposed to Pestalozzi to give up his other plans for the present, and to go to Stanz and take charge of the orphan and destitute children there. Pestalozzi was not the man to refuse such a task as this. "I went," he writes. "I would have gone into the remotest clefts of the mountains to come nearer my aim, and now I really did come nearer."

He established himself with no assistants, and with only one servant, in a convent which was building for the Ursulines. There was but one room fit for occupation when he arrived. Children came flocking in, many of whom were orphans, and could not be otherwise provided for. The one room became a school-room and a dormitory for Pestalozzi and as many children as it would hold. There were soon eighty under Pestalozzi's charge during the day, some of the neighbors taking in children to sleep. Of the eighty, many were beggar children, not accustomed to any control, vicious in their habits, and afflicted with loathsome diseases. Those who had been better off were helpless and exacting. And for all these, Pestalozzi, then over fifty years of age, undertook the management, the clothing, feeding, teaching, and even the performance of the most menial offices. The parents, who looked upon him as the paid official of a hated government, and, moreover, distrusted him as a Protestant, annoyed him in every way they could, and encouraged the children in disorder and discontent. And yet the Protestant was giving an example of love and self-sacrifice worthy of the noblest saint in the Calendar. This love did not lose its reward. By degrees it gained him the affection of the children, and introduced harmony and order into the chaos which at first surrounded him.

The very disadvantages in which he was placed drove him to discoveries he would never otherwise have made. His whole school apparatus consisted of himself and his pupils; so he studied the children themselves, their wants and capacities. "I stood in the midst of them," he says, "pronouncing various sounds, and asking the children to imitate them. Whoever saw it was struck with the effect. It is true it was like a meteor which vanishes in the air as soon as it appears. No one understood its nature. I did not understand it myself. It was the result of a simple idea, or rather, of a fact of human nature, which was revealed to my feelings, but of which I was far from having a clear consciousness." Again he says, "Being obliged to instruct the children by myself, without any assistance, I learnt the art of teaching a great number together; and as I had no other means of bringing the instruction before them than that of pronouncing everything to them loudly and distinctly, I was naturally led to the idea of making them draw, write, or work all at the same time.

"The confusion of so many voices repeating my words suggested the necessity of keeping time in our exercises, and I soon found that this contributed materially to make their impressions stronger and more distinct. Their total ignorance forced me to dwell a long time on the simplest elements, and I was thus led to perceive how much higher a degree of interest and power is obtained by a persevering attention to the elementary parts until they be perfectly familiar to the mind; and what confidence and interest the child is inspired with by the consciousness of complete and perfect attainment, even in the lowest stage of instruction. Never before had I so deeply felt the important bearing which the first elements of every branch of knowledge have upon its complete outline, and what immense deficiencies in the final result of it must arise from the confusion and imperfection of the simplest beginnings. To bring these to maturity and perfection in the child's mind became now a main object of my attention; and the success far surpassed my expectations. The consciousness of energies hitherto unknown to themselves was rapidly developed in the children, and a general sense of order and harmony began to prevail among them. They felt their own powers, and the tediousness of the common school tone vanished like a specter from the room. They were determined to try, they succeeded; they persevered, they accomplished and were delighted. Their mood was not that of laborious learning, it was the joy of unknown powers aroused from sleep; their hearts and minds were elevated by the anticipation of what their powers would enable them to attempt and to effect."

Of course his first difficulty was to arrest the attention of a great number of children. This he overcame by appealing to their senses. Combining this experience with the ideas he had received many years before from Rousseau, he invented his system of object-lessons. He was also driven by his needs to something like a system of monitors, though in an informal way. If a child was found to know anything he was put between two others to whom he might teach it.

Thus, during the short period, not more than a year,

which Pestalozzi spent among the children at Stanz, he settled the main features of the Pestalozzian system.

Sickness broke out among the children, and the wear and tear was too great even for Pestalozzi. He would probably have sunk under his efforts if the French, pressed by the Austrians, had not entered Stanz, in January, 1799, and taken part of the Ursuline Convent for a military hospital. Pestalozzi was, therefore, obliged to break up the school, and he himself went to a medicinal spring on the Gurnigel in the Canton Bern. "Here," he says, "I enjoyed days of recreation. I needed them. It is a wonder that I am still alive. I shall not forget those days as long as I live; they saved me: but I could not live without my work." He came down from the Gurnigel, and began to teach in the primary schools (i. e., schools for children from four to eight years old) of Burgdorf, the second town in the Canton. Here the director was jealous of him, and he met with much opposition. "It was whispered," he tells us, "that I myself could not write nor work accounts, nor even read properly. Popular reports," he adds, "are not always entirely wrong. It is true I could not write nor read nor work accounts well."

A strange account has been left us of his teaching in the school by Ramsauer, then a scholar in it, and afterward one of Pestalozzi's assistants:—

"I got about as much regular schooling as the other scholars," he writes—"that is, none at all; but Pestalozzi's sacred zeal, his devoted love, which caused him to be entirely unmindful of himself, his serious and depressed state of mind, which struck even the children, made the deepest impression on me, and knit my childlike and grateful heart to his forever. Pestalozzi's intention was, that all the instruction given in this school should start from form, number, and language, and should have constant reference to these elements. He taught nothing but drawing, ciphering, and exercises in language. . . . He had not patience to allow things to be gone over a second time, or to put questions (in arithmetic), and in his enormous zeal for the instruction of the whole school, he seemed not to concern himself in the slightest degree for the individual scholar. The best things we had with him were the exercises in language, at least those which he gave us on the paper-hangings of the school-room, which were real exercises in observation. 'Boys,' he would say (he never named the girls), 'what do you see?' Answer—'A hole in the wainscot.' Pestalozzi—'Very good. Now repeat after me—I see a hole in the wainscot. I see a long hole in the wainscot. Through the hole I see the wall. Through the long narrow hole I see the wall,' and so forth. As Pestalozzi, in his zeal, did not tie himself to any particular time, we generally went on until eleven o'clock with whatever we had commenced at eight, and by ten o'clock he was always tired and hoarse. We knew when it was eleven by the noise of the other school children in the street, and then we usually all ran out without bidding good-bye."

After this account of Pestalozzi's instruction, we can hardly wonder that the school rector at Burgdorf was not grateful for his assistance.

In less than a year Pestalozzi left this school in bad health, and joined Krüsi in opening a new school in Burgdorf Castle, for which he afterward (1802) obtained Government aid. Here he was assisted in carrying out his system by Krüsi, Tobler, and Bluss. He now embodied the results of his experience in a work which has obtained great celebrity—"How Gertrude Teaches her Children."

In 1802 Pestalozzi, for once in his life a successful and popular man, was elected a member of a deputation sent by the Swiss people to Paris.

On the restoration of the Cantons in 1804, the Castle of Burgdorf was again occupied by one of the chief magistrates, and Pestalozzi and his establishment were moved to the Monastery of Buchsee. Here the teachers gave the principal direction to another, the since celebrated Fellenburg, "not without my consent," says Pestalozzi, "but to my profound mortification." He therefore soon accepted an invitation from the inhabitants of Yverdun to open an institution there, and within a twelvemonth he was followed by his old assistants, who had found government by Fellenburg less to their taste than no-government by Pestalozzi.

The Yverdun Institute had soon a world-wide reputation. Pestalozzian teachers went from it to Madrid, to Naples, to St. Petersburg. Kings and philosophers joined in doing it honor. But, as Pestalozzi himself has testified, these praises were but as a laurel-wreath encircling a skull. The life of the Pestalozzian institutions had been the love which the old man had infused into all the members, teachers as well as children; but this life was wanting at Yverdun. The establishment was much too large to be carried on successfully without more method and discipline than Pestalozzi, remarkable, as he himself says, for his "unrivalled incapacity to govern," was master of. The assistants began each to take his own line, and even the outward show of unity was soon at an end. Nothing is less interesting or profitable than the details of bygone quarrels, so I will not go into the great feud between Niederer and Schmid, which in its day made a good deal of noise in the scholastic world, as even less important disputes have done, and will do in the world at large. There were, too, many mistakes made at Yverdun. Pestalozzi was mad with enthusiasm to improve elementary education, especially for the poor, throughout Europe. His zeal led him to announce his schemes and methods before he had given them a fair trial; hence many foolish things came abroad as Pestalozzianism, and hindered the reception of principles and practices which better deserved the name. Pestalozzi, too, unfortunately thought that his influence depended on the opinion which was formed of his institution; so he published a highly-colored account of it, and tried to conceal its defects from the strangers by whom he was constantly visited. "His highly active imagination," says Raumer, himself for some time an inmate of the institution, " led him to see and describe as actually existing whatever he hoped sooner or later to realize." The enemies of change made the most of these discrepancies, and this, joined with financial difficulties consequent on Pestalozzi's mismanagement, and with the scandals which arose out of the dissensions of the Pestalozzians, brought his institution to a speedy and unhonored close.

Thus the sun went down in clouds, and the old man, when he died at the age of eighty, in 1827, had seen the apparent failure of all his toils. He had not, however, failed in reality. It has been said of him that his true function was to educate ideas, not children, and when twenty years later the centenary of his birth was celebrated by schoolmasters, not only in his native country, but throughout Germany, it was found that Pestalozzian ideas had been sown, and were bearing fruit, over the greater part of central Europe.

PESTALOZZIANISM.

As it seems to the present writer, the worst part of our educational course—the part which is wrong in theory and pernicious in practice—is our instruction of children, say between the ages of seven and twelve. Before seven years old, there is often no formal instruction, and perhaps there should be none. Pestalozzi would have children systematically taught from the cradle; but I can not help doubting the wisdom, or at least the necessity of this. Nature offers the succession of impressions to the child's senses without any regular order. Art should come to her assistance, says Pestalozzi, and organize a connected series of such impressions. It may well be questioned, however, if the child will be benefited by being put through any course of the kind. Lord Lytton wittily, and in my opinion wisely, applies to this subject the story of the man who thought his bees would make honey faster, if instead of going in search of flowers, they were shut up and had the flowers brought to them. The way in which children turn from object to object, like the bees from flower to flower, is surely an indication to us that Nature herself teaches at this age by an infinite variety of impressions which we should no more attempt to throw into what we call regular order than we should employ a drill-sergeant to teach infants to walk. Of course I do not mean that there is no education for children, however young; but the school is the mother's knee, and the lessons learnt there are other and more valuable than object-lessons.*

The time for teaching, technically so called, comes at last, and what is to be done then? Let us consider briefly what *is* done.

There are in education few maxims which are so universally accepted as this—that education is, if not wholly, at least in a great measure, the development of faculties rather than the imparting of knowledge. On this principle alone is it possible to justify the amount of time given by the higher forms in schools and by undergraduates at the Universities to the study of classics and mathematics. In all the attempts which have been made to depreciate these studies, no one of any authority has disputed that, if they are indeed the best means of training the mind, they should be maintained in their present monopoly, even though the knowledge acquired were sure to drop off, "like the tadpole's tail," when the scholars entered on the business of life. We are agreed, then, that in youth the faculties are to be trained, not the knowledge given, for adult age. But when we come to childhood we forget this principle entirely, and think not so much of cultivating the faculties for youth as of communicating the knowledge which will then come in

---

* See, however, some observations of Mr. Herbert Spencer on the other side.—*Education*, pp. 81, ff.

K

useful. We see clearly enough that it would be absurd to cram the mind of a youth with laws of science or art or commerce which he could not understand, on the ground that the getting-up of these things might save him trouble in after-life. But we do not hesitate to sacrifice childhood to the learning by heart of grammar-rules, Latin declensions, historical dates, and the like, with no thought whatever of the child's faculties, but simply with a view of giving him knowledge (if knowledge it can be called) that will come in useful five or six years afterward. We do not treat youths thus, probably because we have more sympathy with them, or at least understand them better. The intellectual life to which the senses and the imaginations are subordinated in the man, has already begun in the youth. In an inferior degree he can do what the man can do, and understand what the man can understand. He has already some notion of reasoning, and abstraction, and generalization. But with the child it is very different. His active faculties may be said almost to differ in kind from man's. He has a feeling for the sensuous world which he will lose as he grows up. His strong imagination, under no control of the reason, is constantly at work building castles in the air, and investigating the doll or the puppet-show with all the properties of the things they represent. His feelings and affections, easily excited, find an object to love or dislike in every person and thing he meets with. On the other hand, he has no conception of what is abstract, and no interest except in actual known persons, animals, and things.

There is, then, between the child of nine and the youth of fourteen and fifteen a greater difference than between the youth and the man of twenty; and this demands a corresponding difference in their studies. And yet, as matters are carried on now, the child is too often kept to the drudgery of learning by rote mere collections of hard words, perhaps, too, in a foreign language; and absorbed by the present, he gets little comfort from the teacher's *hæc olim meminisse juvabit* [perhaps some time it will be a pleasure to remember these things].

How to educate the child is doubtless the most difficult problem of all, and it is generally allotted to those who are the least likely to find a satisfactory solution.

The earliest educator of the children of many rich parents is the nursemaid—a person not usually distinguished by either intellectual or moral excellence. At an early age, this educator is superseded by the Preparatory School. Taken as a body, the ladies whose pecuniary needs compel them to open " establishments for young gentlemen " (though doubtless possessed of many excellent qualities) can not be said to hold enlarged views, or indeed any views whatever on the subject of education. Their intention is not so much to cultivate the children's faculties as to make a livelihood, and to hear no complaints that pupils who have left them have been found deficient in the expected knowledge by the master of their new school. If any one would investigate the sort of teaching which is considered adapted to the capacity of children at this stage, let him look into a standard work still in vogue ("Mangnall's Questions"), from which the young of both sexes acquire a great quantity and variety of learning; the whole of ancient and modern history and biography, together with the heathen mythology, the planetary system, and the names of all the constellations, lying very compactly in about 300 pages.

Unfortunately, moreover, from the gentility of these ladies, their scholars' bodies are often treated in preparatory schools no less injuriously than their minds. It may be natural in a child to use his lungs and delight in noise, but this can hardly be considered *genteel*, so the tendency is, as far as possible, suppressed. It is found, too, that if children are allowed to run about they get dirty and spoil their clothes, and do not look like "young gentlemen," so they are made to take exercise in a much more genteel fashion, walking slowly two-and-two, *with gloves on.*

At nine or ten years old, boys are commonly put to a school taught by masters. Here they lose sight of their gloves, and learn the use of their limbs; but their minds are not so fortunate as their bodies. The studies of the school have been arranged without any thought of their peculiar needs. The youngest class is generally the largest, often much the largest, and it is handed over to the least competent and worst paid master on the staff of teachers. The reason is, that little boys are found to learn the tasks imposed upon them very slowly. A youth or man who came fresh to the Latin grammar would learn in a morning as much as the master, with great labor, can get into children in a week. It is thought, therefore, that the best teaching should be applied where it will have most result. If any one were to say to the manager of a school, "The master who takes the lowest form teaches badly, and the children learn nothing;" he would perhaps say, "Very likely; but if I paid a much higher salary, and got a better man, they would learn but little." The only thing the school-manager thinks of is, How much do the little boys learn of what is taught in the higher forms? How their faculties are being developed, or whether they have any faculties except for reading, writing, and arithmetic, and for getting grammar rules, etc., by heart, he is not so "unpractical" as to inquire.

Pestalozzi, it has been said, invented nothing new. Most assuredly he did not invent the principle that education is a developing of the faculties rather than an imparting of knowledge. But he did much to bring this truth to bear on early education, and to make it not only received but acted on.

Much has been written about the amount of originality which may be allowed to Pestalozzi, but the question is, after all, of no great importance. We must, at least, concede to him, the merit which he himself claims, of having "lighted upon truths little noticed before, and principles which, though almost generally acknowledged, were seldom carried out in practice."* As Sydney Smith said of Hamilton, "his must be the credit of the man who is so deeply impressed with the importance of what he thinks he has discovered that he will take no denial, but, at the risk of fame and fortune, pushes through all opposition, and is determined the discovery shall not perish, at least for want of a fair trial."

But Pestalozzi is distinguished from other educators not more by what he *did*, than by what he endeavored to do; in other words, his *differentia* [distinguishing characteristic] is rather his aim than his method.

---

* Letters on Early Education, vi. 23.

If we seek for the root of Pestalozzi's system we shall find it, I think, in that which was the motive power of Pestalozzi's career, "the enthusiasm of humanity." Consumed with grief for the degradation of the Swiss peasantry, he never lost faith in their true dignity as men, and in the possibility of raising them to a condition worthy of it. He cast about for the best means of thus raising them, and decided that it could be effected, not by any improvement in their outward circumstances, but by an education which should make them what their Creator intended them to be, and should give them the use and the consciousness of all their inborn faculties. "From my youth up," he says, "I felt what a high and indispensable human duty it is to labor for the poor and miserable; . . . that he may attain to a consciousness of his own dignity through his feeling of the universal powers and endowments which he possesses awakened within him; that he may not only learn to gabble by rote the religious maxim that 'man is created in the image of God, and is bound to live and die as a child of God,' but may himself experience its truth by virtue of the Divine power within him, so that he may be raised, not only above the plowing oxen, but also above the man in purple and silk who lives unworthily of his high destiny."*

Again he says (and I quote at length on the point, as it is indeed the key to Pestalozzianism), "Why have I insisted so strongly on attention to early physical and intellectual education? Because I consider these as merely leading to a higher aim, to qualify the human

---

* Quoted in Barnard, p. 13. [See note, page 194.]

being for the free and full use of all the faculties implanted by the Creator, and to direct all these faculties toward the perfection of the whole being of man, that he may be enabled to act in his peculiar station as an instrument of that All-wise and Almighty Power that has called him into life."*

Believing in this high aim of education, Pestalozzi required a proper early training for all alike. "Every human being," said he, "has a claim to a judicious development of his faculties by those to whom the care of his infancy is confided."†

Pestalozzi therefore most earnestly addressed himself to mothers, to convince them of the power placed in their hands, and to teach them how to use it. "The mother is qualified, and qualified by the Creator Himself, to become the principal agent in the development of her child; . . . and what is demanded of her is—a *thinking love.* . . . God has given to thy child all the faculties of our nature, but the grand point remains undecided—how shall this heart, this head, these hands, be employed? to whose service shall they be dedicated? A question the answer to which involves a futurity of happiness or misery to a life so dear to thee. . . . It is recorded that God opened the heavens to the patriarch of old, and showed him a ladder leading thither. This ladder is let down to every descendant of Adam; it is offered to thy child. But he must be taught to climb it. And let him not attempt it by the cold calculations of the head, or the mere

---

* Letters on Early Education, xxxii. 160.

† Ibid. xxxii. p. 163. For the very striking passage which follows, see Note on p. 194 *infra.*

impulse of the heart; but let all these powers combine, and the noble enterprise will be crowned with success. These powers are already bestowed on him, but to thee it is given to assist in calling them forth."* "Maternal love is the first agent in education. . . . Through it the child is led to love and trust his Creator and his Redeemer."

From the theory of development which lay at the root of Pestalozzi's views of education, it followed that the imparting of knowledge and the training for special pursuits held only a subordinate position in his scheme. "Education, instead of merely considering what is to be imparted to children, ought to consider first what they may be said already to possess, if not as a developed, at least as an involved faculty capable of development. Or if, instead of speaking thus in the abstract, we will but recollect that it is to the great Author of life that man owes the possession, and is responsible for the use, of his innate faculties, education should not only decide what is to be made of a child, but rather inquire, what it was intended that he should become. What is his destiny as a created and responsible being? What are his faculties as a rational and moral being? What are the means for their perfection, and the end held out as the highest object of their efforts by the Almighty Father of all, both in creation and in the page of revelation?"

Education, then, must consist "in a continual benevolent superintendence, with the object of calling forth all the faculties which Providence has implanted; and its province, thus enlarged, will yet be with less difficulty

---

* Letters on Early Education, v. 21.

surveyed from one point of view, and will have more of a systematic and truly philosophical character, than an incoherent mass of exercises—arranged without unity of principle, and gone through without interest—which too often usurps its name."

An education of the latter description he denounced with the zeal of a Luther.

"The present race of schoolmasters," he writes, "sacrifice the essence of true teaching to separate and disconnected teaching in a complete jumble of subjects. By dishing up fragments of all kinds of truths, they destroy the spirit of truth itself, and extinguish the power of self-dependence which without that spirit can not exist."*

With Pestalozzi teaching was not so much to be thought of as training. Training must be found for the child's heart, head, and hand, and the capacities of the heart and head must be developed by practice no less than those of the hand. The heart, as we have seen, is first influenced by the mother. At a later period Pestalozzi would have the charities of the family circle introduced into the school-room (rather ignoring the difference which the altered ratio of the young to the adults makes in the conditions of the problem), and would have the child taught virtue by his affections being exercised and his benevolence guided to action. There is an interesting instance on record of the way in which he himself applied this principle. When he was at Stanz, news arrived of the destruction of Altdorf. Pestalozzi depicted to his scholars the misery of the children there. "Hundreds," said he, "are at this mo-

---

* Quoted by Carl Schmidt, Gesch. d. Pæd., iv. 87.

ment wandering about as you were last year, without a home, perhaps without food or clothing." He then asked them if they would not wish to receive some of these children among them? This, of course, they were eager to do. Pestalozzi then pointed out the sacrifices it would involve on their part, that they would have to share everything with the new comers, and to eat less and work more than before. Only when they promised to make these sacrifices ungrudgingly, he undertook to apply to Government that the children's wish might be granted. It was thus that Pestalozzi endeavored to develop the moral and religious life of the children, which is based on trust and love.

The child's thinking faculty is capable, according to Pestalozzi, of being exercised almost from the commencement of consciousness. Indeed, it has been objected against Pestalozzi's system that he cultivated the mere intellectual powers at the expense of the poetical and imaginative. All knowledge, he taught, is acquired by sensation and observation: sometimes it has been thought that he traces everything originally to the senses; but he seems to extend the word *Anschauung* [contemplation] to every experience of which the mind becomes conscious.*

---

* I dare say I am not the only English reader of German books who has been perplexed by the words *Anschauung* and *anschaulich*. Shelling's definition is as follows: "Anschauung ist jene Handlung des Geistes in welcher er aus Thätigkeit und Leiden, aus unbeschränkter und beschränkter Thätigkeit, in sich selbst ein gemeinschaftliches Produkt schafft," [*Anschauung* is every action of the mind in which it creates out of action and passion, out of unlimited and limited action, a distinct product upon itself]. The word seems used, in fact, for the mind's becoming conscious of any fact immediately by experience, in contradistinction to inferences from symbols. To make instruction *anschaulich*, therefore, is to make the learner acquire knowledge by his direct experiences.

The child, then, must be made to observe accurately, and to reflect on its observations. The best subject-matter for the lessons will be the most ordinary things that can be found. "Not only is there not one of the little incidents in the life of a child, in his amusements and recreations, in his relation to his parents, and friends, and playfellows; but there is actually not anything within the reach of a child's attention, whether it belong to nature or to the employments and arts of life, that may not be made the object of a lesson by which some useful knowledge may be imparted, and, what is still more important, by which the child may not be familiarized with the habit of thinking on what he sees, and speaking after he has thought. The mode of doing this is not by any means to talk much to the child, but to enter into conversation with a child; not to address to him many words, however familiar and well chosen, but to bring him to express himself on the subject; not to exhaust the subject, but to question the child about it, and let him find out and correct the answers. It would be ridiculous to expect that the volatile spirits of a child could be brought to follow any lengthy explanations. The attention is deadened by long expositions, but roused by animated questions. Let these questions be short, clear, and intelligible. Let them not merely lead the child to repeat in the same, or in varied terms, what he has heard just before. Let them excite him to observe what is before him, to recollect what he has learned, and to muster his little stock of knowledge for materials for an answer. Show him a certain quality in one thing, and let him find out the same in others. Tell him that the shape of a ball is called *round*, and if, accordingly, you bring him to point out other objects to which the same property belongs, you have employed him more usefully than by the most perfect discourse on rotundity. In the one instance he would have had to listen and to recollect, in the other he has to observe and to think."* "From observation and memory there is only one step to reflection. Though imperfect, this operation is often found among the early exercises of the infant mind. The powerful stimulus of inquisitiveness prompts to exertions which, if successful or encouraged by others, will lead to a habit of thought."†

Words, which are the signs of things, must never be taught the child till he has grasped the idea of the thing signified.

When an object has been submitted to his senses, he must be led to the consciousness of the impressions produced, and then must be taught the name of the object and of the qualities producing those impressions. Last of all, he must ascend to the definition of the object.

The object-lessons Pestalozzi divided into three great classes, under the heads of—(1) Form; (2) Number; (3) Speech. It was his constant endeavor to make his pupils distinguish between essentials and accidentals, and with his habit of constant analysis, which seems pushed to an extreme that to children would be repulsive, he sought to reduce Form, Number, and Speech to their elements. In his alphabet of Form everything was represented as having the square as its base. In Number all operations were traced back to $1+1$. In Speech the children, in their very cradles, were to be

---

* Letters on Early Education, xxxix. 147.
† Ibid. xx. 92.

taught the elements of sound, as ba, ba, ba, da, da, da, ma, ma, ma, etc. This elementary teaching Pestalozzi considered of the greatest importance, and when he himself instructed he went over the ground very slowly. Buss tells us that when he first joined Pestalozzi the delay over the prime elements seemed to him a waste of time, but that afterward he was convinced of its being the right plan, and felt that the failure of his own education was due to its incoherent and desultory character. "Not only," says Pestalozzi, "have the first elements of knowledge in every subject the most important bearing on its complete outline, but the child's confidence and interest are gained by perfect attainment even in the lowest stage of instruction." By his object-lessons Pestalozzi aimed at—1, enlarging gradually the sphere of a child's intuition, i. e., increasing the number of objects falling under his immediate perception; 2, impressing upon him those perceptions of which he had become conscious, with certainty, clearness, and precision; 3, imparting to him a comprehensive knowledge of language for the expression of whatever had become or was becoming an object of his consciousness, in consequence either of the spontaneous impulse of his own nature, or of the assistance of tuition.

Of all the instruction given at Yverdun, the most successful, in the opinion of those who visited the school, was the instruction in arithmetic. The children are described as performing with great rapidity very difficult tasks in head-calculation. Pestalozzi based his method here, as in other subjects, on the principle that the individual should be brought to knowledge by a road similar to that which the whole race had used in founding the science. Actual counting of things preceded the first Cocker, as actual measuring of land preceded the original Euclid. The child then must be taught to count things, and to find out the various processes experimentally in the concrete before he is given any abstract rule, or is put to any abstract exercises. This plan is now commonly adopted in German schools, and many ingenious contrivances have been introduced by which the combinations of things can be presented to the children's sight.

Next to the education of the affections and the intellect come those exercises in which the body is more prominent. I do not know that there was anything distinctive in Pestalozzi's views and practices in physical education, although he attached the due importance to it which had previously been perceived only by Locke and Rousseau, and in Germany by Basedow and his colleagues of the Philanthropin.

Great pains should be taken with the cultivation of the senses, and finally the artistic faculty (*Kunstcraft*) should be developed, in which the power of the mind and that of the senses are united. Music and drawing played a leading part in Pestalozzi's schools. They were taught to all the children, even the youngest, and were not limited to the conventional two hours a week. It is natural to children to imitate; thus they acquire language, and thus, with proper diction and encouragement, they will find pleasure in attempting to sing the melodies they hear, and to draw the simple objects around them. By drawing, the eye is trained as well as the hand. "A person who is in the habit of drawing, especially from nature, will easily perceive many circumstances which are commonly overlooked, and will form a much more correct impression, even of such objects as he does not stop to examine minutely, than one who has never been taught to look upon what he sees with an intention of reproducing a likeness of it. The attention to the exact shape of the whole, and the proportion of the parts, which is requisite for the taking of an adequate sketch, is converted into a habit, and becomes productive both of instruction and amusement." *

Besides drawing, Pestalozzi recommended modeling, a hint which was afterward worked out by Frœbel in his *Kindergarten.*

Differing from Locke and Basedow, Pestalozzi was no friend to the notion of giving instruction always in the guise of amusement. "I am convinced," says he, "that such a notion will forever preclude solidity of knowledge, and, from want of sufficient exertions on the part of the pupils, will lead to that very result which I wish to avoid by my principle of a constant employment of the thinking powers. A child must very early in life be taught the lesson that exertion is indispensable for the attainment of knowledge." But a child should not be taught to look upon exertion as an evil. He should be encouraged, not frightened into it. "An interest in study is the first thing which a teacher should endeavor to excite and keep alive. There are scarcely any circumstances in which a want of application in children does not proceed from a want of interest; and there are perhaps none in which the want of interest does not originate in the mode of teaching adopted by the teach-

---

* Letters on Early Education, xxiv. 117.

er. I would go so far as to lay it down as a rule, that whenever children are inattentive and apparently take no interest in a lesson, the teacher should always first look to himself for the reason. . . . Could we conceive the indescribable tedium which must oppress the young mind while the weary hours are slowly passing away one after another in occupations which it can neither relish nor understand, could we remember the like scenes which our own childhood has passed through, we should no longer be surprised at the remissness of the school-boy, 'creeping like snail unwillingly to school.' . . . To change all this, 'we must adopt a better mode of instruction, by which the children are less left to themselves, less thrown upon the unwelcome employment of passive listening, less harshly treated for little excusable failings; but more roused by questions, animated by illustrations, interested and won by kindness.

"There is a most remarkable reciprocal action between the interest which the teacher takes and that which he communicates to his pupils. If he is not with his whole mind present at the subject, if he does not care whether he is understood or not, whether his manner is liked or not, he will alienate the affections of his pupils, and render them indifferent to what he says. But real interest taken in the task of instruction—kind words and kinder feelings—the very expression of the features, and the glance of the eye, are never lost upon children."*

In conclusion, I would ask, Have English school-masters nothing to learn from Pestalozzi? Do they aim at

---

* Letters on Early Education, xxx. 150.

a plan of education which shall be founded on a knowledge of human nature, and at modes of instruction which shall develop their pupil's faculties? Perhaps some will be inclined to answer, "Fine words no doubt, and in a sense very true, that education should be the unfolding of the faculties according to the Divine idea; but between this high poetical theory and the dull prose of actual school-teaching, there is a great gulf fixed, and we can not attend to both at the same time." I know full well how different theories and plans of education seem to us when we are at leisure and can think of them without reference to particular pupils, and when all our energy is taxed to get through our day's teaching, and our animal spirits jaded by having to keep order and exact attention among veritable schoolboys who do not answer in all respects to "the young" of the theorists. But whilst admitting most heartily the difference here, as elsewhere, between the actual and the ideal, I think that the dull prose of school-teaching would be less dull and less prosaic if our aim was higher, and if we did not contentedly assume that our present performances are as good as the nature of the case will admit of. Many teachers (I think I might say most) are discontented with the greater number of their pupils, but it is not so usual for teachers to be discontented with themselves. And yet even those who are most averse from theoretical views, which they call unpractical, would admit, as practical men, that their methods are probably susceptible of improvement, and that even if their methods are right, they themselves are by no means perfect teachers. Only let the *desire* of improvement once exist, and the teacher will find a new interest in his work. In part, the treadmill-like monotony so wearing to the spirits will be done away, and he will at times have the encouragement of conscious progress. To a man thus minded, theorists may be of great assistance. His practical knowledge may, indeed, often show him the absurdity of some pompously enunciated principle, and even where the principles seem sound, he may smile at the applications. But the theorist will show him many aspects of his profession, and will lead him to make many observations in it, which would otherwise have escaped him. They will save him from a danger caused by the difficulty of getting anything done in the schoolroom, the danger of thinking more of means than ends. They will teach him to examine what his aim really is, and then whether he is using the most suitable methods to accomplish it.

Such a theorist is Pestalozzi. He points to a high ideal, and bids us measure our modes of education by it. Let us not forget that if we are practical men we are Christians, and as such the ideal set before us is the highest of all. "Be ye perfect, even as your Father in heaven is perfect."*

---

* Raumer reckons up the services Pestalozzi did for education as follows: "He compelled the scholastic world to revise the whole of their task, to reflect on the nature and destiny of man, and also on the proper way of leading him from his youth toward that destiny." Those who wish to study Pestalozzi and his works will find a mass of information, thrown together without any apparent attempt at method, in Henry Barnard's "Pestalozzi and Pestalozzianism." New York, 1859. [This book is no longer published, but it was mainly a reprint from the "American Journal of Education," Vol. VI, already referred to.] This volume contains Tilleard's translation of Raumer's "Pestalozzi," excerpted from the "Geschichte der Padagogik," and published in this country. Besides this, Barnard gives us sketches of Pestalozzi's principal assistants, a translation of "Lienhard und Gertrud," and long extracts from his other writings. I have used chiefly Barnard and Dr. Biber's Life, also article by Palmer in C. A. Schmid's Encyclopædie. An important work (according to Barnard, I have not seen it myself) is R. Christoffel's "Pestalozzis Leben und Ansichten in wortgetreuen Auszugen seiner gesammten Schriften." Zürich, 1847. The little volume of "Letters on Early Education, addressed to Mr. Greaves," was last published in the "Phœnix Library." I have made many quotations from these letters above, and will conclude with this striking passage: "Whenever we find a human being in a state of suffering, and near to the awful moment which is forever to close the scene of his pains and enjoyments in this world, we feel ourselves moved by a sympathy which reminds us, that, however low his earthly condition, here too there is one of our race, subject to the same sensations of alternate joy and grief—born with the same faculties—with the same destination, and the same hopes of immortal life. And as we give ourselves up to that idea, we would fain, if we could, alleviate his sufferings, and shed a ray of light on the darkness of his parting moments. This is a feeling which will come home to the heart of every one—even to the young and the thoughtless, and to those little used to the sight of woe. Why, then, we would ask, do we look with a careless indifference on those who enter life? why do we feel so little interest in the condition of those who enter upon that varied scene, of which we might contribute to enhance the enjoyments, and to diminish the sum of suffering, of discontent, and wretchedness? And that education might do this, is the conviction of all those who are competent to speak from experience. That it ought to do as much, is the persuasion, and that it may accomplish it, is the constant endeavor, of those who are truly interested in the welfare of mankind."

[Pestalozzi's method of teaching is shown directly in C. Reiner's "Lessons on Number, as given in a Pestalozzian school, Cheam, Surrey. The Master's Manual, 12mo, pp. 224. London 1857"; and "Lessons on Form; or an introduction to Geometry. As given in a Pestalozzian school, Cheam, Surrey. 12mo, pp. 215. London 1837." The "Lessons on Objects" in the same series is well known in America as "Sheldon's Object Lessons," having been edited and published by E. A. Sheldon, Ph. D., principal of the State Normal School at Oswego, N. Y.

His system of teaching arithmetic has also been recently reproduced and adapted to modern schools under the name of "Hoose's Pestalozzian Series of Arithmetics," by J. H. Hoose, Ph. D., principal of the State Normal School, at Cortland, N. Y. Dr. Hoose is a strenuous advocate of this method as superior to the "Grubé Method," now so popular.]

IX.

JACOTOT.

Of the inventors of peculiar methods at present known to me, by far the most important, in my judgment, is Jacotot; and if I were not well aware how small an interest English teachers take in Didactics, I should be much surprised that in this country his writings and achievements have received so little attention. It is satisfactory to find, however, that last year some papers on the subject were read at the College of Preceptors by Mr. Joseph Payne, one of the Vice-presidents, and were afterward published in the "Educational Times."* These papers, which will not, I hope, be suffered to lie buried in the pages of a periodical, contain the only good account of Jacotot I have met with, though having long been impressed with the importance of his ideas, I have at different times consulted various foreign books about him.

In the following summary of Jacotot's system, I am largely indebted to Mr. Payne, and to him I refer the reader for a much more luminous account than my shorter space and inferior knowledge of the subject enable me to offer.

Jacotot was born at Dijon, of humble parentage, in 1770. Even as a boy he showed his preference for

---

* For June, July, and September, 1867. [Now found in his "Lectures on the Science and Art of Education," Complete edition, pp. 339-385.]

"self-teaching." We are told that he rejoiced greatly in the acquisition of all kinds of knowledge that could be gained by his own efforts, while he steadily resisted what was imposed on him by authority. He, however, was early distinguished by his acquirements, and at the age of twenty-five was appointed sub-director of the Polytechnic school. Some years afterward he became Professor of "the Method of Sciences at Dijon," and it was here that his method of instruction first attracted attention. "Instead of pouring forth a flood of information on the subject under attention from his own ample stores—explaining everything, and thus too frequently superseding in a great degree the pupil's own investigation of it—Jacotot, after a simple statement of the subject, with its leading divisions, boldly started it as a quarry for the class to hunt down, and invited every member to take part in the chase."* All were free to ask questions, to raise objections, to suggest answers. The Professor himself did little more than by leading questions put them on the right scent. He was afterward Professor of Ancient and Oriental languages, of Mathematics, and of Roman Law; and he pursued the same method, we are told, with uniform success. Being compelled to leave France as an enemy of the Bourbons, he was appointed, in 1818, when he was forty-eight years old, to the Professorship of the French Language and Literature at the University of Louvain. The celebrated teacher was received with enthusiasm, but he soon met with an unexpected difficulty. Many mem-

---

*There is a singular coincidence even in metaphor between Mr. Payne's account of Jacotot's mode of instructing this class and Mr. Wilson's directions for teaching science. (*Essays on a Liberal Education*.) [Mr. Payne thought highly of this paper by Mr. Wilson, and quotes from it on pages 140, 220 of the Reading-Club edition.]

bers of his large class knew no language but the Flemish and Dutch, and of these he himself was totally ignorant. He was, therefore, forced to consider how to teach without talking to his pupils. The plan he adopted was as follows:—He gave the young Flemings copies of Fénelon's "*Télémaque*," with the French on one side, and a Dutch translation on the other. This they had to study for themselves, comparing the two languages, and learning the French by heart. They were to go over the same ground again and again, and as soon as possible they were to give in French, however bad, the substance of those parts which they had not yet committed to memory. This method was found to succeed marvelously. Jacotot attributed its success to the fact that the students had learnt *entirely by the efforts of their own minds*, and that, though working under his superintendence, they had been, in fact, their own teachers. Hence he proceeded to generalize, and by degrees arrived at a series of astounding paradoxes. These paradoxes at first did their work well, and made noise enough in the world, but Jacotot seems to me like a captain, who, in his eagerness to astonish his opponents, takes on board such heavy guns as eventually must sink his own ship.

"*All human beings are equally capable of learning*," said Jacotot. Others had said this before; but no teacher, I suppose, of more than a fortnight's experience, had ever believed it. The truth which Jacotot chose to throw into this more than doubtful form, may perhaps be expressed by saying that the student's power of learning depends, in a great measure, on his *will*, and that where there is no will there is no capacity.

"*Every one can teach; and, moreover, can teach that which he does not know himself.*" I believe this paradox is the property of Jacotot alone. It seems, on the face of it, so utterly absurd, that it seldom answers the purpose of a paradox—seldom draws attention to the truth of which it is a partial, or a perverted, or an exaggerated statement. The answer which Jacotot and his friends made to the scoffs of the unbelieving, was an appeal to facts. Jacotot, they said, not only taught French without any means of communicating with his pupils, but he also taught drawing and music, although quite ignorant on those subjects. Without the least wishing to discredit the honesty of the witnesses who make this assertion, I can only admit the fact with great qualifications. Let us ask ourselves, what is the meaning of the assertion that we can teach what we do not know. First of all, we have to get rid of some ambiguity in the meaning of the word *teach*. To teach, according to Jacotot's idea, is to cause to learn. Teaching and learning are therefore correlatives: where there is no learning there can be no teaching. But this meaning of the word only coincides partially with the ordinary meaning. We speak of the lecturer or preacher as teaching when he gives his hearers an opportunity of learning, and do not say that his teaching ceases the instant they cease to attend. On the other hand, we do not call a parent a teacher because he sends his boy to school, and so causes him to learn. The notion of teaching, then, in the minds of most of us, includes giving information, or showing how an art is to be performed; and we look upon Jacotot's assertion as absurd, because we feel that no one can give information which he does not possess, or show how anything is to be done if he does not himself know. But let us take the Jacototian definition of teaching—causing to learn—and then see how far a person can cause another to learn that of which he himself is ignorant.

Subjects which are *taught* may be divided into three great classes:—1, Facts; 2, reasonings, or generalization from facts, i. e., science; 3, actions which have to be performed by the learner, i. e., arts.

1. We learn some facts by what the Pestalozzians call intuition, i. e., by direct experience. It may be as well to make the number of them as large as possible. No doubt there are no facts which are *known* so perfectly as these. For instance, a boy who has tried to smoke, knows the fact that tobacco is apt to produce nausea, much better than another who has picked up the information at second-hand. An intelligent master may suggest experiments, even in matters about which he himself is ignorant, and thus, in Jacotot's sense, he teaches things which he does not know. But some facts can not be learnt in this way, and then a Newton is helpless either to find them out for himself, or to teach them to others without knowing them. If the teacher does not know in what county Tavistock is, he can only learn from those who do, and the pupils will be no cleverer than their master. Here, then, I consider that Jacotot's pretensions utterly break down. "No," the answer is; "the teacher may give the pupil an atlas, and direct the boy to find out for himself; thus the master will teach what he does not know." But, in this case, he is a teacher only so far as he knows. For what he does not know, he hands over the pupil to the maker of the map,

who communicates with him, not orally, but by ink and paper. The master's ignorance is simply an obstacle to the boy's learning; for the boy would learn sooner the position of Tavistock, if it were shown him on the map. "That's the very point," says the disciple of Jacotot. "If the boy gets the knowledge without any trouble, he is likely to forget it again directly. 'Lightly come, lightly go.' Moreover, his faculty of observation will not have been exercised." It may, indeed, be well not to allow the knowledge even of facts, to come too easily; though I doubt whether the difficulties which arise from the master's ignorance will generally be the most advantageous. Still there is obviously a limit. If we gave boys their lessons in cipher, and offered a prize to the first decipherer, one would probably be found at last, and meantime all the boys' powers of observation, etc., would have been cultivated by comparing like signs in different positions, and guessing at their meaning: but the boys' time might have been better employed. Many eminent authorities consider that the memory is assisted by dictionary work, but all are agreed that, at least in the case of beginners, the outlay of time is too great for the advantage obtained. Jacotot's plan of teaching a language which the master did not know, was to put a book, with, say, "*Arma virumque cano*," etc., on one side, and "I sing arms and the man," etc., on the other, and to require the pupil to puzzle over it till he found out which word answered to which. I contend that in this case the teacher was the translator; and though from the roundabout way in which the knowledge was communicated the pupil derived some benefit, the benefit was hardly sufficient to make up for the expenditure of time involved.

I hold, then, that Jacotot did not teach facts of which he was ignorant, except in the sense in which the parent who sends his boy to school may be said to teach him. All Jacotot did was to direct the pupil to learn, sometimes in a very awkward fashion, from somebody else.*

When we come to science, we find all the best authorities agree that the pupil should be led to principles, if possible, and not have the principles brought to him. Mr. Wilson of Rugby, Professor Tyndall, Mr. H. Spencer, have all spoken eloquently on this subject, and shown how valuable scientific teaching is, when thus conducted, in drawing out the faculties of the mind. But although a schoolboy may be led to great scientific discoveries by any one who knows the road, he will have no more chance of making them with an ignorant teacher, than he would have had in the days of the Ptolemies. Here again, then, I can not understand how the teacher can teach what he does not know. He may, indeed, join his pupil in investigating principles, but he must either keep with the pupil or go in advance of him. In the first case he is only a fellow-pupil; in the second, he teaches only that which he knows.

Finally, we come to arts, and we are told that Jacotot taught drawing and music, without being either a draughtsman or a musician. In art everything depends on *rightly directed practice.* The most consummate artist

---

* Here Jacotot's notion of teaching reminds one of the sophism quoted by Montaigne—"A Westphalia ham makes a man drink. Drink quenches thirst. Therefore a Westphalia ham quenches thirst."

can not communicate his skill, and is often inferior as a teacher to one whose attention is more concentrated on the mechanism of the art. Perhaps it is not even necessary that the teacher should be able to do the exercises himself, if only he knows how they should be done; but he seldom gets credit for this knowledge, unless he can show that he knows how the thing should be done, by doing it. Lessing tells us that Raphael would have been a great painter even if he had been born without hands. He would not, however, have succeeded in getting mankind to believe it. I grant then that the teacher of art need not be a first-rate artist, and in some very exceptional cases, need not be an artist at all; but, if he can not perform the exercises he gives his pupil, he must at least *know how they should be done*. But Jacotot claims perfect ignorance. We are told that he "taught" drawing by setting objects before his pupils, and making them imitate them on paper as best they could. Of course the art originated in this way, and a person with great perseverance, and (I must say, in spite of Jacotot) with more than average ability, would make considerable progress with no proper instruction; but he would lose much by the ignorance of the person calling himself his teacher. An awkward habit of holding the pencil will make skill doubly difficult to acquire, and thus half his time might be wasted. Then, again, he would hardly have a better eye than the Cimabues and Bellinis of early art, so the drawing of his landscape would not be less faulty than theirs. To consider music. I am told that a person who is ignorant of music can teach, say, the piano or the violin. This assertion, I confess, seems to me to go beyond the region of paradox into that of utter nonsense. In music, talent often surmounts all kinds of difficulties; but it would have taxed the genius of Mozart himself to become a good player on the violin and piano, without being shown how to stop and finger.*

I have thus carefully examined Jacotot's pretensions to teach what he did not know, because I am anxious that what seems to me the rubbish should be cleared away from his principles, and should no longer conceal those parts of his system which are worthy of general attention.

At the root of Jacotot's Paradox lay a truth of very great importance. The highest and best teaching is not that which makes the pupils passive recipients of other people's ideas (not to speak of the teaching which conveys mere words without any ideas at all), but that which guides and encourages the pupils in working for themselves and thinking for themselves. The master, as Mr. Payne well says, can no more think, or practice, or see for his pupil, than he can digest for him, or walk for him. The pupil must owe everything to his own exertions, which it is the function of the master to encourage and direct. Perhaps this may seem very obvious truth, but obvious or not it has been very generally neglected. The Jesuits, who were the best masters of the old school, did little beyond communicating facts, and insisting on their pupils committing these facts to

---

* This assertion is probably too strong. Mozart would have learnt to play (and he could only have played *well*) on the violin and piano, if he had been shut up by himself with those instruments. But he would not have learnt so rapidly or so well as if he had been shown how to set to work. His fingering would always have been clumsy; he would have been hampered by a bad mechanism in his violin-playing, and he would have had a wretched "bow-arm."

memory. Their system of lecturing has indeed now passed away, and boys are left to acquire facts from school-books instead of from the master. But this change is merely accidental. The essence of the teaching still remains. Even where the master does not confine himself to hearing what the scholars have learnt by heart, he seldom does more than offer explanations. He measures the teaching rather by the amount which has been put before the scholars—by what he has done for them and shown them—than by what they have learned. But this is not teaching of the highest type. When the votary of Dullness in the "Dunciad" is rendering an account of his services, he arrives at this climax:

> For thee explain a thing till all men doubt it,
> And write about it, Goddess, and about it.

And in the same spirit Mr. Wilson stigmatizes as synonymous "the most stupid and most *didactic* teaching."

All the eminent authorities on education have a very different theory of the teacher's functions. "Education," says Pestalozzi, "instead of merely considering what is to be imparted to children, ought to consider first what *they already possess;* not merely their developed faculties, but also their innate faculties capable of development." The master's attention, then, is not to be fixed on his own mind and his own store of knowledge, but on his pupil's mind and on its gradual expansion. He must, in fact, be not so much a *teacher* as a *trainer*. Here we have the view which Jacotot intended to enforce by his paradox; for we may possibly train faculties which we do not ourselves possess. Sayers' trainer brought up his man to face Heenan, but he could not have done so himself. The sportsman trains his pointer and his hunter to perform feats which are altogether out of the range of his own capacities. Now, "training is the cultivation bestowed on any set of faculties with the object of developing them" (Wilson), and to train any faculty, you must set it to work. Hence it follows, that as boys' minds are not simply their memories, the master must aim at something more than causing his pupils to remember facts. Jacotot has done good service to education by giving prominence to this truth, and by showing in his method how other faculties may be cultivated besides the memory.

"*Tout est dans tout*" ("All is in all"), is another of Jacotot's paradoxes. I do not propose discussing it as the philosophical thesis which takes other forms, as "Every man is a microcosm," etc., but merely to inquire into its meaning as applied to didactics.

If you asked an ordinary Frenchman who Jacotot was, he would probably answer, Jacotot was a man who thought you could learn everything by getting up Fénelon's "*Télémaque*" by heart. By carrying your investigation further, you would find that this account of him required modification, that the learning by heart was only part, and a very small part, of what Jacotot demanded from his pupils, but you would also find that entire mastery of "*Télémaque*" was his first requisite, and that he managed to connect everything he taught with that "model-book." Of course, if "*tout est dans tout*," everything is in *Télémaque;* and, said an objector, "also in the first book of *Télémaque*," and in *the first word*. Jacotot went through a variety of subtilities to show that all "*Télémaque*" is contained in the word *Calypso*, and perhaps he would have been equally successful, if he had been required to take only the first letter instead of the first word. The reader is amused rather than convinced by these discussions, but he finds them not without fruit. They bring to his mind very forcibly a truth to which he has hitherto probably not paid sufficient attention. He sees that all knowledge is connected together, or (what will do equally well for our present purpose) that there are a thousand links by which we may bring into connection the different subjects of knowledge. If by means of these links we can attach in our minds the knowledge we acquire to the knowledge we already possess, we shall learn faster and more intelligently, and at the same time we shall have a much better chance of retaining our new acquisitions. The memory, as we all know, is assisted even by artificial association of ideas, much more by natural. Hence the value of "*tout est dans tout,*" or, to adopt a modification suggested by Mr. Payne, of the connection of knowledge. Suppose we know only one subject, but know that thoroughly, our knowledge, if I may express myself algebraically, can not be represented by ignorance plus the knowledge of that subject. We have acquired a great deal more than that. When other subjects come before us, they may prove to be so connected with what we had before, that we may almost seem to know them already. In other words, when we know a little thoroughly, though our actual possession is small, we have potentially a great deal more.

Jacotot's practical application of his "*tout est dans tout*" was as follows: "*Il faut apprendre quelque chose, et y rapporter tout le reste.*" ("The pupil must learn something thoroughly, and refer everything to that.") For language he must take a model-book, and become thoroughly master of it. His knowledge must not be a verbal knowledge only, but he must enter into the sense and spirit of the writer. Here we find that Jacotot's practical advice coincides with that of many other great authorities, who do not base it on the same principle. The Jesuits' maxim was, that their pupils should always learn something thoroughly, however little it might be. Pestalozzi, as I have mentioned, insisted on the children going over the elements again and again till they were completely master of them. "Not only," says he, "have the first elements of knowledge in every subject the most important bearing on its complete outline; but the child's confidence and interest are gained by *perfect attainment* even in the lowest stage of instruction." Ascham, Ratich, and Comenius all required a model-book to be read and re-read till words and thoughts were firmly fixed in the pupil's memory. Jacotot probably never read Ascham's "Schoolmaster." If he had done so, he might have appropriated some of Ascham's words as exactly conveying his own thoughts. Ascham, as we saw, recommended that a short book should be thoroughly mastered, each lesson being worked over in different ways a dozen times at the least. "Thus is learned easily, sensibly, by little and little, not only all the hard congruities of grammar, the choice of aptest words, the right framing of words and sentences, comeliness of figures, and forms fit for every matter and proper for every tongue; but that which is greater also—in marking daily and following diligently thus the best authors, like invention of arguments, like order in disposition, like utterance in elocution, is easily gathered up; whereby your scholar shall be brought not only to like eloquence, but also to all true understanding and right judgment, both for writing and speaking." The voice seems Jacotot's voice, though the hand is the hand of Ascham.

But if Jacotot agrees so far with earlier authorities, there is one point in which he seems to differ from them. He makes great demands on the memory, and requires six books of "*Télémaque*" to be learned by heart. On the other hand, Montaigne said, "*Savoir par cœur est ne pas savoir*" [To know by heart is not to know at all]; which is echoed by Rousseau, H. Spencer, etc. Ratich required that nothing should be learnt by heart. Protests against "loading the memory," "saying without book," etc., are everywhere to be met with, and nowhere more vigorously expressed than in Ascham. He says of the grammar-school boys of his time, that "their whole knowledge, by learning without the book, was tied only to their tongue and lips, and never ascended up to the brain and head, and therefore was soon spit out of the mouth again. They learnt without book everything, they understood within the book little or nothing." But these protests were really directed at verbal knowledge, when it is made to take the place of knowledge of the thing signified. We are always too ready to suppose that words are connected with ideas, though both old and young are constantly exposing themselves to the sarcasm of Mephistopheles:—

> . . . eben wo Begriffe fehlen,
> Da stallt ein Wort zur rechten Zeit sich ein.*

---

* . . . just where meaning fails, a word
Comes patly in to serve your turn.
Theodore Martin's Trans.

M

Against this danger Jacotot took special precautions. The pupil was to undergo an examination in everything connected with the lesson learnt, and the master's share in the work was to convince himself, from the answers he received, that the pupil thoroughly grasped the meaning, as well as remembered the words, of the author. Still the six books of "*Télémaque*," which Jacotot gave to be learnt by heart, was a very large dose, and Mr. Payne is of opinion that he would have been more faithful to his own principles if he had given the first book only.

There are three ways in which the model-book may be studied. 1st. It may be read through rapidly again and again, which was Ratich's plan and Hamilton's; or, 2d, each lesson may be thoroughly mastered, read in various ways a dozen times at the least, which was Ascham's plan; or, 3d, the pupil may begin always at the beginning, and advance a little further each time, which was Jacotot's plan. This last could not, of course, be carried very far. The repetitions, when the pupil had got on some way in the book, could not always be from the beginning; still every part was to be repeated so frequently that *nothing could be forgotten.* Jacotot did not wish his pupils to learn simply in order to forget, but to learn in order to remember forever. "We are learned," said he, "not so far as we have learned, but only so far as we remember." He seems, indeed, almost to ignore the fact that the act of learning serves other purposes than that of making learned, and to assert that to forget is the same as never to have learned, which is a palpable error. We necessarily forget much that passes through our minds, and yet its effect remains. All grown people have arrived at some opinions, convictions, knowledge, but they can not call to mind every spot they trod on in the road thither. When we have read a great history, say, or traveled through a fresh country, we have gained more than the number of facts we happen to remember. The mind seems to have formed an acquaintance with that history or that country, which is something different from the mere acquisition of facts. Moreover, our interests, as well as our ideas, may long survive the memory of the facts which originally started them. We are told that one of the old judges, when a barrister objected to some dictum of his, put him down by the assertion, "Sir, I have forgotten more law than ever you read." If he wished to make the amount forgotten a measure of the amount remembered, this was certainly fallacious, as the ratio between the two is not a constant quantity. But he may have meant that this extensive reading had left its result, and that he could see things from more points of view than the less traveled legal vision of his opponent. That *power* acquired by learning may also last longer than the knowledge of the thing learned is sufficiently obvious.

The advantages derived from having learnt a thing are, then, not entirely lost when the thing itself is forgotten. This leads me to speak, though at the risk of a digression, on the present state of opinion on this matter. In setting about the study of any subject, we may desire (1) the knowledge of that subject; or (2) the mental vigor derivable from learning it; or (3) we may hope to combine these advantages. Now, in spite of the aphorism which connects knowledge and power together, we find that these have become the badges of opposite parties. One party would make knowledge the end of education. Mr. Spencer assumes as a law of nature that the study which conveys useful knowledge must also give mental vigor; so he considers that the object of education should be to impart useful knowledge, and teach us in what way to treat the body, to treat the mind, to manage our affairs, to bring up a family, to behave as a citizen, etc., etc. The old school, on the other hand, which I may call the English party, as it derives its strength from some of the peculiar merits and demerits of the English character, heartily despises knowledge, and would make the end of education power only.

As the most remarkable outcome of this idea of education, we have the Cambridge mathematical tripos.

The typical Cambridge man studies mathematics, not because he likes mathematics, or derives any pleasure from the perception of mathematical truth, still less with the notion of ever using his knowledge; but either because, if he is "a good man," he hopes for a fellowship, or because, if he can not aspire so high, he considers reading the thing to do, and finds a satisfaction in mental effort just as he does in a constitutional to the Gogmagogs. When such a student takes his degree, he is by no means a highly cultivated man; but he is not the sort of a man we can despise for all that. He has in him, to use one of his own metaphors, a considerable amount of *force*, which may be applied in any direction. He has great power of concentration and sustained mental effort even on subjects which are distasteful to him. In other words, his mind is under the control of his will, and he can bring it to bear promptly and vigorously on anything put before him. He will sometimes be half through a piece of work, while an average Oxonian (as we Cambridge men conceive of him at least) is thinking about beginning. But his training has taught him to value mental force without teaching him to care about its application. Perhaps he has been working at the gymnasium, and has at length succeeded in "putting up" a hundredweight. In learning to do this, he has been acquiring strength for its own sake. He does not want to put up hundredweights, but simply to be able to put them up, and his reward is the consciousness of power. Now the tripos is a kind of competitive examination in putting up weights. The student who has been training for it has acquired considerable mental vigor, and when he has put up his weight he falls back on the consciousness of strength which he seldom thinks of using. Having put up the heavier, he despises the lighter weights. He rather prides himself on his ignorance of such things as history, modern languages, and English literature. He "can get those up in a few evenings," whenever he wants them. He reminds me, indeed, of a tradesman who has worked hard to have a large balance at his banker's. This done, he is satisfied. He has neither taste nor desire for the things which make wealth valuable; but when he sees other people in the enjoyment of them, he hugs himself with the consciousness that he can write a check for such things whenever he pleases.

I confess that this outcome of the English theory of education does not seem to me altogether satisfactory. But we have, as yet, no means of judging what will be the outcome of the other theory which makes knowledge the end of education. Its champions confine themselves at present to advising that a variety of sciences be taught to boys, and maintain a rather perplexing silence as to how to teach them. Mr. Spencer, as we have seen, requires that a boy should be taught how to behave in every relation of manhood, and he also tells us how to teach—elementary geometry. Still these advocates of knowledge are acquiring a considerable amount of influence, and there seems reason to fear lest halting between the two theories, our education, instead of combining knowledge and power, should attain to neither.

Our old-fashioned school-teaching, confined as it was to a grammatical drill in the classical languages, did certainly give something of the power which comes from concentrated effort. The Eton Latin Grammar does not indeed seem to me a well-selected model-book, but many a man has found the value of knowing even that book thoroughly. Now, however, a cry has been raised for useful information. It is shameful, we are told, that a boy leaving school should not know the names of the capitals of Europe, and should never have heard of the Habeas Corpus and the Bill of Rights, etc., etc. The schoolmaster is beginning to give way. He admits homœopathic doses of geographical, historical, and scientific epitomes and of modern languages: and perhaps between these stools the unlucky schoolboy will come to the ground; his accurate knowledge of Latin grammar will be exchanged for "some notion" of a variety of things, and in the end his condition will be best described by varying a famous sarcasm, and saying, that if he knew a little of good hard work, he would know a little of everything.

The reader will by this time begin to suspect that I am an educational Tory after all, even a reactionary Tory. This I deny, but I am probably not free from those prejudices which beset Englishmen, especially Cambridge men and schoolmasters, and I confess I look with dismay on the effort which is being made to introduce a large number of subjects into our school-course, and set up knowledge rather than power as the goal of education.*

But can not these be combined? May we not teach such subjects as shall give useful knowledge and power too? On this point the philosopher and the schoolmaster are at issue. The philosopher says, It is desirable that we should have the knowledge of such and such sciences—therefore teach them. The schoolmaster says, It may be desirable to know those sciences, but boys can not learn them. The knowledge acquired by boys will never be very valuable in itself. We must, therefore, consider it a means rather than an end. We must think first of mental discipline; for this boys must thoroughly master what they learn, and this thoroughness absolutely requires that the young mind should be applied to very few subjects; and, though we are quite ready to discuss which subjects afford the best mental training, we can not allow classics to be thrust out till

---

*In this matter the testimony of Lord Stanley is very valuable. "If teaching is, as I believe, better on the whole in the higher than in the lower classes (of society) it is chiefly on this account—not that *more* is taught at an early age, but *less;* that time is taken, that the wall is not run up in haste; that the bricks are set on carefully, and the mortar allowed time to dry. And so the structure, whether high or low, is likely to stand." (From a speech reported in the *Evening Mail*, December 9, 1864.)

some other subjects have been proved worthy to reign in their stead.

Unless I am mistaken, the true ground of complaint against the established education is, that it fails to give, not knowledge, but the desire of knowledge. A literary education which leaves no love of reading behind, can not be considered entirely successful.

As I have said elsewhere, I would admit a natural science into the curriculum in order to give the mind some training in scientific processes, and some interest in scientific truth. I would also endeavor to cultivate a fondness for English literature* and the fine arts; but, whatever the subject taught, I consider that, for educational purposes, the power and the desire to acquire knowledge, are to be valued far before knowledge itself.

How does this conclusion bear upon the matter I set out with, the function of memory in education?

Classicists, scientific men, and all others, are agreed about the value of memory, and must therefore desire that its powers should not be squandered on the learning of facts which, for want of repetition, will be soon lost, or facts which will prove of little value if retained. But in estimating facts, we must think rather of their educational value than of their bearing upon after-life. We must make the memory a storehouse of such facts as are good material for the other powers of the mind to work with; and, that the facts may serve this purpose, they must be such as the mind can thoroughly grasp and han-

---

* The claims of English literature in education have been urged by Professor Seeley with a force which seems to me irresistible. (See *Macmillan's Magazine* for November, 1867.)

dle, and such as may be connected together. "To instruct," as Mr. Payne reminds us, is *instruere*, "to put together in order, to build or construct." We must be careful, then, not to cram the mind with isolated, or as Mr. Spencer calls them, *unorganizable* facts—such facts, e. g., as are taught to young ladies.*

A great deal of our children's memory is wasted in storing facts of this kind, which can never form part of any organism. We do not teach them geography (*earth-knowledge*, as the Germans call it), but the names of places. Our "history" is a similar, though disconnected study. We leave our children ignorant of the land, but insist on their getting up the "landmarks." And, perhaps, from a latent perception of the uselessness of such work, neither teachers nor scholars ever think of these things as learnt to be remembered. Latin grammar is gone through again and again, and a boy feels that the sooner he gets it into his head, the better it will be for him; but who expects that the lists of geographi-

---

* I do not pretend myself to have fathomed the mystery of what *is* taught to young ladies, but I follow the best authorites on the subject. "'I can not remember the time,' said Maria Bertram, 'when I did not know a great deal that Fanny has not the least notion of *yet*. How long ago is it, aunt, since we used to repeat the chronological order of the kings of England, with the dates of their accessions, and most of the principal events of their reigns?' 'Yes,' added Julia, 'and of the Roman emperors as low as Severus, besides a great deal of the heathen mythology, and all the metals, semi-metals, planets, and distinguished philosophers.' Very true, indeed, my dears,' replied the aunt, ' but you are blessed with wonderful memories. . . . Remember that if you are ever so forward and clever yourselves, you should always be modest; for, as much as you know already, there is a great deal more for you to learn.' 'Yes, I know there is,' said Julia, 'till I am seventeen.'" (Miss Austen's *Mansfield Park*.) And, fortunately for the human race, the knowledge vanishes away as soon as that grand climacteric is passed, though perhaps we must regret that often nothing but sheer vacuity is left in its place.

cal and historical names which are learnt one half-year will be remembered the next? I have seen it asserted, that when a boy leaves school he has already forgotten nine-tenths of what he has been taught, and I dare say that estimate is quite within the mark.

By adopting the principles of Jacotot, we shall avoid a great deal of this waste. We shall give some thorough knowledge with which fresh knowledge may be connected.

Perfect familiarity with a subject is something beyond the mere understanding it, and being able with difficulty to reproduce what we have learned. A Cambridge man getting up book-work for the tripos, does not indeed attempt to learn it by heart, without understanding it; but when his mind has thoroughly mastered the steps of the reasoning, he goes over it again and again, till he uses, in fact, hardly any faculty but his memory in writing it out. If he has to think during the operation, he considers that piece of book-work not properly got up.* By thus going over the same thing again and

---

* As an instance of the use of memory in mathematics, and also of the power acquired by perfect attainment, I may mention a case which came under my own observation. A "three days" man, not by any means remarkable for mathematical ability, had got up the book-work of his subject very exactly, but had never done a problem. In the three days' problem paper, to his no small surprise, he got out several of them. A friend who was afterward a good wrangler, ventured to doubt his having done a particular problem. "It came out very easily," said the three days' man, "from such and such a formula." "You are right," said the wrangler, "I worked it out in a much clumsier way myself. *I never thought of that formula.*" I may mention here a fact which, whether it is *à propos* [to the purpose] or not, will be interesting to musicians. The late Professor Walmisley, of Cambridge, told me that when his godfather Attwood was Mozart's pupil, Mozart always had Bach's Forty-eight Preludes and Fugues on his piano, and hardly played anything else.

again, we acquire a thorough command over our knowledge, and the feeling perfectly at home, even within narrow borders, gives a consciousness of strength. An old adage tells us that the Jack-of-all-trades is master of none; but the master of one trade will have no difficulty in extending his insight and capacity beyond it. To use an illustration, which is of course an illustration merely, I would kindle knowledge in children, like fire in a grate. A stupid servant, with a small quantity of wood, spreads it over the whole grate. It blazes away, goes out, and is simply wasted. Another, who is wiser or more experienced, kindles the whole of the wood at one spot, and the fire, thus concentrated, extends in all directions. Thus would I concentrate the beginning of knowledge; and although I could not expect to make much show for a time, I should trust that afterward the fire would extend, almost of its own accord.

I proceed to give Jacotot's directions for carrying out the rule, "*Il faut apprendre quelque chose, et y rapporter tout le reste.*"

1. LEARN—i. e., learn so as to know thoroughly, perfectly, immovably (*imperturbablement*), as well six months or twelve months hence, as now—SOMETHING—something which fairly represents the subject to be acquired, which contains its essential characteristics. 2. REPEAT that "something" incessantly (*sans cesse*), i. e., every day, or very frequently, from the beginning without any omission, so that no part may be forgotten. 3. REFLECT upon the matter thus acquired, so as by degrees to make it a possession of the mind as well as of the memory, so that, being appreciated as a whole, and appreciated in its minutest parts, what is as yet unknown, may be *referred*

to it and interpreted by it. 4. VERIFY, or test, general remarks, e. g., grammatical rules, etc., made by others, by comparing them with the facts (i. e., the words and phraseology) which you have learnt yourself.*

In conclusion, I will give some account of the way in which reading, writing, and the mother-tongue were taught on the Jacototian system.

The teacher takes a book, say Edgeworth's "Early Lessons," points to the first word, and names it, "Frank." The child looks at the word and also pronounces it. Then the teacher does the same with the first two words, "Frank and;" then with the three first, "Frank and Robert," etc. When a line or so has been thus gone over, the teacher asks which word is Robert? What word is that (pointing to one)? 'Find me the same word in this line' (pointing to another part of the book). When a sentence has been thus acquired, the words already known are analyzed into syllables, and these syllables the child must pick out elsewhere. Finally, the same thing is done with letters. When the child can read a sentence, that sentence is put before him written in small-hand, and the child is required to copy it. When he has copied the first word, he is led, by the questions of the teacher, to see how it differs from the original, and then he tries again. The pupil must always correct himself, guided only by questions. This sentence must be worked at till the pupil can write it pretty well from memory. He then tries it in larger characters. By carrying out this plan, the children's powers of observation and making comparisons are

---

* I take this paragraph verbatim from Mr. Payne.

strengthened, and the arts of reading and writing are said to be very readily acquired.

For the mother-tongue, a model-book is chosen and thoroughly learned. Suppose "Rasselas" is selected. The pupil learns by heart a sentence, or a few sentences, and to-morrow adds a few more, still repeating from the beginning. The teacher, after two or three lessons of learning and repeating, takes portions—any portion—of the matter, and submits it to the crucible of the pupil's mind:—Who was Rasselas? Who was his father? What is the father of waters? Where does it begin its course? Where is Abyssinia? Where is Egypt? Where was Rasselas placed? What sort of a person was Rasselas? What is 'credulity'? What are the 'whispers of fancy,' 'the promises of youth,' etc.? What was there peculiar in the position of Rasselas? Where was he confined? Describe the valley. How would you have liked to live there? Why so? Why not? etc."

A great variety of written exercises is soon joined with the learning by heart. Pieces must be written from memory, and the spelling, pointing, etc., corrected by the pupil himself from the book. The same piece must be written again and again, till there are no mistakes to correct. "This," says Mr. Payne, who has himself taught in this way, "is the best plan for spelling that has been devised." Then the pupil may write an analysis, may define words, distinguish between synonyms, explain metaphors, imitate descriptions, write imaginary dialogues or correspondence between the characters, etc.

Besides these, a great variety of grammatical exercises may be given, and the force of prefixes and affixes may be found out by the pupils themselves, by collection and comparison. "The resources even of such a book as 'Rasselas,'" says Mr. Payne, "will be found all but exhaustless, while the training which the mind undergoes in the process of thoroughly mastering it, the acts of analysis, comparison, induction, and deduction, performed so frequently as to become a sort of second nature, can not but serve as an excellent preparation for the subsequent study of English literature."

We see, from these instances, how Jacotot sought to imitate the method by which young children and self-taught men teach themselves. All such proceed from objects to definitions, from facts to reflections and theories, from examples to rules, from particular observations to general principles. They pursue, in fact, however unconsciously, the *method of investigation*, the advantages of which are thus set out in a passage from Burke's treatise on the Sublime and Beautiful:—

"I am convinced," says he, "that the method of teaching which approaches most nearly to the method of investigation is incomparably the best; since, not content with serving up a few barren and lifeless truths, it leads to the stock on which they grew; it tends to set the reader (or learner) himself in the track of invention, and to direct him into those paths in which the author has made his own discoveries."

"For Jacotot, I think the claim may, without presumption, be maintained, that he has, beyond all other teachers, succeeded in co-ordinating the method of elementary teaching with the method of investigation" (Payne).

The latter part of his life, which did not end till

1840, Jacotot spent in his native country—first at Valenciennes, and then at Paris. To the last he labored indefatigably, and with a noble disinterestedness, for what he believed to be the "intellectual emancipation" of his fellow-creatures. For a time, his system made great way in France, but the practices introduced by it were probably unworthy of its principles, and have been abandoned. The University of France, in 1852, recommended more attention to its principles:* but I have not observed any reference to Jacotot in Mr. Arnold's recent report.

---

* "The professors have been directed to instruct their students in the secret movements of thought, not as heretofore by long expositions that can set at work only the mind of the professor, but, following the example that excellent teachers have revived from Socrates by questions that at every instant make the intelligence of the students share in the analysis, and, so to speak, in the discovery of the laws of reason." This is the quotation from the Report to the Emperor in 1853, on which M. Achille Guillard seems to found the assertion in the text. The quotation, however, recommends a return to Socrates, not Jacotot.—(*Nouvelle Biographie, Générale. Jacotot.*)

X.

HERBERT SPENCER.

I once heard it said by a teacher of great ability that no one without practical acquaintance with the subject could write anything worth reading on education. My own opinion differs very widely from this. I am not, indeed, prepared to agree with another authority, much given to paradox, that the actual work of education unfits a man for forming enlightened views about it, but I think that the outsider, coming fresh to the subject, and unencumbered by tradition and prejudice, may hit upon truths which the teacher, whose attention is too much engrossed with practical difficulties, would fail to perceive without assistance, and that, consequently, the theories of intelligent men, unconnected with the work of education, deserve our careful, and, if possible, our impartial consideration.

One of the most important works of this kind which has lately appeared, is the treatise of Mr. Herbert Spencer. So eminent a writer has every claim to be listened to with respect, and in this book he speaks with more than his individual authority. The views he has very vigorously propounded are shared by a number of distinguished scientific men; and not a few of the unscientific believe that in them is shadowed forth the education of the future.

It is perhaps to be regretted that Mr. Spencer has not kept the tone of one who investigates the truth in a subject of great difficulty, but lays about him right and left, after the manner of a spirited controversialist. This, no doubt, makes his book much more entertaining reading than such treatises usually are, but, on the other hand, it has the disadvantage of arousing the antagonism of those whom he would most wish to influence. When the man who has no practical acquaintance with education, lays down the law *ex cathedra* [from the bench], garnished with sarcasm at all that is now going on, the schoolmaster, offended by the assumed tone of authority, sets himself to show where these theories would not work, instead of examining what basis of truth there is in them, and how far they should influence his own practice.

I shall proceed to examine Mr. Spencer's proposals with all the impartiality I am master of.

The great question, whether the teaching which gives the most valuable knowledge is the same as that which best disciplines the faculties of the mind, Mr. Spencer dismisses briefly. "It would be utterly contrary to the beautiful economy of nature," he says, "if one kind of culture were needed for the gaining of information, and another kind were needed as a mental gymnastic." But it seems to me that different subjects must be used to train the faculties at different stages of development. The processes of science, which form the staple of education in Mr. Spencer's system, can not be grasped by the intellect of a child. "The scientific discover does the work, and when it is done the schoolboy is called in to witness the result, to learn its chief features by heart, and to repeat them when called upon, just as he is called on to name the mothers of the patriarchs, or to give an account of the Eastern campaigns of Alexander the Great." (*Pall Mall Gazette*, Feb. 8, 1867.) This, however, affords but scanty training for the mind. We want to draw out the child's interests, and to direct them to worthy objects. We want not only to teach him, but to enable and encourage him to teach himself; and, if following Mr. Spencer's advice, we make him get up the species of plants, "which amount to some 320,000," and the varied forms of animal life, which are "estimated at some 2,000,000," we may, as Mr. Spencer tells us, have strengthened his memory as effectually as by teaching him languages; but the pupil will, perhaps, have no great reason to rejoice over his escape from the horrors of the "As in Præsenti," and "Propria quæ Maribus." The consequences will be the same in both cases. We shall disgust the great majority of our scholars with the acquisition of knowledge, and with the use of the powers of their mind. Whether, therefore, we adopt or reject Mr. Spencer's conclusion, that there is one sort of knowledge which is universally the most valuable, I think I must deny that there is one sort of knowledge which is universally, and at every stage in education, the best adapted to develop the intellectual faculties. Mr. Spencer himself acknowledges this elsewhere. "There is," says he, "a certain sequence in which the faculties spontaneously develop, and a certain kind of knowledge, which each requires during its development. It is for us to ascertain this sequence, and supply this knowledge."

Mr. Spencer discusses more fully "the relative value of knowledges," and this is a subject which has hitherto not met with the attention it deserves. It is not sufficient for us to prove of any subject taught in our schools that the knowledge or the learning of it is valuable. We must also show that the knowledge or the learning of it is of at least as great value as that of anything else that might be taught in the same time. "Had we time to master all objects we need not be particular. To quote the old song—

> Could a man be secure
> That his life would endure,
> As of old for a thousand long years,
> What things he might know !
> What deeds he might do !
> And all without hurry or care !

But we that have but span-long lives must ever bear in mind our limited time for acquisition."

To test the value of the learning imparted in education we must look to the end of education. This Mr. Spencer defines as follows: "To prepare us for complete living, is the function which education has to discharge, and the only rational mode of judging of an educational course is to judge in what degree it discharges such function." For complete living we must know "in what way to treat the body; in what way to treat the mind; in what way to manage our affairs; in what way to bring up a family; in what way to behave as a citizen; in what way to utilize those sources of happiness which nature supplies—how to use all our faculties to the greatest advantage of ourselves and others." There are a number of sciences, says Mr. Spencer, which throw light on these subjects. It should, therefore, be the business of education to impart these sciences.

But, if there were (which is far from being the case)

a well-defined and well-established science in each of these departments, those sciences would not be understandable by children, nor would any individual have time to master the whole of them, or even "a due proportion of each." The utmost that could be attempted would be to give young people some knowledge of the *results* of such sciences and the rules derived from them. But to this Mr. Spencer would object that it would tend, like the learning of languages, "to increase the already undue respect for authority."

To consider Mr. Spencer's divisions in detail, we come first to knowledge that leads to self-preservation:

"Happily, that all-important part of education which goes to secure direct self-preservation, is, in part, already provided for. Too momentous to be left to our blundering, Nature takes it into her own hands." But Mr. Spencer warns us against such thwartings of Nature as that by which "stupid school-mistresses commonly prevent the girls in their charge from the spontaneous physical activites they would indulge in, and so render them comparatively incapable of taking care of themselves in circumstances of peril."

Indirect self-preservation, Mr. Spencer believes, may be much assisted by a knowledge of physiology. "Diseases are often contracted, our members are often injured, by causes which superior knowledge would avoid." I believe these are not the only grounds on which the advocates of physiology urge its claim to be admitted into the curriculum; but these, if they can be established, are no doubt very important. Is it true, however, that doctors preserve their own life and health by their knowledge of physiology? I think the matter is open to dispute. Mr. Spencer does not. He says very truly, that many a man would blush if convicted of ignorance about the pronunciation of Iphigenia, or about the labors of Hercules, who, nevertheless, would not scruple to acknowledge that he had never heard of the Eustachian tubes, and could not tell the normal rate of pulsation. "So terribly," adds Mr. Spencer, "in our education does the ornamental override the useful!" But this is begging the question. At present classics form part of the instruction given to every gentleman, and physiology does not. This is the simpler form of Mr. Spencer's assertion about the labors of Hercules, and the Eustachian tubes, and no one denies it. But we are not so well agreed on the comparative value of these subjects. In his Address at St. Andrews, Mr. Mill showed that he at least was not convinced of the uselessness of classics, and Mr. Spencer does not tell us how the knowledge of the normal state of pulsation is useful; how, to use his own test, "it influences action." However, whether we admit the claims of physiology or not, we shall probably allow that there are certain physiological facts and rules of health, the knowledge of which would be of great practical value, and should therefore be imparted to every one. Here the doctor should come to the schoolmaster's assistance, and give him a manual from which to teach them.

Next in order of importance, according to Mr. Spencer, comes the knowledge which aids indirect self-preservation by facilitating the gaining of a livlihood. Here Mr. Spencer thinks it necessary to prove to us that such sciences as mathematics and physics and biology underlie all the practical arts and business of life. No one will think of joining issue with him on this point; but the question still remains, what influence should this have on education? "Teach science," says Mr. Spencer. "A grounding in science is of great importance, both because it prepares for all this (business of life,) and because rational knowledge has an immense superiority over empirical knowledge." Should we teach all sciences to every body? This is clearly impossible. Should we, then, decide for each child what is to be his particular means of money-getting, and instruct him in those sciences which will be most useful in that business or profession? In other words, should we have a separate school for each calling? The only attempt of this kind which has been made is, I believe, the institution of *Handelschulen* (commercial schools) in Germany. In them, youths of fifteen or sixteen enter for a course of two or three years' instruction which aims exclusively at fitting them for commerce. But, in this case, their general education is already finished. With us, the lad commonly goes to work at the business itself quite as soon as he has the faculties for learning the sciences connected with it. If the school sends him to it with a love of knowledge, and with a mind well disciplined to acquire knowledge, this will be of more value to him than any special information.

As Mr. Spencer is here considering science merely with reference to its importance in earning a livelihood, it is not beside the question to remark, that in a great number of instances, the knowledge of the science which underlies an operation confers no practical ability whatever. No one sees the better for understanding the structure of the eye and the undulatory theory of light.

In swimming and rowing, a senior wrangler has no advantage over a man who is entirely ignorant about the laws of fluid pressure. As far as money-getting is concerned, then, science will not be found to be universally serviceable. Mr. Spencer gives instances, indeed, where science would prevent very expensive blundering; but the true inference is, not that the blunderers should learn science, but that they should mind their own business, and take the opinion of scientific men about theirs. "Here is a mine," says he, "in the sinking of which many shareholders ruined themselves, from not knowing that a certain fossil belonged to the old red sandstone, below which no coal is found." Perhaps they were misled by the little knowledge which Pope tells us is a dangerous thing. If they had been entirely ignorant, they would surely have called in a professional geologist, whose opinion would have been more valuable than their own, even though geology had taken the place of classics in their schooling. "Daily are men induced to aid in carrying out inventions which a mere tyro in science could show to be futile." But these are men whose function it would always be to lose money, not make it, whatever you might teach them.* I have great doubt, therefore, whether the learning of sciences will ever be found a ready way of making a fortune. But directly we get beyond the region of pounds, shillings, and pence, I agree most cordially with Mr. Spencer that a rational knowledge has an immense superiority over empirical knowledge. And, as a part of their education, boys

---

* "The brewer," as Mr. Spencer himself tells us, "if his business is very extensive, finds it pay to keep a chemist on the premises"—pay a good deal better, I suspect, than learning chemistry at school.

should be taught to distinguish the one from the other, and to desire rational knowledge. Much might be done in this way by teaching, not all the sciences and nothing else, but the main principles of some one science, which would enable the more intelligent boys to understand and appreciate the value of "a rational explanation of phenomena." I believe this addition to what was before a literary education has already been made in some of our leading schools, as Harrow, Rugby, and the City of London.*

Next, Mr. Spencer would have instruction in the proper way of rearing off-spring form a part of his curriculum. There can be no question of the importance of this knowledge, and all that Mr. Spencer says of the lamentable ignorance of parents is, unfortunately, no less undeniable. But could this knowledge be imparted early in life? Young people would naturally take but little interest in it. It is by parents, or at least by those who have some notion of the parental responsibility, that this knowledge should be sought. The best way in which we can teach the young will be so to bring them up that, when they themselves have to rear children, the remembrance of their own youth may be a guide and not a beacon to them. But more knowledge than this is

---

* Mr. Helps, who by taste and talent is eminently literary, put in this claim for science more than twenty years ago. "The higher branches of method can not be taught at first; but you may begin by teaching orderliness of mind. Collecting, classifying, contrasting, and weighing facts are some of the processes by which method is taught. . . . Scientific method may be acquired without many sciences being learnt; but one or two great branches of science must be accurately known" (*Friends in Council, Education*.) Mr. Helps, though by his delightful style he never gives the reader any notion of over-compression, has told us more truth about education in a few pages than one sometimes meets with in a complete treatise.

necessary, and I differ from Mr. Spencer only as to the proper time for acquiring it.

Next comes the knowledge which fits a man for the discharge of his functions as a citizen, a subject to which Dr. Arnold attached great importance at the time of the first Reform Bill, and which deserves our attention all the more in consequence of the second. But what knowledge are we to give for this purpose? One of the subjects which seem especially suitable is history. But history, as it is now written, is, according to Mr. Spencer, useless. "It does not illustrate the right principles of political action." "The great mass of historical facts are facts from which no conclusions can be drawn—unorganizable facts, and, therefore, facts of no service in establishing principles of conduct, which is the chief use of facts. Read them if you like for amusement, but do not flatter yourself they are instructive." About the right principles of political action we seem so completely at sea that perhaps, the main thing we can do for the young is to point out to them the responsibilities which will hereafter devolve upon them, and the danger, both to the state and the individual, of just echoing the popular cry, without the least reflection, according to our present usage. But history, as it is now written by great historians, may be of some use in training the young both to be citizens and men. "Reading about the fifteen decisive battles, or all the battles in history, would not make a man a more judicious voter at the next election," says Mr. Spencer. But is this true? The knowledge of what has been done in other times, even by those whose coronation renders them so distasteful to Mr. Spencer, is knowledge which influences a man's whole character, and may, therefore, affect particular acts, even when we are unable to trace the connection. As it has been often said, the effect of reading history is, in some respects the same as that of traveling. Any one in Mr. Spencer's vein might ask, "If a man has seen the Alps, of what use will that be to him in weighing out groceries?" Directly, none at all; but indirectly, much. The traveled man will not be such a slave to the petty views and customs of his trade as the man who looks on his county town as the center of the universe. The study of history, like traveling, widens the student's mental vision, frees him, to some extent, from the bondage of the present, and prevents his mistaking conventionalities for laws of nature. It brings home to him, in all its force, the truth that "there are also people beyond the mountain" (*Hinter dem Berge sind auch Leute*), that there are higher interests in the world than his own business concerns, and nobler men than himself, or the best of his acquaintance. It teaches him what men are capable of, and thus gives him juster views of his race. And to have all this truth worked into the mind contributes, perhaps, as largely to "complete living" as knowledge of the Eustachian tubes, or of the normal rate of pulsation.*

I think, therefore, that the works of great historians

---

* Mr. Mill (who, by the way, would leave history entirely to private reading, *Address at St. Andrews*, p. 21) has pointed out that "there is not a fact in history which is not susceptible of as many different explanations as there are possible theories of human affairs," and that "history is not the foundation but the verification of the social science." But he admits that "what we know of former ages, like what we know of foreign nations is, with all its imperfectness, of much use, by correcting the narrowness incident to personal experience." (Dissertations, i., 112.)

and biographers, which we already possess, may be usefully employed in education. It is difficult to estimate the value of history according to Mr. Spencer's idea, as it has yet to be written; but I venture to predict than if boys, instead of reading about the history of nations in connection with their leading men, are required to study only "the progress of society," the subject will at once lose all its interest for them; and, perhaps, many of the facts communicated will prove, after all, no less unorganizable than the fifteen decisive battles.

Lastly, we come to that "remaining division of human life which includes the relaxations and amusements filling leisure hours." Mr. Spencer assures us that he will yield to none in the value he attaches to æsthetic culture and its pleasures; but if he does not value the fine arts less, he values science more; and painting, music, and poetry would receive as little encouragement under his dictatorship as in the days of the Commonwealth. As the fine arts and belles-lettres occupy the leisure part of life, so should they occupy the leisure part of education." This language is rather obscure; but the only meaning I can attach to it is, that music, drawing, poetry, etc., may be taught if time can be found when all other knowledges are provided for. This reminds me of the author whose works are so valuable that they will be studied when Shakespeare is forgotten—but not before. Any one of the sciences which Mr. Spencer considers so necessary might employ a lifetime. Where, then, shall we look for the leisure part of education when education includes them all?*

---

* It is difficult to treat seriously the arguments by which Mr. Spencer endeavors to show that a knowledge of science is necessary for the prac-

But if, adopting Mr. Spencer's own measure, we estimate the value of knowledge by its influence on action, we shall probably rank "accomplishments" much higher than they have hitherto been placed in the schemes of educationists. Knowledge and skill connected with the business of life are, of necessity, acquired in the discharge of business. But the knowledge and skill which make our leisure valuable to ourselves, and a source of pleasure to others, can seldom be gained after the work of life is begun. And yet every day a man may benefit by possessing such an ability, or may suffer from the want of it. One whose eyesight has been trained by

---

tice or the enjoyment of the fine arts. Of course, the highest art of every kind is based on science, that is, on truths which science takes cognizance of and explains; but it does not therefore follow that "without science there can be neither perfect production nor full appreciation." Mr. Spencer tells us of mistakes which John Lewis and Rossetti have made for want of science. Very likely: and had those gentlemen devoted much of their time to science we should never have heard of their blunders—or of their pictures either. If they were to paint a piece of woodwork, a carpenter might, perhaps, detect something amiss in the mitering. If they painted a wall, a bricklayer might point out that with their arrangement of stretchers and headers the wall would tumble down for want of a proper bond. But even Mr. Spencer would not wish them to spend their time in mastering the technicalities of every handicraft, in order to avoid these inaccuracies. It is the business of the painter to give us form and color as they reveal themselves to the eye, not to prepare illustrations of scientific text-books. The physical sciences, however, are only part of the painter's necessary acquirements, according to Mr. Spencer. "He must also understand how the minds of spectators will be affected by the several peculiarities of his work—a question in psychology!" Still more surprising is Mr. Spencer's dictum about poetry. "Its rhythm, its strong and numerous metaphors, its hyperboles, its violent inversions, are simply exaggerations of the traits of excited speech. To be good, therefore, poetry must pay attention to those laws of nervous action which excited speech obeys." It is difficult to see how poetry can pay attention to anything. The poet, of course, must not violate those laws, but, if he *has paid attention* to them in composing, he will do well to present his MS. to the local newspaper.

drawing and painting finds objects of interest all around him, to which other people are blind. A primrose by the river's brim is, perhaps, more to him who has a feeling for its form and color than even to the scientific student, who can tell all about its classification and component parts. A knowledge of music is often of the greatest practical service, as by virtue of it, its possessor is valuable to his associates, to say nothing of his having a constant source of pleasure and a means of recreation which is most precious as a relief from the cares of life. Of far greater importance is the knowledge of our best poetry. One of the first reforms in our school-course would have been, I should have thought, to give this knowledge a much more prominent place; but Mr. Spencer consigns it, with music and drawing, to "the leisure part of education." Whether a man who was engrossed by science, who had no knowledge of the fine arts except as they illustrated scientific laws, no acquaintance with the lives of great men, or with any history but sociology, and who studied the thoughts and emotions expressed by our great poets merely with a view to their psychological classification—whether such a man could be said to "live completely" is a question to which every one, not excepting Mr. Spencer himself, would probably return the same answer. And yet this is the kind of man which Mr. Spencer's system would produce where it was most successful.

Let me now briefly sum up the conclusions arrived at, and consider how far I differ from Mr. Spencer. I believe that there is no one study which is suited to train the faculties of the mind at every stage of its development, and that when we have decided on the necessity of this or that knowledge, we must consider further what is the right time for acquiring it. I believe that intellectual education should aim, not so much at communicating facts, however valuable, as at showing the boy what true knowledge is, and giving him the power and the *disposition* to acquire it. I believe that the exclusively scientific teaching which Mr. Spencer approves would not effect this. It would lead at best to a very one-sided development of the mind. It might fail to engage the pupil's interest sufficiently to draw out his faculties, and in this case the net outcome of his school-days would be no larger than at present. Of the knowledges which Mr. Spencer recommends for special objects, some, I think, would not conduce to the object, and some could not be communicated early in life. (1.) For indirect self-preservation we do not require to know physiology, but the result of physiology. (2.) The science which bears on special pursuits in life has not in many cases any pecuniary value, and although it is most desirable that every one should study the science which makes his work intelligible to him, this must usually be done when his schooling is over. The school will have done its part if it has accustomed him to the intellectual processes by which sciences are learned, and has given him an intelligent appreciation of their value.* (3.) The right way of rearing and training children

---

* Speaking of law, medicine, engineering, and the industrial arts, Mr. Mill remarks: "Whether those whose specialty they are will learn them as a branch of intelligence or as a mere trade, and whether having learnt them, they will make a wise and conscientious use of them, or the reverse, depends less on the manner in which they are taught their profession, than upon what sort of mind they bring to it—what kind of intelligence and of conscience the general system of education has developed in them."—Address at St. Andrews, p. 6.

should be studied indeed, but not by the children themselves. (4.) The knowledge which fits a man to discharge his duties as a citizen is of great importance, and, as Dr. Arnold pointed out, is likely to be entirely neglected by those who have to struggle for a livelihood. The schoolmaster should, therefore, by no means neglect this subject with those of his pupils whose schooldays will soon be over; but, probably, all that he can do is to cultivate in them a sense of the citizen's duty, and a capacity for being their own teachers.* (5.) The knowledge of poetry, belles-lettres, and the fine arts, which Mr. Spencer hands over to the leisure part of education, is the only knowledge in his programme which I think should most certainly form a prominent part in the curriculum of every school.

I therefore differ, though with great respect, from the conclusions at which Mr. Spencer has arrived. But I heartily agree with him that we are bound to inquire into the relative value of knowledges, and if we take, as I should willingly do, Mr. Spencer's test, and ask how does this or that knowledge influence action (including in our inquiry its influence on mind and character, through which it bears upon action), I think we should banish from our schools much that has hitherto been taught in them, besides those old tormenters of youth (laid, I fancy, at last—*requiescant in pace* [let them rest in peace])—the *Propria quæ Maribus* [Things appropriate to men] and its kindred absurdities. What we *should* teach is, of course, not so easily decided as what we *should not*.

---

* Vide Mill.—Address, p. 67.

I now come to consider Mr. Spencer's second chapter, in which, under the heading of "Intellectual Education," he gives an admirable summing up of the main principles in which the great writers on the subject have agreed, from Comenius downward. These principles are, perhaps, not all of them unassailable, and even where they are true, many mistakes must be expected before we arrive at the best method of applying them; but the only reason that can be assigned for the small amount of influence they have hitherto exercised is, that most teachers are as ignorant of them as of the abstrusest doctrines of Kant and Hegel.

In stating these principles Mr. Spencer points out that they merely form a commencement for a science of education. "Before educational methods can be made to harmonize in character and arrangement with the faculties in the mode and order of unfolding, it is first needful that we ascertain with some completeness how the faculties *do* unfold. At present we have acquired on this point only a few general notions. These general notions must be developed in detail—must be transformed into a multitude of specific propositions before we can be said to possess that *science* on which the *art* of education must be based. And then, when we have definitely made out in what succession and in what combinations the mental powers become active, it remains to choose out of the many possible ways of exercising each of them, that which best conforms to its natural mode of action. Evidently, therefore, it is not to be supposed that even our most advanced modes of teaching are the right ones, or nearly the right ones." It is not to be wondered at that we have no science of education. Those who have been able to observe the phenomena have had no interest in generalizing from them. Up to the present time the schoolmaster has been a person to whom boys were sent to learn Latin and Greek. He has had, therefore, no more need of a science than the dancing-master. But the present century, which has brought in so many changes will not leave the state of education as it found it. Latin and Greek, if they are not dethroned in our higher schools, will have their despotism changed for a very limited monarchy. A course of instruction certainly without Greek and perhaps without Latin will have to be provided for middle schools. Juster views are beginning to prevail of the schoolmaster's function. It is at length perceived that he has to assist the development of the human mind, and, perhaps by-and-by, he may think it as well to learn all he can of that which he is employed in developing. When matters have advanced as far as this, we may begin to hope for a science of education. In Locke's days he could say of physical science that there was no such science in existence. For thousand of years the human race had live in ignorance of the simplest laws of the world it inhabited. But the true method of inquiring once introduced, science has made such rapid conquests, and acquired so great importance, that some of our ablest men seem inclined to deny, if not the existence, at least the value, of any other kind of knowledge. So, too, when teachers seek by actual observation to discover the laws of mental development, a science may be arrived at which, in its influence on mankind, would, perhaps, rank before any we now possess.

Those who have read the previous Essays will have seen in various forms most of the principles which Mr.

Spencer enumerates, but I gladly avail myself of his assistance in summing them up.

1. We should proceed from the simple to the complex, both in our choice of subjects and in the way in which each subject is taught. We should begin with but few subjects at once, and, successively adding to these, should finally carry on all subjects abreast.

Each larger concept is made by a combination of smaller ones, and presupposes them, If this order is not attended to in communicating knowledge, the pupil can learn nothing but words, and will speedily sink into apathy and disgust.

That we must proceed from the known to the unknown is something more than a corollary to the above;* because not only are new concepts formed by the combination of old, but the mind has a liking for what it knows, and this liking extends itself to all that can be connected with its object. The principle of using the known in teaching the unknown is so simple, that all teachers who really endeavor to make anything understood, naturally adopt it. The traveler who is describing what he has seen and what we have not seen tells us that it is in one particular like this object, and in another like that object, with which we are already familiar. We combine these different concepts we possess, and so get some notion of things about which we were previously ignorant. What is required in our teaching is that the use of the known should be employed more systematically. Most teachers think of boys who have no school learning as

---

* Mr. Spencer does not mention this principle in his enumeration, but, no doubt, considers he implies it.

entirely ignorant. The least reflection shows, however, that they know already much more than schools can ever teach them. A sarcastic examiner is said to have handed a small piece of paper to a student, and told him to write *all he knew* on it. Perhaps many boys would have no difficulty in stating the sum of their school learning within very narrow limits; but with other knowledge a child of five years old, could he write, might soon fill a volume. Our aim should be to connect the knowledge boys bring with them to the school-room with that which they are to acquire there. I suppose all will allow, whether they think it a matter of regret or otherwise, that hardly anything of the kind has hitherto been attempted. Against this state of things I can not refrain from borrowing Mr. Spencer's eloquent protest. " Not recognizing the truth that the function of books is supplementary—that they form an indirect means to knowledge when direct means fail, a means of seeing through other men what you can not see for yourself, teachers are eager to give second-hand facts in place of first-hand facts. Not perceiving the enormous value of that spontaneous education which goes on in early years, not perceiving that a child's restless observation, instead of being ignored or checked, should be diligently ministered to and made as acurate and complete as possible, they insist on occupying its eyes and thoughts with things that are, for the time being, incomprehensible and repugnant. Possessed by a superstition which worships the symbols of knowledge instead of the knowledge itself, they do not see that only when his acquaintance with the objects and processes of the household, the street, and the fields, is becoming tolerably exhaustive, only then should a child be introduced to the new sources of information which books supply, and this not only because immediate cognition is of far greater value than mediate cognition, but also because the words contained in books can be rightly interpreted into ideas only in proportion to the antecedent experience of things."* While agreeing heartily in the spirit of this protest, I doubt whether we should wait till the child's acquaintance with the objects and processes of the household, the street, and the fields, is becoming tolerably exhaustive before we give him instruction from books. The point of time which Mr. Spencer indicates is, at all events, rather hard to fix, and I should wish to connect book-learning as soon as possible with the learning that is being acquired in other ways. Thus might both the books, and the acts and objects of daily life, win an additional interest. If, e. g., the first reading books were about the animals, and later on about trees and flowers which the children constantly meet with, and their attention were kept up by large colored pictures, to which the text might refer, the children would soon find both pleasure and advantage in reading, and they would look at the animals and trees with a keener interest from the additional knowledge of them they had derived from books. This is, of course, only one small application of a very influential principle.

---

* After remarking on the wrong order in which subjects are taught, he continues, "What with perceptions unnaturally dulled by early thwartings, and a coerced attention to books, what with the mental confusion produced by teaching subjects before they can be understood, and in each of them giving generalizations before the facts of which they are the generalizations, what with making the pupil a mere passive recipient of others' ideas and not in the least leading him to be an active inquirer or self-instructor, and what with taxing the faculties to excess, there are very few minds that become as efficient as they might be."

One marvelous instance of the neglect of this principle is found in the practice of teaching Latin grammar before English grammar. Respect for the high authority of Professor Kennedy, who would not have English grammar taught at all, prevents my expressing myself as strongly as I should like in this matter. As Professor Seeley has so well pointed out, children bring with them to school the knowledge of language in its concrete form. They may soon be taught to observe the language they already know, and to find, almost for themselves, some of the main divisions of words in it. But, instead of availing himself of the child's previous knowledge, the schoolmaster takes a new and difficult language, differing as much as possible from English; a new and difficult science, that of grammar, conveyed, too, in a new and difficult terminology; and all this he tries to teach at the same time. The consequence is that the science is destroyed, the terminology is either misunderstood, or, more probably, associated with no ideas, and even the language for which every sacrifice is made, is found, in nine cases out of ten, never to be acquired at all.*

* A class of boys whom I once took in Latin Delectus denied, with the utmost confidence, when I questioned them on the subject, that they were any such things in English as verbs and substantives. On another occasion, I saw a poor boy of nine or ten caned, because, when he had said that *proficiscor* was a deponent verb, he could not say what a deponent verb was. Even if he had remembered the inaccurate grammar definition expected of him, "A deponent verb is a verb with a passive form and an active meaning," his comprehension of *proficiscor* would have been no greater. It is worth observing that, even when offending grievously in great matters against the principle of connecting fresh knowledge with the old, teachers are sometimes driven to it in small. They find that it is better for boys to see that *lignum* is like *regnum*, and *laudare* like *amare*, than simply to learn that *lignum* is of the Second Declension, and *laudare* of the First Conjugation. If boys had to learn, by mere effort of memory, the particular declension and conjugation of Latin words before they were

2. "All development is an advance from the indefinite to the definite."

I do not feel very certain of the truth of this principle, or of its application, if true. Of course, a child's intellectual conceptions are at first vague, and we should not forget this; but it is rather a fact than a principle.

3. "Our lessons ought to start from the concrete, and end in the abstract." What Mr. Spencer says under this head well deserves the attention of all teachers. "General formulas which men have devised to express groups of details, and which have severally simplified their conceptions by uniting many facts into one fact, they have supposed must simplify the conceptions of a child also. They have forgotten that a generalization is simple only in comparison with the whole mass of particular truths it comprehends; that it is more complex than any one of these truths taken simply; that only, after many of these single truths have been acquired, does the generalization ease the memory and help the reason; and that, to a mind not possessing these single truths, it is necessarily a mystery.* Thus, confounding two kinds of simplification, teachers have constantly erred by setting out with "first principles," a proceeding essentially, though not apparently, at variance with the primary rule (of proceeding from the simple to the complex), which implies that the mind should be intro-

---

taught anything about declensions or conjugations, this would be as sensible as the method adopted in some other instances, and the teachers might urge, as usual, that the information would come in useful afterward.

*"General terms are, as it were, but the indorsements upon the bundles of our ideas; they are useful to those who have collected a number of ideas, but utterly useless to those who have no collections ready for classification."—Edgeworth's Practical Education, 1. 91.

duced to principles through the medium of examples, and so should be led from the particular to the general, from the concrete to the abstract." In conformity with this principle, Pestalozzi made the actual counting of things precede the teaching of abstract rules in arithmetic. Basedow introduced weights and measures into the school, and Mr. Spencer describes some exercise in cutting out geometrical figures in cardboard as a preparation for geometry. The difficulty about such instruction is that it requires apparatus, and apparatus is apt to get lost or out of order. But, if apparatus is good for anything at all, it is worth a little trouble. There is a tendency in the minds of many teachers to depreciate "mechanical appliances." Even a decent blackboard is not always to be found in our higher schools. But, though such appliances will not enable a bad master to teach well, nevertheless, other things being equal, the master will teach better with them than without them. There is little credit due to him for managing to dispense with apparatus. An author might as well pride himself on being saving in pens and paper.

4. "The genesis of knowledge in the individual must follow the same course as the genesis of knowledge in the race." This is a thesis on which I have no opinion to offer. It was, I believe, first maintained by Pestalozzi.

5. From the above principle Mr. Spencer infers that every study should have a purely experimental introduction, thus proceeding through an empirical stage to a rational.

6. A second conclusion which Mr. Spencer draws is that, in education, the process of self-development

should be encouraged to the utmost. Children should be led to make their own investigations, and to draw their own inferences. They should be told as little as possible, and induced to discover as much as possible. I quite agree with Mr. Spencer that this principle can not be too strenuously insisted on, though it obviously demands a high amount of intelligence in the teacher. But if education is to be a training of the faculties, if it is to prepare the pupil to teach himself, something more is needed than simply to pour in knowledge and make the pupil reproduce it. The receptive and reproductive faculties form but a small portion of a child's powers, and yet the only portion which many schoolmasters seek to cultivate. It is, indeed, not easy to get beyond this point; but the impediment is in us, not in the children. "Who can watch," asks Mr. Spencer, "the ceaseless observation, and inquiry, and inference, going on in a child's mind, or listen to its acute remarks in matters within the range of its faculties, without perceiving that these powers it manifests, if brought to bear systematically upon studies *within the same range*, would readily master them without help? This need for perpetual telling results from our stupidity, not from the child's. We drag it away from the facts in which it is interested, and which it is actively assimilating of itself. We put before it facts far too complex for it to understand, and therefore distasteful to it. Finding that it will not voluntarily acquire these facts, we thrust them into its mind by force of threats and punishment. By thus denying the knowledge it craves, and cramming it with knowledge it can not digest, we produce a morbid state of its faculties, and a consequent disgust for knowledge in general. And when, as a result, partly of the stolid indolence we have brought on, and partly of still-continued unfitness in its studies, the child can understand nothing without explanation, and becomes a mere passive recipient of our instruction, we infer that education must necessarily be carried on thus. Having by our method induced helplessness, we make the helplessness a reason for our method." It is, of course, much easier to point out defects than to remedy them: but every one who has observed the usual indifference of school-boys to their work, and the waste of time consequent on their inattention, or only half-hearted attention, to the matter before them, and then thinks of the eagerness with which the same boys throw themselves into the pursuits of their play-hours, will feel a desire to get at the cause of this difference; and, perhaps, it may seem to him partly accounted for by the fact that their school-work makes a monotonous demand on a single faculty—the memory.

7. This brings me to the last of Mr. Spencer's principles of intellectual education. Instruction must excite the interest of the pupils, and therefore be pleasurable to them. "Nature has made the healthful exercise of our faculties both of mind and body pleasurable. It is true that some of the highest mental powers as yet but little developed in the race, and congenitally possessed in any considerable degree only by the most advanced, are indisposed to the amount of exertion required of them. But these in virtue of their very complexity will in a normal course of culture come last into exercise, and will, therefore, have no demands made on them until the pupil has arrived at an age

when ulterior motives can be brought into play, and an indirect pleasure made to counterbalance a direct displeasure. With all faculties lower than these, however, the immediate gratification consequent on activity is the normal stimulus, and under good management the only needful stimulus. When we have to fall back on some other, we must take the fact as evidence that we are on the wrong track. Experience is daily showing with greater clearness that there is always a method to be found productive of interest—even of delight—and it ever turns out that this is the method proved by all other tests to be the right one."

As far as I have had the means of judging, I have found that the majority of teachers reject this principle. If you ask them why, most of them will you that it is impossible to make school-work interesting to children. A large number also hold that it is not desirable. Let us consider these two points separately.

Of course, if it is not possible to get children to take interest in anything they could be taught in school, there is an end of the matter. But no one really goes as far as this. Every teacher finds that some of the things boys are taught they like better than others, and perhaps that one boy takes to one subject and another to another, and he also finds, both of classes and individuals, that they always get on best with what they like best. The utmost that can be maintained is, then, that some subjects which must be taught will not interest the majority of the learners. And if it be once admitted that it is desirable to make learning pleasant and interesting to our pupils, this principle will influence us to some extent in the subjects we select for teaching, and still more in the methods by which we endeavor to teach them. I say we shall be guided *to some extent* in the selection of subjects. There are theorists who assert that nature gives to young minds a craving for their proper aliment, so that they should be taught only only what they show an inclination for. But surely our natural inclinations in this matter, as in others, are neither on the one hand to be ignored, nor on the other to be uncontrolled by such motives as our reason dictates to us. We at length perceive this in the physical nurture of our children. Locke directs that children are to have very little sugar or salt. "Sweetmeats of all kinds are to be avoided," says he, " which, whether they do more harm to the maker or eater is not easy to tell." (Ed. § 20.) Now, however, doctors have found out that young people's taste for sweets should in moderation be gratified, that they require sugar as much as they require any other kind of nutriment. But no one would think of feeding his children entirely on sweetmeats, or even of letting them have an unlimited supply of plum-puddings and hardbake. If we follow out this analogy in nourishing the mind, we shall, to some extent gratify a child's taste for "stories," whilst we also provide a large amount of more solid fare. But although we should certainly not ignore our children's likes and dislikes in learning, or in anything else, it is easy to attach too much importance to them. Dislike very often proceeds from mere want of insight into the subject. When a boy has "done" the First Book of Euclid without knowing how to judge of the size of an angle, or the Second Book without forming any conception of a rectangle, no one can be surprised at his not liking Euclid. And then the failure which is really due to bad teaching is attributed by the master to the stupidity of his pupils, and by the pupil to the dullness of the subject. If masters really desired to make learning a pleasure to their pupils, I think they would find that much might be done to effect this without any alteration in the subjects taught.

But the present dullness of school-work is not without its defenders. They insist on the importance of breaking in the mind to hard work. This can only be done, they say, by tasks which are repulsive to it. The schoolboy does not like, and ought not to like, learning Latin grammar any more than the colt should find pleasure in running round in a circle: the very fact that these things are not pleasant makes them beneficial. Perhaps a certain amount of such training may train *down* the mind and qualify it for some drudgery from which it might otherwise revolt; but if this result is attained, it is attained at the sacrifice of the intellectual activity which is necessary for any higher function. As Carlyle says, when speaking of routine work generally, you want nothing but a sorry nag to draw your sand-cart; your high-spirited Arab will be dangerous in such a capacity. But who would advocate for all colts a training which should render them fit for nothing but such humble toil? I have spoken elsewherere on this subject, and here I will merely express my strong conviction that boys' minds are frequently dwarfed, and their interests in intellectual pursuits blighted, by the practice of employing the first years of their school life in learning by heart things which it is quite impossible for them to understand or care for. Teachers set out by assuming that little boys can not understand anything, and that all we can do with them is to keep them quiet and cram them with forms which will come in useful at a later age. When the boys have been taught on this system for two or three years, their teacher complains that they are stupid and inattentive, and that so long as they can say a thing by heart they never trouble themselves to understand it. In other words, the teacher grumbles at them for doing precisely what they have been taught to do, for repeating words without any thought of their meaning.

In this very important matter I am fully alive to the difference between theory and practice. It is so easy to recommend that boys should be got to understand and take an interest in their work—so difficult to carry out the recommendation! Grown people can hardly conceive that words which have in their minds been associated with familiar ideas from time immemorial, are mere sounds in the mouths of their pupils. The teacher thinks he is begining at the begining if he says that a transitive verb must govern an accusative, or that all the angles of a square are right angles. He gives his pupils credit for innate ideas up to this point, at all events, and advancing on this supposition he finds that he can get nothing out of them but memory-work, so he insists on this that his time and theirs may not seem to be wholly wasted. The great difficulty of teaching well, however, is after all but a poor excuse for contentedly teaching badly, and it would be a great step in advance if teachers in general were as dissatisfied with themselves as they usually are with their pupils.*

---

* Mr. Spencer and Professor Tyndall appeal to the results of experience as justifying a more rational method of teaching. Speaking of geometrical deductions, Mr. Spencer says: " It has repeatedly occurred that those who have been stupefied by the ordinary school-drill—by its ab-

I do not purpose following Mr. Spencer through his chapters on moral and physical education. In practice I find I can draw no line between moral and religious education; so the discussion of one without the other has not for me much interest. Mr. Spencer has some very valuable remarks on physical education which I could do little more than extract, and I have already made too many quotations from a work which will be in the hands of most of my readers.

Mr. Spencer differs very widely from the great body of our schoolmasters. I have ventured in turn to differ on some points from Mr. Spencer; but I am none the less conscious that he has written not only one of the most readable, but also one of the most important books on education in the English language.

[The best edition of Spencer's "Education" is Appleton's, price in cloth $1.25, in paper 50 cts. It is also published in the Humboldt Library at 15 cts.]

---

stract formulas, its wearisome tasks, its cramming—have suddenly had their intellects roused by thus ceasing to make them passive recipients, and inducing them to become active discoverers. The discouragement caused by bad teaching having been diminished by a little sympathy, and sufficient perseverance excited to achieve a first success, there arises a revolution of feeling affecting the whole nature. They no longer find themselves incompetent; they, too, can do something. And gradually, as success follows success, the incubus of despair disappears, and they attack the difficulties of their other studies with a courage insuring conquest."

XI.

THOUGHTS AND SUGGESTIONS.

One of the great wants of middle-class education at present, is an ideal to work toward. Our old public schools have such an ideal. The model public schoolman is a gentleman who is an elegant Latin and Greek scholar. True, this may not be a very good ideal, and some of our ablest men, both literary and scientific, are profoundly dissatisfied with it. But, so long as it is maintained, all questions of reform are comparatively simple. In middle class schools, on the other hand, there is no *terminus ad quem* [end to work toward]. A number of boys are got together, and the question arises, not simply *how* to teach, but *what* to teach. Where the masters are not university men, they are, it may be, not men of broad views or high culture. Of course no one will suppose me ignorant of the fact that a great number of teachers who have never been at a university, are both enlightened and highly cultivated; and also that many teachers who have taken degrees, even in honors, are neither. But, speaking broadly of the two classes, I may fairly assume that the non-university men are inferior in these respects to the graduates. If not, our universities should be reformed on Carlyle's "live-coal" principle, without further loss of time. Many non-university masters have been engaged in teaching ever since they were boys themselves, and teaching is a very narrowing occupation. They are apt therefore to be careless of general principles, and to aim merely at storing their pupils' memory with *facts*—facts about language, about history, about geography, without troubling themselves to consider what is and what is not worth knowing, or what faculties the boys have, and how they should be developed. The consequence is their boys get up, for the purpose of forgetting with all convenient speed, quantities of details about as instructive and entertaining as the *Propria quæ maribus*, such as the division of England under the Heptarchy, the battles in the wars of the Roses, and lists of geographical names. Where the masters are university men, they have rather a contempt for this kind of cramming, which makes them do it badly, if they attempt it at all: but they are driven to this teaching in many cases because they do not know what to substitute in its place. Their own education was in classics and mathematics. Their pupils are too young to have much capacity for mathematics, and they will leave school too soon to get any sound knowledge of classics, so the strength of the teaching ought clearly not to be thrown into these subjects. But the master really knows no other. He soon finds that he is not much his pupils' superior in acquaintance with the theory of the English language or with history and geography. There are not many men with sufficient strength of will to study whilst their energies are taxed by teaching, and standard books are not always within reach: so the master is forced to content himself with hearing lessons in a perfunctory way out of dreary school-books. Hence it comes to pass that he goes on teaching subjects of which he himself is ignorant, subjects, too, of which he does not recognize the importance, with an enlightened disbelief in his own method of tuition. He finds it up-hill work, to be sure—labor of Sisyphus, in fact—and is conscious that his pupils do not get on, however hard he may try to drive them; but he never hoped for success in his teaching, so the want of it does not distress him. I may be suspected of caricature, but not, I think, by university men who have themselves had to teach anything besides classics and mathematics.

If there is any truth in what I have been saying, school-teaching, in subjects other than classics and mathematics (which I am not now considering), is very commonly a failure. And a failure it must remain until boys can be got to work with a will, in other words, to feel interest in the subject taught. I know there is a strong prejudice in some people's minds against the notion of making learning pleasant. They remind us that school should be a preparation for after-life. After-life will bring with it an immense amount of drudgery. If, they say, things at school are made too easy and pleasant (words, by the way, very often and very erroneously confounded), school will cease to give the proper discipline: boys will be turned out not knowing what hard work is, which, after all, is the most important lesson that can be taught them. In these views I sincerely concur, so far as this, at least, that we want boys to work hard and vigorously to go through necessary drudgery, i. e., labor in itself disagreeable. But this result is not attained by such a system as I have described. Boys do not learn to work *hard*, but in a dull, stupid way, with most of their faculties lying dormant, and though they

P

are put through a vast amount of drudgery, they seem as incapable of throwing any energy into it, as prisoners on the tread-mill. I think we shall find, on consideration, that no one succeeds in any occupation unless that occupation is interesting, either in itself or from some object that is to be obtained by means of it. Only when such an interest is aroused is energy possible. No one will deny that, as a rule, the most successful men are those for whom their employment has the greatest attractions. We should be sorry to give ourselves up to the treatment of a doctor who thought the study of disease mere drudgery, or a dentist who felt a strong repugnance to operating on teeth. No doubt, the successful man in every pursuit has to go through a great deal of drudgery, but he has a general interest in the subject, which extends, partially at least, to its most wearisome details; his energy, too, is excited by the desire of what the drudgery will gain for him.*

---

* On this subject I can quote the authority of a great observer of the mind—no less a man, indeed, than Wordsworth. He speaks of the "grand elementary principle of pleasure, by which man knows, and feels, and lives, and moves. We have no sympathy," he continues, " but what is propagated by pleasure—I would not be misunderstood—but wherever we sympathize with pain, it will be found that the sympathy is produced and carried on by subtle combinations with pleasure. We have no knowledge, that is, no general principles drawn from the contemplation of particular facts, but what has been built up by pleasure, and exists in us by pleasure alone. The man of science, the chemist, and mathematician, whatever difficulties and disgusts they may have to struggle with, know and feel this. However painful may be the objects with which the anatomist's knowledge may be connected, he feels that his knowledge is pleasure, and *when he has no pleasure he has no knowledge.*"—Preface to second edition of *Lyrical Ballads.* If we accept Professor Bain's doctrine, "States of pleasure are connected with an *increase,* and states of pain with a *diminution,* of some or all of the vital functions," it will follow that the healthy discharge of the functions, either of the mind or the body, must be pleasurable. However, I merely suggest this for consideration.

Observe, that although I would have boys take pleasure in their work, I regard the pleasure as a *means*, not an end. If it could be proved that the mind was best trained by the most repulsive exercises, I should most certainly enforce them. But I do not think that the mind *is* benefited by galley-slave labor: indeed, hardly any of its faculties are capable of such labor. We can compel a boy to learn a thing by heart, but we can not compel him to wish to understand it; and the intellect does not act without the will. Hence, when anything is required which can not be performed by the memory alone, the driving system utterly breaks down; and even the memory, as I hope to show presently, works much more effectually in matters about which the mind feels an interest. Indeed, the mind without sympathy and interest is like the sea-anemone when the tide is down, an unlovely thing, closed against external influences, enduring existence as best it can. But let it find itself in a more congenial element, and it opens out at once, shows altogether unexpected capacities, and eagerly assimilates all the proper food that comes within its reach. Our school-teaching is often little better than an attempt to get sea-anemones to flourish on dry land.

We see, then, that a boy, before he can throw energy into study, must find that study *interesting in itself, or in its results*.

Some subjects, properly taught, are interesting in themselves.

Some subjects may be interesting to older and more thoughtful boys, from a perception of their usefulness.

All subjects may be made interesting by emulation.

Hardly any effort is made in some schools to interest

the younger children in their work, and yet no effort can be, as the Germans say, more "rewarding." The teacher of children has this advantage, that his pupils are never dull and listless, as youths are apt to be. If they are not attending to him, they very soon give him notice of it, and if he has the sense to see that their inattention is his fault, not theirs, this will save him much annoyance and them much misery. He has, too, another advantage, which gives him the power of gaining their attention—their emulation is easily excited. In the Waisenhaus at Halle I once heard a class of very young children, none of them much above six years old, perform feats of mental arithmetic quite beyond their age (I wished their teacher had not been so successful), and I well remember the pretty eagerness with which each child held out a little hand and shouted, "*Mich!*" [Me!] to gain the privilege of answering.

Then again, there are many subjects in which children take an interest. Indeed, all visible things, especially animals, are much more to them than to us. A child has made acquaintance with all the animals in the neighborhood, and can tell you much more about the house and its surroundings than you know yourself. But all this knowledge and interest you would wish forgotten directly he comes into school. Reading, writing, and figures are taught in the driest manner. The first two are in themselves not uninteresting to the child, as he has something to do, and young people are much more ready to do anything than to learn anything. But when lessons are given the child to learn, they are not about things concerning which he has ideas, and feels an interest, but you teach him the Catechism—mere sounds—and, that Alfred (to him only a name) came to the throne in 871, though he has no notion what the throne is, or what 871 means. The child learns the lesson with much trouble and small profit, bearing the infliction with what patience he can, till he escapes out of school, and begins to learn much faster on a very different system.

An attempt has been made by the Pestalozzians to remedy all this. They insist strongly on the necessity of teaching children about *things*, and of appealing to their senses. But, to judge from the Cheam manual,* they have succeeded merely in proving that lessons on things may be made as tiresome as any other lessons. They hold up an object, say a piece of sponge, and run through all the adjectives which can possibly be applied to it. "This is sponge. Sponge is an animal product. Sponge is amorphous. Sponge is porous. Sponge is absorbent," etc., etc. I have no practical acquaintance with this method, but confess I do not like the look of it from a distance.†

We can not often introduce into the school the thing, much less the animal, which children would care to see, but we can introduce what will please the children as well, in some cases even better, viz., good pictures. A teacher who could draw boldly on the blackboard, would have no dfficulty in arresting the children's attention. But, of course, few can do this. Pictures must, therefore, be provided for him. A good deal has been done of late years in the way of illustrating children's books, and even childhood must be the happier for such pictures as

---

* [See note, page 195.]

† Mr. Herbert Spencer has conclusively shown Pestalozzian practices are often at variance with Pestalozzian principles.—*Education*, Chap. II.

those of Tenniel and Harrison Weir. But, it seems well understood that these gentlemen are incapable of doing anything for children beyond affording them innocent amusement, and we should be as much surprised at seeing their works introduced into that region of asceticism, the English school-room, as if we ran across one of Raphael's Madonnas in a Baptist chapel.

I had the good fortune, some years ago, to be present at the lessons given by a very excellent teacher to the youngest class, consisting both of boys and girls, at the first *Burger-schule* of Leipzig. In Saxony the schooling which the state demands for each child, begins at six years old, and lasts till fourteen. These children were, therefore, between six and seven. In one year, a certain Dr. Vater taught them to read, write, and reckon. His method was as follows:—Each child had a book with pictures of objects, such as a hat, a slate, etc. Under the picture was the name of the object in printing and writing characters, and also a couplet about the object. The children having opened their books, and found the picture of a hat, the teacher showed them a hat, and told them a tale connected with one. He then asked the children questions about his story, and about the hat he had in his hand—What was the color of it? etc. He then drew a hat on the blackboard, and made the children copy it on their slates. Next he wrote the word "hat," and told them that for people who could read this did as well as the picture. The children then copied the word on their slates. The teacher proceded to analyze the word "hat." "It is made up," said he, "of three sounds, the most important of which is the *a*, which comes in the middle." In all cases the vowel sound was first ascertained in every syllable, and then was given an approximation to the consonantal sounds before and after. The couplet was now read by the teacher, and the children repeated it after him. In this way the book had to be worked over and over till the children were perfectly familiar with everything in it. They had been already six months thus employed when I visited the school, and knew the book pretty thoroughly. To test their knowledge, Dr. Vater first wrote a number of capitals at random, on the board, and called out a boy to tell him words having these capitals as initials. This boy had to call out a girl to do something of the kind, she a boy, and so forth. Everything was done very smartly, both by master and children. The best proof I saw of their accuracy and quickness was this: the master traced words from the book very rapidly with a stick on the blackboard, and the children always called out the right word, though I often could not follow him. He also wrote with chalk words which the children had never seen, and made them name first the vowel sounds, then the consonantal, then combine them.

I have been thus minute in my description of this lesson, because it seems to me an admirable example of the way in which children between six and eight years of age should be taught. The method was arranged and the book prepared by the late Dr. Vogel, who was then Director of the school. Its merits, as its author pointed out to me, are:—1. That it connects the instruction with objects of which the child has already an idea in his mind, and so associates new knowledge with old; 2. That it gives the children plenty to *do* as well as to learn, a point on which the Doctor was very emphatic; 3. That it makes the children go over the same matter in various ways, till they have *learnt a little thoroughly*, and then applies their knowledge to the acquirement of more. Here the Doctor seems to have followed Jacotot. But though the method was no doubt a good one, I must say its success at Leipzig was due at least as much to Dr. Vater as to Dr. Vogel. This gentleman had been taking the youngest class in this school for twenty years, and, whether by practice or natural talent, he had acquired precisely the right manner for keeping children's attention. He was energetic without bustle and excitement, and quiet without a suspicion of dullness or apathy. By frequently changing the employment of the class, and requiring smartness in everything that was done, he kept them all on the alert. The lesson I have described was followed without pause by one in arithmetic, the two together occupying an hour and three-quarters, and the interest of the children never flagged throughout.

It is then possible to teach children, at this stage at least, without making them hate their work, and dread the sound of the school-bell.

I will suppose a child to have passed through such a course as this by the time he is eight or nine years old. He can now read and copy easy words. What we next want for him is a series of good reading books, about things in which he takes an interest. The language must of course be simple, but the matter so good that neither master nor pupils will be disgusted by its frequent repetition.

The first volume may very well be about animals—

dogs, horses, etc., of which large pictures should be provided, illustrating the text. The first cost of these pictures would be considerable, but as they would last for years, the expense to the friends of each child taught from them, would be a mere trifle.

The books placed in the hands of the children, should be well printed, and strongly bound. In the present penny-wise system, school-books are given out in cloth, and the leaves are loose at the end of a fortnight, so that children get accustomed to their destruction, and treat it as a matter of course. This ruins their respect for books, which is not so unimportant a matter as it may at first appear.

After each reading lesson, which should contain at least one interesting anecdote, there should be columns of all the words which occurred for the first time in that lesson. These should be arranged according to their grammatical classification, not that the child should be taught grammar, but this order is as good as any other, and by it the child would learn to observe certain differences in words almost unconsciously. As good reading is best learnt by imitation, the lesson should first be read aloud by the master. It will sometimes be a useful exercise to make the children prepare a lesson beforehand, and give an account of the substance of it before opening their books, "Accustoming boys to read aloud what they do not first understand," says Dr. Franklin, "is the cause of those even set tones so common among readers, which, when they have once got a habit of using, they find so difficult to correct; by which means, among fifty readers we scarcely find a good one."*

---

* Essays: Sketch of an English School.

As a change reading-book, Æsop's Fables may now be used, and an edition with such illustrations as Tenniel's will be well worth the additional outlay.

Easy descriptive and narrative poetry should be learnt by heart in this form. That the children may repeat it well, they should get their first notions of it from the master *viva voce* [orally]. According to the usual plan, they get it up with false emphasis and false stops, and the more thoroughly they have learnt the piece, the more difficulty the master has in making them say it properly.

Every lesson should be worked over in various ways. The columns of words at the end of the reading lessons may be printed with writing characters, and used for copies. To write an upright column either of words or figures is an excellent exercise in neatness. The columns will also be used as spelling lessons, and the children may be questioned about the meaning of the words. The poetry, when thoroughly learned, may sometimes be written from memory. Sentences from the book may be copied either directly or from the blackboard, and afterward used for dictation.

Dictation lessons are often given very badly. The boys spell nearly as many words wrong as right, and if even all the blunders are corrected, little more pains is taken to impress the right way on their memory than the wrong. But the chief use of dictation is to fix in the memory by practice words already known. Another mistake is for the master to keep repeating the sentence the boys are writing. He should first read the piece straight through, that the boys may know what they are writing about. Then he should read it by clauses, slowly and distinctly, waiting a sufficient time between the clauses, but never repeating them. This exercises the boys' attention, and accustoms their ear to the form of good sentences—an excellent preparation for composition. Where the dictation lesson has been given from the reading-book, the boys may afterward take the book and correct either their own exercises or one another's.*

Boys should as soon as possible be accustomed to write out fables, or the substance of other reading lessons, in their own words. They may also write descriptions of things with which they are familiar, or any event which has recently happened, such as a country excursion. Every one feels the necessity, on grounds of practical utility at all events, of boys being taught to express their thoughts neatly on paper, in good English and with correct spelling. Yet this is a point rarely reached before the age of fifteen or sixteen, often never reached at all. The reason is, that written exercises must be carefully looked over by the master, or they are done in a slovenly manner. Any one who has never taught in a school will say, "Then let the master carefully look them over." But the expenditure of time and trouble this involves on the master is so great that in the end he is pretty sure either to have few exercises written, or to neglect to look them over. The only remedy is for the master not

---

*Mr. R. Robinson, in his *Manual of Method and Organization*, gives some good hints for impressing on boys' memories the words they have spelt wrong. An exercise-book, he says, should always be used for the dictation lesson, and of every word in which a boy blunders, he should afterward make a line at the end of the book, writing the word as many times as it will go in the line. Now and then the master may turn to these words, and examine the boy in them, and by comparing different books, he will see which words are most likely to be wrongly spelt.

to have many boys to teach, and not to be many hours in school. Even then, unless he set apart a special time every day for correcting exercises, he is likely to find them "increase upon him."

The course of reading-books, accompanied by large illustrations, may go on to many other things which the children see around them, such as trees and plants, and so lead up to instruction in natural history and physiology. But in imparting all knowledge of this kind, we should aim, not at getting the children to remember a number of facts, but at opening their eyes, and extending the range of their interests.

Hitherto I have supposed the children to have only three books at the same time; viz., a reading-book about animals and things, a poetry book, and Æsop's Fables. With the first commences a series culminating in works of science; with the second a series that should lead up to Milton and Shakespeare; the third should be succeeded by some of our best writers in prose.

But many schoolmasters will shudder at the thought of a child's spending a year or two at school without ever hearing of the Heptarchy or Magna Charta, and without knowing the names of the great towns in any country of Europe. I confess I regard this ignorance with great equanimity. If the child, or the youth even, takes no interest in the Heptarchy and Magna Charta, and knows nothing of the towns but their names, I think him quite as well off without this knowledge as with it —perhaps better, as such knowledge turns the lad into a "wind-bag," as Carlyle might say, and gives him the appearance of being well-informed without the reality. But I neither despise a knowledge of history and geog-

.phy, nor do I think that these studies should be neglected for foreign languages or science; and it is because I should wish a pupil of mine to become in the end thoroughly conversant in history and geography, that I should, if possible, conceal from him the existence of the numerous school manuals on these subjects.

We will suppose that a parent meets with a book which he thinks will be both instructive and entertaining to his children. But the book is a large one, and would take a long time to get through; so, instead of reading any part of it to them or letting them read it for themselves, he makes them *learn the index by heart*. The children do *not* find it entertaining; they get a horror of the book, which prevents their ever looking at it afterward, and they forget the index as soon as they possibly can. Just such is the sagacious plan adopted in teaching history and geography in schools, and such are the natural consequences. Every student knows that the use of an epitome is to *systematize* knowledge, not to communicate it, and yet, in teaching, we give the epitome first, and allow it to precede, or rather to supplant, the knowledge epitomized. The children are disgusted, and no wonder. The subjects, indeed, are interesting, but not so the epitomes. I suppose if we could see the skeletons of the Gunnings, we should not find them more fascinating than any other skeletons.

The first thing to be aimed at, then, is to excite the children's interest. Even if we thought of nothing but the acquiring of information, this is clearly the true method. What are the facts which we remember? Those in which we feel an interest. If we are told that So-and-so has met with an accident, or failed in business, we forget it directly, unless we know the person spoken of. Similarly, if I read anything about Addison or Goldsmith, it interests me, and I remember it, because they are, so to speak, friends of mine; but the same information about Sir Richard Blackmore or Cumberland would not stay in my head for four-and-twenty hours. So, again, we naturally retain anything we learn about a foreign country in which a relation has settled, but it would require some little trouble to commit to memory the same facts about a place in which we had no concern. All this proceeds from two causes. First, that the mind retains that in which it takes an interest, and, secondly, that one of the principal helps to memory is the association of ideas. These were, no doubt, the ground reasons which influenced Dr. Arnold in framing his plan of a child's first history-book. This book, he says, should be a picture book of the memorable deeds which would best appeal to the child's imagination. They should be arranged in order of time, but with no other connection. The letterpress should simply, but fully, tell the *story* of the action depicted. These would form starting-points of interest. The child would be curious to know more about the great men whose acquaintance he had made, and would associate with them the scenes of their exploits; and thus we might actually find our children anxious to learn history and geography! I am sorry that even the great authority of Dr. Arnold has not availed to bring this method into use. Such a book would, of course, be dear. Bad pictures are worse than none at all: and Goethe tells us that his appreciation of Homer was for years destroyed by his having been shown, when a child, absurd pictures (*Fratzenbilder*) of the Homeric heroes. The book would, therefore, cost six or eight shillings at least; and who would give this sum for an account of single actions of a few great men, when he might buy the lives of all great men, together with ancient and modern history, the names of the planets, and a great amount of miscellaneous information, all for half-a-crown in " Mangall's Questions ? "

However, if the saving of a few shillings is more to be thought of than the best method of instruction, the subject hardly deserves our serious consideration.

It is much to be regretted that books for the young are so seldom written by distinguished authors. I suppose that of the three things which the author seeks—money, reputation, influence—the first is not often despised, nor the last considered the least valuable. And yet both money and influence are more certainly gained by a good book for the young, than by any other. The influence of "Tom Brown," however different in kind, is probably not smaller in amount, than that of "Sartor Resartus."

An improvement, I hope, has already begun. Miss Yonge's "Golden Deeds" is just the sort of a book that I have been recommending. Professor Huxley has lately published an elementary book on Physiology, and Professor Kingsley has promised us a "Boys' History of England."

What we want is a Macaulay for boys, who shall handle historical subjects with that wonderful art displayed in the "Essays"—the art of elaborating all the more telling portions of the subject, outlining the rest, and suppressing everything that does not conduce to heighten the general effect. Some of these essays, such as the

"Hastings" and "Clive," will be read with avidity by the elder boys; but as Macaulay did not write for children, he abounds in words to them unintelligible. Had he been a married man, we might perhaps have had such a volume of historical sketches for boys as now we must wish for in vain. But there are good story-tellers left among us, and we might soon expect such books as we desiderate, if it were clearly understood what is the right sort of book, and if men of literary ability and experience would condescend to write them. At present, teachers who have a "connection" make compendiums, which last only as long as the "connection" that floats them: and literary men, if they wish to make money out of the young, hand over works written for adults, to some underling, who epitomizes them for schools. Of Mr. Knight, who has done so much for sound education, I should have expected better things; but he tells us in a volume of some 500 pages, called "Knight's School History of England," condensed from his large history *under his superintendence,* that he trusts no event of importance in our annals has been omitted. This seems to me like trusting that the work is valueless for all purposes of rational instruction.

If in these latter days "the individual withers, and the world is more and more," we must not expect our children to enter into this. Their sympathy and their imagination can be aroused, not for nations, but for individuals; and this is the reason why some biographies of great men should precede any history. These should be written after Macaulay's method. There should be no attempt at completeness, but what is most important and interesting about the man should be narrated in detail, and the rest lightly sketched, or omitted altogether. Painters understand this principle, and in taking a portrait, very often depict a man's features minutely without telling all the truth about the buttons on his waistcoat. But, because in a literary picture each touch takes up additional space, writers seem to fear that the picture will be distorted unless every particular is expanded or condensed in the same ratio. As a model for our biographies, we may take "Plutarch's Lives," which should be read as soon as boys are old enough to *like* them.*

At the risk of wearisome repetition, I must again say, that I care as little about driving "useful knowledge" into a boy, as the most ultra Cambridge-man could wish; but I want to get the boy to have wide sympathies, and to teach himself; and I should therefore select the great men from very different periods and countries, that his net of interest (if I am allowed the metaphor) may be spread in all waters.

When we have thus got our boys to form the acquaintance of great men, they will have certain associations connected with many towns and countries. Constant reference should be made to the map, and the boy's

---

* "There is no profane study better than Plutarch: all other learning is private, fitter for universities than cities; fuller of contemplation than experience; more commendable in students themselves than profitable unto others. Whereas stories are fit for every place, reach to all persons, serve for all times; teach the living, revive the dead; so far excelling all other books, as it is better to see learning in noble men's lives than to read it in philosopher's writings. Now for the author ... I believe I might be bold to affirm that he hath written the profitablest story of all authors; ... being excellent in wit, learning, and experience, he hath chosen the special acts of the best persons of the famousest nations of the world."—Sir Thomas North's Dedication to Queen Elizabeth of his translation of Plutarch.

knowledge and interest will thus make settlements in different parts of the globe. These may be extended by a good book of travels, especially of voyages of discovery. There are, no doubt, many such books suitable for the purpose, but the only one I have met with is Miss Hack's "Winter Evenings; or Tales of Travelers," which has been a great favorite with children for the last five-and-twenty years at least. This is a capital book, but the very childish conversations interpolated in the narratives would disgust a boy a little too old for them, much more than they would an adult reader. In studying such travels, the map should, of course, be always in sight; and outline maps may be filled up by the boys, as they learn about the places in the traveler's route. Any one who has had the management of a school library knows how popular "voyage and venture" is with the boys who have passed the stage in which the picture-books of animals were the main attraction. Captain Cook, Mungo Park, and Admiral Byron are heroes without whom boyhood would be incomplete; but as boys are engrossed by the adventures and never trouble themselves about the map, they often remember the incidents without knowing where they happened.

Of course school geographies never mention such people as celebrated travelers: if they did, it would be impossible to give all the principal geographical names in the world within the compass of two hundred pages.

What might be fairly expected from such a course of teaching as I have here suggested?

At the end of a year and a half or two years from the age, say, of nine, the boy would read aloud well, he would write fairly, he would spell all common English words correctly; he would have had his interest excited or increased in common objects, such as animals, trees, and plants; he would have made the acquaintance of some great men, and traced the voyages of some great travelers; he would be able to say by heart some of the best simple English poetry, and his ear would be familiar with the sound of good English prose. Above all, he would *not* have learned to look upon books and school-time as the torment of his life, nor have fallen into the habit of giving them as little of his attention as he could reconcile with immunity from the cane. The benefit of this *negative* result, at all events, might prove incalculable.

XII.

MORAL AND RELIGIOUS EDUCATION.

ALL who are acquainted with the standard treatises on the theory of education, and also with the management of schools, will have observed that moral and religious training occupies a larger and more prominent space in theory than in practice. On consideration, we shall find perhaps that this might naturally be expected. Of course we are all agreed that morality is more important than learning, and masters, who are many of them clergymen, will hardly be accused of underestimating the value of religion. Why, then, does not moral and religious training receive a larger share of the master's attention? The reason I take to be this. Experience shows that it depends directly on the master whether a boy acquires knowledge, but only indirectly, and in a much less degree, whether he grows up a good and religious man. The aim which engrosses most of our time is likely to absorb an equal share of our interest; and thus it happens that masters, especially those who never associate on terms of intimacy with their pupils out of school, throw energy enough into making boys *learn*, but seldom think at all of the development of their character, or about their thoughts and feelings in matters of religion. This statement may indeed be exaggerated, but no one who has the means of judging will assert that it is altogether without foundation. And yet, although a master can be more certain of sending out his pupils well taught than well principled, his influence on their character is much greater than it might appear to a superficial observer. I intend speaking presently of formal religious instruction. I refer now to the teacher's indirect influence. The results of his formal teaching vary as its amount, but he can apply no such gauge to his informal teaching. A few words of earnest advice or remonstrance, which a boy hears at the right time from a man whom he respects, may affect that boy's character for life. Here everything depends, not on the words used, but on the feeling with which they are spoken, and on the way in which the speaker is regarded by the hearer. In such matters the master has a much more delicate and difficult task than in mere instruction. The words, indeed, are soon spoken, but that which gives them their influence is not soon or easily acquired. Here, as in so many other instances, we may in a few minutes throw down what it has cost us days—perhaps years—to build up. An unkind word will destroy the effects of long-continued kindness. Boys always form their opinion of a man from the worst they know of him. Experience has not yet taught them that good people have their failings, and bad people their virtues. If the scholars find the master at times harsh and testy, they can not believe in his kindness of heart and care for their welfare. They do not see that he may have an ideal before him to which he is partly, though not wholly, true. They judge him by his demeanor in his least guarded moments—at times when he is jaded and dissatisfied with the results of his labors.

At such times the bonds of sympathy between him and his pupils hang loose. He is conscious only of his power and of his mental superiority. Feeling almost a contempt for the boys' weakness, he does not care for their opinion of him, or think for an instant what impression he is making by his words and conduct. He gives full play to his *arbitrium*, and says or does something which seems to the boys to reveal him in his true character, and which causes them ever after to distrust his kindness.

When we consider the way in which masters endeavor to gain influence, we shall find that they may be divided roughly into two parties, whom I will call, as a matter of convenience, realists and idealists. A teacher of the *real* party endeavors to appear to his pupils precisely as he is. He will hear of no restraint except that of decorum. He believes that if he is as much the superior of his pupils as he ought to be, his authority will take care of itself, without his casting round it a wall of artificial reserve. "Be natural," he says; "get rid of affectations and shams of all kinds; and then, if there is any good in you, it will tell on those around you. Whatever is bad, would be felt just as surely in disguise; and the disguise would only be an additional source of mischief." The idealists, on the other hand, wish their pupils to think of them as they ought to be, rather than as they are. They urge against the realists that our words and actions can not always be in harmony with our thoughts and feelings, however much we may desire to make them so. We must, therefore, they say, reconcile ourselves to this fact; and since our words and actions are more under our control than our thoughts and feelings, we must make them as nearly as possible what they should be, instead of debasing them to involuntary thoughts and feelings which are not worthy of us. Then, again, the idealist teacher may say, "The young require some one to look up to. In my better moments I am not altogether unworthy of their respect, but if they knew all my weaknesses, they would naturally, and perhaps justly, despise me. For their sakes, therefore, I must keep my weaknesses out of sight, and the effort to do this demands a certain reserve in all our intercourse."

I suppose an excess of either realism or idealism might lead to mischievous results. The "real" man might be wanting in self-restraint, and might say and do things which, though not wrong in themselves, might have a bad effect on the young. Then, again, the lower and more worldly side of his character might show itself in too strong relief, and his pupils seeing this mainly, and supposing that they understood him entirely, might disbelieve in his higher motives and religious feeling. On the other hand, the idealists are, as it were, walking on stilts. They gain no real influence by their separation from their pupils, and they are always liable to an accident which may expose them to their ridicule.

I am, therefore, though with some limitation, in favor of the natural school. I am well aware, however what an immense demand this system makes on the master who desires to exercise a good influence on the moral and religious character of his pupils. If he would have his pupils know him as he is, if he would have them think as he thinks, feel as he feels, and believe as he believes, he must be, at least in heart and aim, worthy of their imitation. He must (with reverence be it spoken) enter, in his humble way, into the spirit of the perfect Teacher, who said, "For their sakes I sanctify myself, that they also may be sanctified in truth." Are we prepared to look upon our calling in this light? I believe that the school-teachers of this country need not fear comparison with any other body of men, in point of morality and religious earnestness; but I dare say many have found, as I have, that the occupation is a very *narrowing* one, that the teacher soon gets to work in a groove, and from having his thoughts so much occupied with routine work, especially with small fault findings and small corrections, he is apt to settle down insensibly into a kind of moral and intellectual stagnation—Philistinism, as Mr. Matthew Arnold would call it—in which he cares as little for high aims and general principles as his most commonplace pupil. Thus it happens sometimes that a man who set out with the notion of developing all the powers of his pupils' minds, thinks in the end of nothing but getting them to work out equations and do Latin exercises without false concords; and the clergyman even who began with a strong sense of his responsibility, and a confident hope of influencing the boys' belief and character at length is quite content if they conform to discipline, and give him no trouble out of school-hours. We may say of a really good teacher what Wordsworth says of the poet; in his work he must neither

> lack that first great gift, the vital soul,
> Nor general truths, which are themselves a sort
> Of elements and agents, underpowers,
> Subordinate helpers of the human mind.—*Prelude*, i. 9.

But the "vital soul" is too often crushed by excessive

routine labor, and then when general truths, both moral and intellectual, have ceased to interest us, our own education stops, and we become incapable of fulfilling the highest and most important part of our duty in educating others.

It is, then, the duty of the teacher to resist gravitating into this state, no less for his pupils' sake than for his own. The ways and means of doing this I am by no means competent to point out; so I will merely insist on the importance of teachers not being overworked—a matter which has not, I think, hitherto, received due attention.

We can not expect intellectual activity of men whose minds are compelled "with pack-horse constancy to keep the road" hour after hour, till they are too jaded for exertion of any kind. The man himself suffers, and his work, even his easiest work, suffers also. It may be laid down, as a general rule, that no one can teach long and teach well. All satisfactory teaching and management of boys absolutely require that the master should be *in good spirits.* When the " genial spirits fail," as they must from an overdose of monotonous work, everything goes wrong directly. The master has no longer the power of keeping the boys' attention. and has to resort to punishments even to preserve order. His gloom quenches their interest and mental activity, just as fire goes out before carbonic acid; and in the end teacher and taught acquire, not without cause, a feeling of mutual aversion.

And another reason why the master should not spend the greater part of his time in formal teaching is this— his doing so compels him to neglect the informal but very important teaching he may both give and receive by making his pupils his companions.

I fear I shall be met here by an objection which has only too much force in it. Most Englishmen are at a loss how to make any use of leisure. If a man has no turn for thinking, no fondness for reading, and is without a hobby, what good shall his leisure do him? He will only pass it in insipid gossip, from which any easy work would be a relief. That this is so, in many cases, is a proof, to my mind, of the utter failure of our ordinary education; and perhaps an improved education may some day alter what now seems a national peculiarity. Meantime the mind, even of Englishmen, is more than a "succedaneum for salt,"* and its tendency to bury its sight ostrich-fashion, under a heap of routine work, must be strenuously resisted, if it is to escape its deadly enemies, stupidity and ignorance.

I have elsewhere expressed what I believe is the common conviction of those who have seen something both of large schools and of small, viz., that the moral atmosphere of the former is, as a rule, by far the more wholesome;† and also that each boy is more influenced by his

---

* "That you are wife
To so much bloated flesh, *as scarce hath soul
Instead of salt to keep it sweet,* I think
Will ask no witness to prove."
BEN JONSON: *The Devil is an Ass*, Act i,, sc. 3.

† I have quoted De Quincy on this subject (*supra*, p. 85, *note*). Here is the testimony of a schoolmaster to the same effect. Mr. Hope, in his amusing "Book about Dominies," says, that a school of from twenty to a hundred boys is too large to be altogether under the influence of one man, and too small for the development of a healthy condition of public opinion among the boys themselves. "In a community of fifty boys, there will always be found so many bad ones who will be likely to carry things their own way. Vice is more unblushing in small societies than in large ones. *Fifty*

companions than by his master. More than this, I believe that in many, perhaps in most, schools, one or two boys affect the tone of the whole body more than the master.* What are called Preparatory Schools labor under this immense disadvantage, that their ruling spirits are mere children without reflection or sense of responsibility. But where the leading boys are virtually young men, these may be made a medium through which the mind of the master may act upon the whole school. They can enter into the thoughts, feelings, and aims of the master on the one hand, and they know what is said and done among the boys on the other. The master must, therefore, know the elder boys intimately, and they must know him. This consummation, however, will not be arrived at without great tact and self-denial on the part of the master. The youth, who is "neither man nor boy," is apt to be shy and awkward, and is not by any means so easy to entertain as the lad who chatters freely of the school's cricket or foot-ball, past, present, and to come. But the master who feels

---

boys will be more easily leavened by the wickedness of five, than five hundred by that of fifty. It would be too dangerous an ordeal to send a boy to a school where sin appears fashionable, and where, if he would remain virtuous, he must shun his companions. There may be middle-sized schools which derive a good and healthy tone from the moral strength of their masters, or the good example of a certain set of boys, but I doubt if there are many. Boys are so easily led to do right or wrong, that we should be very careful at least to set the balance fairly" (p. 107); and again he says (p. 170), "The moral tone of a middle-sized school will be peculiarly liable to be at the mercy of a set of bold and bad boys."

*"The moral tone of the school is made what it is, not nearly so much by its rules and regulations or its masters, as by the leading characters among the boys. They mainly determine the public opinion amongst their schoolfellows—their personal influence is incalculable." I quote these words of a master whose opinion is respected by all who know him, because I have been thought to express myself so strongly on this point.

how all-important is the *tone* of the school, will not grudge any pains to influence those on whom it chiefly depends.

But, allowing the value of all these indirect influences, can we afford to neglect direct formal religious instruction? We have most of us the greatest horror of what we call a secular education, meaning thereby an education without formal religious teaching. But this horror seems to affect our theory more than our practice. Few parents ever inquire what religious instruction their sons get at Eton, Harrow, or Westminster. I am told that, in amount at least, it is quite insignificant; and I can myself vouch for the fact, that once upon a time the lower forms at one of these had no religious instruction except a weekly lesson in Watts' "Scripture History." Even in some national schools, where the managers would rather close their doors altogether than accept the "Conscience-clause," the religious instruction is confined to teaching the Catechism by heart, and using the Bible as a reading-book.

In this matter we differ very widely from the Germans. All their classes have a "religion-lesson" (*Religionstunde*) nearly every day, the younger children in the German Bible, the elder in the Greek Testament or Church History; and in all cases the teacher is careful to instruct his pupils in the tenets of Luther or Calvin. The Germans may urge that if we believe a set of doctrines to be a fitting expression of Divine revelation, it is our first duty to make the young familiar with those doctrines. I can not say, however, that I have been favorably impressed by the religion-lessons I have heard given in German schools. I do not deny that dogmatic teaching is necessary, but the first thing to cultivate in the young is reverence; and reverence is surely in danger if you take a class in "religion" just as you take a class in grammar. Emerson says somewhere, that to the poet, the saint, and the philosopher, all distinction of sacred and profane ceases to exist, all things become alike sacred. As the schoolboy, however, does not as yet come under any one of these denominations, if the distinction ceases to exist for him, all things will become alike profane.

I believe that religious instruction is conveyed in the most impressive way when it is connected with worship. Where the prayers are joined with the reading of Scripture, and with occasional simple addresses, and where the congregation have responses to repeat, and psalms and hymns to sing, there is reason to hope that boys will increase, not only in knowledge, but in wisdom and reverence too. Without asserting that the Church of England service is the best possible for the young, I hold that any form for them should at least resemble it in its main features, should be as varied as possible, should require frequent change of posture, and should give the congregation much to say and sing. The Church of Rome is wise, I think, in making more use than we do of litanies. The service, whatever its form, should be conducted with great solemnity, and the boys should not sit or kneel so close together that the badly disposed may disturb their neighbors who try to join in the act of worship. If good hymns are sung, these may be taken occasionally as the subject of an address, so that attention may be drawn to their meaning. Music should be carefully attended to, and the danger of irreverence at practice guarded against by never using sacred words more than is necessary, and by impressing on the singers the sacredness of everything connected with Divine worship. Questions combined with instruction may sometimes keep up boys' attention better than a formal sermon. Though common prayer should be frequent, this should not be supposed to take the place of private prayer. In many schools boys have hardly an opportunity for private prayer. They kneel down, perhaps, with all the talk and play of their schoolfellows going on around them, and sometimes fear of public opinion prevents their kneeling down at all. A schoolmaster can not teach private prayer, but he can at least see that there is opportunity for it.

These observations of mine only touch the surface of this most important subject, and do not point the way to any efficient religious education. In fact, I believe that education to piety, as far as it lies in human hands, must consist almost entirely in the influence of the pious superior over his inferiors.*

In conclusion, I wish to say a word on the education of opinion. Helps lays great stress on preparing the way to moderation and open-mindedness, by teaching boys that all good men are not of the same way of thinking. It is indeed a miserable error to lead a young person to suppose that his small ideas are a measure of

---

* "What is education? It is that which is imbibed from the moral atmosphere which a child breathes. It is the involuntary and unconscious language of its parents and of all those by whom it is surrounded, and not their set speeches and set lectures. It is the words which the young hear fall from their seniors when the speakers are off their guard: and it is by these unconscious expressions that the child interprets the hearts of its parents. That is education."—" Drummond's Speeches in Parliament."

the universe, and that all who do not accept his formularies are less enlightened than himself. If a young man is so brought up, he either carries intellectual blinkers all his life, or, what is far more probable, he finds that something he has been taught is false, and forthwith begins to doubt everything. On the other hand, it is a necessity with the young to believe, and we could not, even if we would, bring a youth into such a state of mind as to regard everything about which there is any variety of opinion as an open question. But he may be taught reverence and humility; he may be taught to reflect how infinitely greater the facts of the universe must be than our poor thoughts about them, and how inadequate are words to express even our imperfect thoughts. Then he will not suppose that all truth has been taught him in his formularies, nor that he understands even all the truth of which those formularies are the imperfect expression.*

---

* In what I have said on this subject, the incompleteness which is noticeable enough in the preceding essays, has found an appropriate climax. I see, too, that if any one would take the trouble, the little I have said might easily be misinterpreted. I am well aware, however, that if the young mind will not readily assimilate sharply defining religious formulæ still less will it feel at home among the "immensities" and "veracities." The great educating force of Christianity I believe to be due to this, that it is not a set of abstractions or vague generalities, but that in it God reveals himself to us in a Divine Man, and raises us through our devotion to Him. I hold therefore that religious teaching for the young should neither be vague nor abstract. Mr. Froude, in commenting on the use made of hagiology in the Church of Rome, has shown that we lose much by not following the Bible method of instruction. (See "Short Studies: Lives of the Saints and Representative Men.")

APPENDIX.

CLASS MATCHES.

With young classes I have tried the Jesuits' plan of matches [see page 23], and have found it answer exceedingly well. The top boy and the second pick up sides (in schoolboy phrase), the second boy having first choice. The same sides may be kept till the superiority of one of them is clearly established, when it becomes necessary to pick up again. The matches, if not too frequent, prove an excellent break to the monotony of school-work. A subject well suited for them (as Franklin pointed out) is spelling. The boys are told that on a certain day there will be a match in the spelling of some certain class of words—say words of one syllable, or the preterites of verbs. For the match the sides are arranged in lines opposite one another; the dux of one side questions the dux of the other, the second boy the second, and so forth. The match may be conducted *viva voce,* or, better still, by papers previously written. Each boy has to bring on paper a list of the right sort of words. Suppose six is the number required, he will write a column with a few to spare, as some of his words may be disallowed by the umpire, i. e., the master. The master takes the first boy's list, and asks the top boy on the opposite side to spell the words. When he fails, the owner of the list has to correct him, and gets a mark for doing so. Should the owner of the list himself make a mistake, his opponent scores even if he is wrong also. When the master has gone through all the lists in this way, he adds up the marks, and announces which side has won. The method has the great merit of stimulating the lower end of the form as well as the top; for it usually happens that the match is really decided by the lower boys, who make the most mistakes. Of course the details and the subjects of such matches admit of almost endless variation.

DOCTRINALE ALEXANDRI DE VILLA DEI.

This celebrated grammar [see page 35] was written by a Franciscan of Brittany, about the middle of the thirteenth century. It is in leonine verses. To the verses is attached a commentary, which is by no means superfluous. The book begins thus:

> Scribere clericulis paro Doctrinale novellis,
> Pluraque doctorum sociabo scripta meorum.
> Jamque legent pueri pro nugis Maximiani
> Quæ veteres sociis nolebant pandere caris.

(Maximianus, says the commentary, was a *scriptor fabularum.*)

> Presens huic operi sit gratia Pneumatis almi:
> Me juvat: et faciat complere quod utile fiat.
> Si pueri primo nequeunt attendere plene,
> Hic tamen attendat, qui doctoris est vice fungens,
> Atque legens pueris laica lingua reserabit,
> Et pueris etiam pars maxima plana patebit.
> Voces in primis, quas par casus variabis,
> Ut levius protero, te declinare docebo.
>   etc.   etc.

R

If Alexander kept his promise, he certainly had no faculty for making things easy. Take, e. g., his notion of teaching the singular of the first declension:

> Rectus *as*, *es*, *a*, dat declinatio prima,
> Atque per *am* propria quædam ponuntur hebræa;
> Dans *œ* dipthongon genitivis atqua dativis.
> *Am* servat quartus, tamen *an* aut *en* reperimus,
> Cum rectus fit in *as* vel in *es*, vel cum dat *a* Græcus,
> Rectus in *a* Græci facit *an* quarto breviari.
> Quintus in *a* dabitur, post *es* tamen *e* reperitur.
> *A* sextus, tamen *es* quandoque per *e* dare debes
> *Am* recti repetes, quinto sextum sociando.

I read this wonderful grammar (not much of it, however) with great satisfaction. Our researches sometimes bring a feeling of despondency, and we think that knowledge comes, but wisdom lingers. But here is some evidence to the contrary. Part of the knowledge given by Alexander about the first declension has, happily, never come even to most teachers of the present day; and, however unsatisfactory may be our condition with regard to wisdom, we certainly are in advance of those masters who used the "Doctrinale."

LILY'S GRAMMAR.

In some respects further simplification has since been effected, as, e. g., in the matter of genders. The "Short Introduction of Grammar," commonly called the "King's Book," and afterward "Lily's Grammar," [see page 35], made this startling assertion:—" Genders of nounes be seven: the masculine, the feminine, the neuter, the commune of two, the commune of three, the doubtful, and the epicene." The ingenious authors seem not to have discovered any Latin substantive which they were able *tergeminis tollere honoribus;* so they take rather unfair advantage of the fact that adjectives in *x* do not vary in the *nominative*, and give this example of the common of three—"The commune of three is declined with hic, hæc, and hoc: as hic, hæc, and hoc, Felix, Happy." In justice to the old book, I must say, however, that some of the later simplifications were so managed as to be doubtful improvements. Lily's Grammar put the preposition *a* before *all* ablatives. This was simplified into the blunder of putting it before *none*, and teaching boys, e. g., that *Domino* alone was Latin for "by a lord." The old grammar had an optative mood with *utinam* (*Utinam sim*, "I pray God I be;" *Utinam essem*, "Would God I were," etc.) and a subjunctive with *cum* (*cum sim*, "when I am," etc.) These gave place to the mysterious announcement of the Eton Grammar, "The subjunctive mood is declined like the potential." The old book has besides Lily's Carmen de Moribus, the Apostles' Creed, etc., in Latin verse. The following classical version of the Lord's Prayer is curious, and reminds one of Rennaissance architecture:—

> O Pater omnipotens, clarique habitator Olympi,
> Laudetur merito nomen honore tuum.
> Adveniat regnum. Tua sit rata ubique voluntas,
> Fiat et in terris, sicut in arce poli.
> Da nobis hodie panem, et nos exime noxæ,
> Ut veniam nostris hostibus usque damus.
> Nec sine tentando Stygius nos opprimat Error;
> Fac animas nostras ut mala nulla ligent.
> Amen.

Our Lord's command, "Go teach all nations," is thus rendered:—

Ite per extremas ô vos mea viscera gentes:
Cunctos doctrinam rite docete meam.
Inque Patris, Natique et Flatus nomine Sancti
Mortales undis sponte lavate sacris.

COLET.

From "Joannis Coleti theologi, olim Decani Divi Pauli, editio, una cum quibusdam G. Lilli Grammatices Rudimentis, etc. Antuerpiæ 1530." [See page 35.] After the accidence of the eight parts of speech, he says:

"Of these eight parts of speech, in order well construed, be made reasons and sentences and long orations. But how and in what manner, and with what constructions of words, and all the varieties, and diversities, and changes in Latin speech (which be innumerable), if any man will know, and by that knowledge attain to understand Latin books, and to speak and to write clean Latin, let him, above all, busily learn and read good Latin authors of chosen poets and orators, and note wisely how they wrote and spake; and study always to follow them, desiring none other rules but their examples. For in the beginning men spake not Latin because such rules were made, but, contrarywise, because men spake such Latin, upon that followed the rules, and were made. That is to say, Latin speech was before the rules, and not the rules before the Latin speech. Wherefore, well beloved masters and teachers of grammar, after the parts of speech sufficiently known in our schools, read and expound plainly unto your scholars, good authors, and show to them [in] every word, and in every sentence, what they shall note and observe, warning them busily to follow and do like both in writing and in speaking; and be to them your own self also, speaking with them the pure Latin very present, and leave the rules; for reading of good books, diligent information of learned masters, studious advertence and taking heed of learners, hearing eloquent men speak, and finally, busy imitation with tongue and pen, more availeth shortly to get the true eloquent speech, than all the traditions, rules, and precepts of masters."

MULCASTER.

Richard Mulcaster, who, in the second half of the sixteenth century, was the first head-master of Merchant Tailors' School, and in 1596 became headmaster of St. Paul's School, was a celebrated man in his day, and was highly esteemed by Bishop Andrews, who had been his pupil, and always kept a portrait of him hung up in his study. Mulcaster has left us two curious books on education, the "Positions," and the "Elementarie" [see page 45]. The following defense of the use of English by the learned, is from the latter:—

"Is it not a marvelous bondage to become servants to one tongue, for learning's sake, the most part of our time, with loss of most time, whereas we may have the very same treasure in our own tongue with the gain of most time? our own bearing the joyful title of our liberty and freedom, the Latin tongue remembering us of our thraldom and bondage? I love Rome, but London better; I favor Italy, but England more: I honor the Latin, but I worship the English. . . . I honor foreign tongues, but wish my own to be partaker of their honor. Knowing them, I wish my own tongue to resemble their grace. I confess their furniture, and wish it were ours. . . . The diligent labor of learned countrymen did so enrich those tongues, and not the tongues themselves; though they proved very pliable, as our tongue will prove, I dare assure it, of knowledge, if our learned countrymen will put to their labor. And why not, I pray you, as well in English as either Latin or any tongue else? Will ye say it is needless? sure that will not hold. If loss of time, while ye be pilgrims to learning, by lingering about tongues be no argument of need; if lack of sound skill while the tongue distracteth sense more than half to itself, and that most of all in a simple student or a silly wit, be no argument of need, then ye say somewhat which pretend no need. But because we needed not to lose any time unless we listed, if we had such a vantage, in the course of study, as we now lose while we travail in tongues; and because our understanding also were most full in our natural speech, though we know the foreign exceedingly well— methink *necessity* itself doth call for *English,* whereby all that gaiety may be had at home which makes us gaze so much at the fine stranger."

Among various objections to the use of English which he answers, he comes to this one:—

"But will ye thus break off the common conference with the learned foreign?"

To this his answer is not very forcible:—

" The conference will not cease while the people have

cause to interchange dealings, and without the Latin it may well be continued: as in some countries the learneder sort and some near cousins to the Latin itself do already wean their pens and tongues from the use of the Latin, both in written discourse and spoken disputation into their own natural, and yet no dry nurse being so well appointed by the milch nurse's help."

Further on he says:—

"The Emperor Justinian said, when he made the Institutes of force, that the students were happy in having such a foredeal [i. e., advantage—German *Vortheil*] as to hear him at once, and not to wait four years first. And doth not our languaging hold us back four years and that full, think you? . . . [But this is not all.] Our best understanding is in our natural tongue, and all our foreign learning is applied to our use by means of our own; and without the application to particular use, wherefore serves learning? . . . [As for dishonoring antiquity], if we must cleave to the eldest and not the best, we should be eating acorns and wearing old Adam's pelts. But why not all in English, a tongue of itself both deep in conceit and frank in delivery? I do not think that any language, be it whatsoever, is better able to utter all arguments either with more pith or greater plainness than our English tongue is. . . . It is our accident which restrains our tongue and not the tongue itself, which will strain with the strongest and stretch to the furthest, for either government if we were conquerors, or for cunning if we were treasurers; not any whit behind either the subtle Greek for couching close, or the stately Latin for spreading fair."

There is much more in the same strain, but I have already quoted enough to show how vigorously a learned man and a schoolmaster in the sixteenth century took the side of the vernacular against the Latin language. The "Elementaire" is now, of course, a scarce book. There are two copies of it in the British Museum, but none that I have been able to discover of the "Positions."

WORDS AND THINGS.

This antithesis between words and things which constantly occurs in educational literature, from the sixteenth century onward [see page 45], is not very exact. Sometimes the antithesis so expressed is really between the material world and abstract ideas. In this case the study of things which affect the senses is opposed to the study of grammar, logic, rhetoric, etc. Sometimes by *words* is understood the expression of ideas in different languages, and by *things* the ideas themselves. This is the antithesis of those who depreciate linguistic study, and say that it is better to acquire fresh ideas than various ways of expressing the same idea. Of course it may be shown, that linguistic study does more for us than merely giving us various ways of expressing ideas, but I will not here discuss the matter. Besides the disputants who use one or other of these antitheses, many of those who find fault with the attention bestowed on words in education, mean generally words learned by rote, and not connected with ideas at all.

Several of our greatest writers have declared in one sense or other against "words." First, both in time and importance, we have Milton:

"The end of all learning is to repair the ruins of our first parents by regaining to know God aright, and out of that knowledge to love Him, to imitate Him, to be like Him, as we may the nearest by possessing our souls of true virtue, which being united to the heavenly grace of faith, makes up the highest perfection. But because our understanding can not in this body found itself but on sensible things, nor arrive so clearly to the knowledge of God, and things invisible as by orderly conning over the visible and inferior creature, the same method is necessarily to be followed in all discreet teaching. And seeing every nation affords not experience and tradition enough for all kinds of learning, therefore we are chiefly taught the language of those people who have at any time been most industrious after wisdom: so that language is but the instrument conveying to us things useful to be known. And though a linguist should pride himself to have all the tongues that Babel cleft the world into, yet if he have not studied solid things in them, as well as the words and lexicons, he were nothing so much to be esteemed a learned man, as any yeoman or tradesman completely wise in his mother dialect only."*

Soon after we find Cowley complaining of the loss which children make of their time at most schools, employing, or rather casting away, six or seven years in the learning of words only; and he designs a school in which *things* should be taught together with language. (*Proposition for the Advancement of Experimental Philosophy.*) Both Milton and Cowley wished that boys should read

---

*Tract to Hartlib. [School Room Classics, vi, pp. 7, 8.]

such Latin books as would instruct them in husbandry, etc., and so combine linguistic knowledge with "real" knowledge.

In the fourth book of the "Dunciad," the most consummate master of words thus uses his power to satirize verbal education:—

> Then thus since man from beast by words is known,
> Words are man's province, words we teach alone.
> * * * * *
> To ask, to guess, to know, as they commence,
> As fancy opens the quick springs of sense,
> We ply the memory, we loan the brain,
> Bind rebel wit, and double chain on chain,
> Confine the thought to exercise the breath,
> And keep them in the pale of words till death.
>
> (Lines 148 ff.)

Cowper, too, says:—

> And is he well content his son should find
> No nourishment to feed his growing mind
> But conjugated verbs, and nouns declined?
> For such is all the mental food purveyed
> By public hackneys in the schooling trade;
> Who feed a pupil's intellect with store
> Of syntax truly, but with little more;
> Dismiss their cares when they dismiss their flock;
> Machines themselves, and governed by a clock.
> Perhaps a father blessed with any brains
> Would deem it no abuse or waste of pains,
> 'T' improve this diet, at no great expense,
> With sav'ry truth and wholesome common sense;
> To lead his son, for prospects of delight,
> To some not steep tho' philosophic height,
> Thence to exhibit to his wondering eyes
> Yon circling worlds, their distance and their size,
> The moons of Jove and Saturn's belted ball,
> And the harmonious order of them all;
> To show him in an insect or a flower
> Such microscopic proof of skill and power,
> As, hid from ages past, God now displays
> To combat atheists with in modern days;
> To spread the earth before him, and commend,
> With designation of the finger's end,

Its various parts to his attentive note,
Thus bringing home to him the most remote:
To teach his heart to glow with generous flame,
Caught from the deeds of men of ancient fame.*

On the other side we have Dr. Johnson:—

"The truth is, that the knowledge of external nature and the sciences which that knowledge requires or includes, are not the great or the frequent business of the human mind. Whether we provide for action or for conversation, whether we wish to be useful or pleasing, the first requisite is the religious and moral knowledge of right and wrong: the next is an acquaintance with the history of mankind, and with those examples which may be said to embody truth and prove by events the reasonableness of opinions. Prudence and justice are virtues and excellences of all times and of all places; we are perpetually moralists, but we are geometricians only by chance. Our intercourse with intellect, not nature, is necessary; our speculations upon matter are voluntary and at leisure. Physiological learning is of such rare emergency, that one may know another half his life without being able to estimate his skill in hydrostatics or astronomy; but his moral and prudential character immediately appears. Those authors, therefore, are to be read at schools that supply most axioms of prudence, most principles of moral truth, and most materials for conversation; and these purposes are best served by poets, orators, and historians."†

In more recent times the increasing importance of natural science has drawn many of the best intellects

---

* Tirocinium.

† Life of Milton.

into its service. Linguistic and literary instruction now finds few supporters in theory, though its friends have not yet made much alteration in their practice. Our last two School Commissions have recommended a compromise between the claims of literature and natural science. Both reports state clearly the importance of a training in language and literature, to which our present theorists hardly seem to do justice. The Public Schools Report says:—

"Grammar is the logic of common speech, and there are few educated men who are not sensible of the advantages they gained, as boys, from the steady practice of composition and translation, and from their introduction to etymology. The study of literature is the study, not indeed of the physical, but of the intellectual and moral world we live in, and of the thoughts, lives, and characters of those men whose writings or whose memories succeeding generations have thought it worth while to preserve."*

The Commissioners on Middle Schools express a similar opinion:—

"The 'human' subjects of instruction, of which the study of language is the beginning, appear to have a distinctly greater educational power than the 'material.' As all civilization really takes its rise in human intercourse, so the most efficient instrument of education appears to be the study which most bears on that intercourse, the study of human speech. Nothing appears to develop and discipline the whole man so much as the study which assists the learner to understand the thoughts, to enter into the feelings, to appreciate the

---

* Public Schools Report, i. 28. § 8.

moral judgments of others. There is nothing so opposed to true cultivation, nothing so unreasonable, as excessive narrowness of mind; and nothing contributes to remove this narrowness so much as that clear understanding of language which lays open the thoughts of others to ready appreciation. Nor is equal clearness of thought to be obtained in any other way. Clearness of thought is bound up with clearness of language, and the one is impossible without the other. When the study of language can be followed by that of literature, not only breadth and clearness, but refinement becomes attainable. The study of history in the full sense belongs to a still later age: for till the learner is old enough to have some appreciation of politics, he is not capable of grasping the meaning of what he studies. But both literature and history do but carry on that which the study of language has begun, the cultivation of all those faculties by which man has contact with man."*

AXIOMATIC TRUTHS OF METHODOLOGY.†

1. The method of nature is the archetype of all methods, and especially of the method of learning languages.

2. The classification of the objects of study should mark out to teacher and learner their respective spheres of action.

3. The ultimate objects of the study should always be

---

* Middle Schools Report, ii. 22.

† [Compare page 46.]

kept in view, that the end be not forgotten in pursuit of the means.

4. The means ought to be consistent with the end.

5. Example and practice are more efficient than precept and theory.

6. Only one thing should be taught at one time; and an accumulation of difficulties should be avoided, especially in the beginning of the study.

7. Instruction should proceed from the known to the unknown, from the simple to the complex, from concrete to abstract notions, from analysis to synthesis.

8. The mind should be impressed with the idea before it takes cognizance of the sign that represents it.

9. The development of the intellectual powers is more important than the acquisition of knowledge; each should be made auxiliary to the other.

10. All the faculties should be equally exercised, and exercised in any way consistent with the exigencies of active life.

11. The protracted exercise of the faculties is injurious: a change of occupation renews the energy of their action.

12. No exercise should be so difficult as to discourage exertion, nor so easy as to render it unnecessary; attention is secured by making study interesting.

13. First impressions and early habits are the most important, because they are the most enduring.

14. What the learner discovers by mental exertion is better known than what is told him.

15. Learners should not do with their instructor what they can do by themselves, that they may have time to do with him what they can not do by themselves.

16. The monitorial principle multiplies the benefits of public instruction. By teaching we learn.

17. The more concentrated is the professor's teaching, the more comprehensive and efficient his instruction.

18. In a class, the time must be so employed, that no learner shall be idle, and the business so contrived, that learners of different degrees of advancement shall derive equal advantage from the instructor.

19. Repetition must mature into a habit what the learner wishes to remember.

20. Young persons should be taught only what they are capable of clearly understanding, and what may be useful to them in after-life.*

FROM "JANUA LINGUARUM." †

480. Of Journeys and Passages.—Let a traveler go straightway whither he is going without turnings; let him not turn or stray out of the way into by-wayes. 481. Let him not leave the highway for a foot-path; unless it be a beaten path or a way much used, or that the guide or companion know the way . . . 483. A forked way or carfax (bivium aut quadrivium) is deceitful and uncertain. . . . 486. Boots are fit for one that goeth far from home, or shoes of raw leather because of the mire and dirt; and a broad hat or cover of the head because of the sunne, and a cloak to keep from

---

*From Marcel on Language. London, 1853. As M. Marcel shows a thorough mastery of his subject, he may be trusted as giving the commonly received conclusions.

† [See pp. 75-78.]

rain, and a staffe to rely or lean upon, for it is a help and a support. 487. There is likewise need of provision to make expenses, and to bear the charges, or at least of letters of exchange. 488. But of patience withall; for it happeneth or cometh to pass sometimes to be all the night abroad or in the open aire. 489. Wheresoever or in what place soever thou be consider with whom thou art. 490. For robbers and thieves seek for a prey or bootie; pirates a spoil; yea, which is more, a guest or stranger is not sure or out of danger from his host. (Latrones enim prædantur: piratæ spoliant: imo in hospitio non hospes ab hospite tutus.) 491. Bags, packs, or fardles, wherein they carry their own things or baggage trussed; are a budget, a wallet, cap case, a pouch, a sachell, a male, a purse, a bag of leather. 492. To be more ready, do not burden nor charge or aggravate thyself with lets. 493. If there be necessity to make haste, it's better to use running horses or swift geldings or hunting nags than post-horses. 494. Being returned home safe and sound, thine shall receive and entertain thee with joy and gladness.—(*Edition of* 1639, p. 84.)

LOCKE ON POETRY.*

"If he have a poetic vein, it is to me the strangest thing in the world that the father should desire or suffer it to be cherished or improved. Methinks the parents should labor to have it stifled and suppressed as much as may be; and I know not what reason a father can have

---

* See page 104.]

to wish his son a poet, who does not desire to have him bid defiance to all other callings and business: which is not yet the worst of the case; for if he prove a successful rhymer, and gets once the reputation of a wit, I desire it to be considered what company and places he is like to spend his time in, nay, and estate too; for it is very seldom seen that any one discovers mines of gold or silver in Parnassus. It is a pleasant air, but a barren soil; and there are very few instances of those who have added to their patrimony by anything they have reaped from thence. Poetry and gaming, which usually go together, are alike in this too, that they seldom bring any advantage but to those who have nothing else to live on. Men of estates almost constantly go away losers; and it is well if they escape at a cheaper rate than their whole estates, or the greatest part of them. If, therefore, you would not have your son the fiddle to every jovial company, without whom the sparks could not relish their wine, nor know how to pass an afternoon idly; if you would not have him waste his time and estate to divert others, and contemn the dirty acres left him by his ancestors, I do not think you will much care he should be a poet, or that his schoolmaster should enter him in versifying."—(§ 174.)

FROM THE "EVENING HOUR OF A HERMIT."*

What man is, what he needs, what elevates him and degrades him, what strengthens him and weakens him,

---

* [See page 165.]

such is the knowledge needed both by shepherds of the people, and by the inmate of the most lowly hut.

Everywhere humanity feels this want. Everywhere it struggles to satisfy it with labor and earnestness. For the want of it men live restless lives, and at death they cry aloud that they have not fulfilled the purposes of their being. Their end is not the ripening of the perfect fruits of the year, which in full completion are laid away for the repose of the winter. . . .

The powers of conferring blessings on humanity are not a gift of art or of accident. They exist with their fundamental principles in the inmost nature of all men. Their development is the universal need of humanity.

Central point of life, individual destiny of man, thou art the book of *Nature*. In thee lieth the power and the plan of that wise teacher; and every school education not erected upon the principles of human development leads astray.

The happy infant learns by this road what his mother is to him; and thus grows within him the actual sentiment of love and gratitude before he can understand the words Duty or Thanks. . . . The truth which rises from our inmost being is universal human truth, and would serve as a truth for the reconciliation of those who are quarreling by thousands over its husks.

Man, it is thyself, the inner consciousness of thy powers, which is the object of the education of nature.

The general elevation of these inward powers of the human mind to a pure human wisdom is the universal purpose of the education even of the lowest man. The practice, application, and use of these powers and this wisdom under special circumstances and conditions of humanity, is education for a professional or social condition. These must always be kept subordinate to the general object of human training. . . .

Nature develops all the human faculties by practice, and their growth depends upon their exercise. . . .

Men, fathers, force not the faculties of your children into paths too distant before they have attained strength by exercise; and avoid harshness and over-fatigue. . .

(You leave the right order) when, before making them sensitive to truth and wisdom by the real knowledge of actual objects, you engage them in the thousand-fold confusions of word-learning and opinions; and lay the foundation of their mental character and of the first determination of their powers, not with truth and actual obligations, but with sounds and speech and words. . . .

God is the nearest resource for humanity. . . .

To suffer pain and death and the grave, without God, thy nature, educated to mildness, goodness, and feeling has no power. . . .

Believe in thyself, O man; believe in the inward intelligence of thine own soul; thus shalt thou believe in God and immortality.

Faith in the fatherhood of God is faith in immortality. . . .

Faith in my own father, who is a child of God, is a training for my faith in God.

Faith in God sanctifies and strengthens the bond between parents and children, between subjects and princes. Unbelief dissolves all bonds, destroys all blessing.

Freedom rests on justice, justice on love; therefore even freedom rests on love.

The true disposition of the child is the right source of freedom resting on justice, as the true disposition of the father is the source of all power of government which is exalted enough to do justice and to love freedom. And the source of justice and of all blessing for the world, the source of love and brotherly feeling among men, rests on the great thought of religion that we are children of God, and that belief of this truth is the sure ground of all blessing for the world. . . .

That men have lost the disposition of children toward God is the greatest misfortune of the world, inasmuch as it renders impossible all God's fatherly education of them; and the restoring of this lost childlike disposition is the redemption of the lost children of God upon earth.

The Man of God who, with suffering and death, restored to mankind the universally lost feeling of the child's disposition toward God, is the Redeemer of the World. He is the great sacrificed Priest of the Lord. He is the Mediator between God and God-forgetting mankind. His teaching is pure justice, educating people's philosophy; it is the revelation of God to His lost race of children.

FROM RAMSAUER.

As many hundred times in the course of the year as foreigners visited the Pestalozzian Institution [see page 174], so many hundred times did Pestalozzi allow himself in his enthusiasm to be deceived by them. On the arrival of every fresh visitor, he would go to the teachers in whom he placed most confidence, and say to them, "This is an important personage, who wants to become acquainted with all we are doing. Take your best pupils and their analysis-books (copy-books in which the lessons were written out), and show him what we can do, and what we wish to do." Hundreds and hundreds of times there came to the Institution silly, curious, and often totally uneducated persons, who came because it was the fashion. On their account we usually had to interrupt the class instruction, and hold a kind of examination. In 1814, the aged Prince Esterhazy came. Pestalozzi ran all over the house, calling out, "Ramsauer, Ramsauer, where are you! Come directly, with your best pupils, to the Maison Rouge (the hotel at which the Prince had alighted). He is a person of the highest importance and of infinite wealth; he has thousands of serfs in Hungary and Austria. He is certain to build schools and set free his serfs, if he is made to take an interest in the matter." I took about fifteen pupils to the hotel. Pestalozzi presented me to the Prince with these words, "This is the teacher of these scholars, a young man who, fifteen years ago, migrated with other poor children from the Canton of Appenzell and came to me. He received an elementary education according to his aptitudes, without let or hindrance. Now he is a teacher himself. Thus you see that there is as much ability in the poor as in the richest, frequently more, but it is seldom developed, and even then not methodically. It is for this reason that the improvement of the popular schools is so highly important. But he will show you everything we do better than I could. I will, therefore, leave him with you for the present." I now examined the pupils, taught, explained, and bawled, in my zeal, till I was quite hoarse, believing that the Prince was thoroughly convinced about everything. At the end of an hour Pestalozzi returned. The Prince expressed his pleasure at what he had seen. He then took leave, and Pestalozzi, standing on the top of the stairs of the hotel, said, "He is quite convinced, quite convinced, and will certainly establish schools on his Hungarian estates." When we had descended the stairs, Pestalozzi said, "Whatever ails my arm! It is so painful! Why, see, it is quite swollen; I can't bend it!" And in truth his wide sleeve was now too small for his arm. I looked at the key of the house-door of the Maison Rouge, and said to Pestalozzi, "Look here! you struck yourself against this key when we were going to the Prince an hour ago!" On closer observation, it appeared that Pestalozzi had actually bent the key by hitting his elbow against it. In the first hour afterward he had not noticed the pain for the excess of his zeal and his joy.*

HELPS, STEPHEN, ETC.†

Mr. Helps, in his admirable essay on reading, in "Friends in Council," makes some observations which, although they refer to the reading of grown persons, may be applied to early education as well. He would have every one "take something for the main stem and

---

*For an account of Ramsauer, see Barnard's Pestalozzi.
† [Compare pages 206, 207.]

trunk of their culture, whence branches might grow out in all directions, seeking light and air for the parent tree, which it is hoped might end in becoming something useful and ornamental, and which, at any rate, all along will have had life and growth in it."

He concludes his remarks on the connection of knowledges as follows:—

"In short, all things are so connected together that a man who knows one subject well, can not, if he would, have failed to have acquired much besides; and that man will not be likely to keep fewer pearls who has a string to put them on, than he who picks them up and throws them together without method. This, however, is a very poor metaphor to represent the matter; for what I would aim at producing, not merely holds together what is gained, but has vitality in itself—is always growing. And anybody will confirm this who, in his own case, has had any branch of study or human affairs to work upon; for he must have observed how all he meets seems to work in with, and assimilate itself to, his own peculiar subject. During his lonely walks, or in society, or in action, it seems as if this one pursuit were something almost independent of himself, always on the watch, and claiming its share in whatever is going on."

Sir James Stephens also made some excellent remarks to the same effect in his lecture on "Desultory and Systematic Reading," delivered at Exeter Hall:—

"By sound—that is solid—learning," (he said), "I mean such knowledge as relates to useful and substantial things, and as in itself is compact, coherent, all of a piece—having its several parts fitted into each other, and mutually sustaining and illustrating one another."

We must with a firm hand draw our own meridian line in the world of learning:—

"For learning is a world, not a chaos. The various accumulations of human knowledge are not so many detached masses. They are all connected parts of one great system of truth, and though that system be infinitely too comprehensive for any one of us to compass, yet each component member of it bears to every other component member relations which each of us may, in his own department of study, search out and discover for himself. A man is really and soundly learned in exact proportion to the number and to the importance of those relations which he has thus carefully examined and accurately understood."

In discussing the advantage of learning one subject thoroughly, we must not overlook the valuable testimony of Professor De Morgan.

"When the student has occupied his time in learning a moderate portion of many different things, what has he acquired—extensive knowledge or useful habits? Even if he can be said to have varied learning, it will not long be true of him, for nothing flies so quickly as half-digested knowledge; and when this is gone, there remains but a slender portion of useful power. A small quantity of learning quickly evaporates from a mind which never held any learning except in small quantities; and the intellectual philosopher can perhaps explain the following phenomenon—that men who have given deep attention to one or more liberal studies, can learn to the end of their lives, and are able to retain and apply very small quantities of other kinds of knowledge; while those who have never learnt much of any one thing seldom acquire new knowledge after they attain to years of maturity, and frequently lose the greater part of that which they once possessed."

I am indebted for this quotation to Mr. Payne's pamphlet, "The Curriculum of Modern Education, etc." 1866.* This pamphlet contains a most interesting discussion of the questions—Many subjects or few? and, Shall language or science have precedence? In considering these matters, Mr. Payne has an advantage possessed by at present by very few Englishmen—knowledge derived both from teaching, and from studying the theory of teaching. *Vide* his evidence before Middle Schools Commission.

MANGNALL'S QUESTIONS.

The long-continued success of this book is a melancholy proof of the stupidity which is at work, vigorously destroying the intelligence of youthful minds. When I referred to "Mangnall" [see page 179], I did so from what I remember of my own early lessons. On getting the book to see if it was as bad as I thought, I am almost driven to the supposition that it was written as a satire on the instruction generally given to children, and that it has imposed on as the *Epistolæ Obscurorum Virorum* did on some of the Roman clergy. The edition now in use begins as follows:—

"*Name some of the most Ancient Kingdoms.*—Chaldea, Babylonia, Assyria, China in Asia, and Egypt in Africa.

---

* [Now published in his "Lectures," Complete Edition, pp. 237-280.]

Nimrod, the grandson of Ham, is supposed to have founded the first of the these B. C. 2221, as well as the famous cities of Babylon and Nineveh: his kingdom being within the fertile plains of Chaldea, Chalonitis, and Assyria, was of small extent, compared with the vast empires that afterward arose from it, but included several large cities. In the portion called Babylonia, were the cities of Babylon, Barsita, Idacarra, and Vologsia, etc."

This is the opening of an historical sketch which in twelve pages brings matters down to A. D. 1849. The information given about Greece is of this kind:—

"*What progress did the Greeks make in the Arts?*—From the time of Cyrus to that of Alexander, they were gradually improving: warriors, statesmen, philosophers, poets, historians, painters, architects, and sculptors form a glorious phalanx in this golden age of literature; and the history of Greece at this period is equally important and instructive.

"*Name the chief Grecian Poets.*—Homer, Hesiod, Archilochus, Tyrtæus, Alcæus, Sappho, Simonides, Æschylus, Euripides, Sophocles, Anacreon, Pindar and Menander.

"*Name the chief Philosophers.*—Thales, Solon, Pythagoras, Heraclitus, Anaxagoras, Socrates, Empedocles, Plato, Aristotle, and Zeno.

"*Name the chief Lawgivers.*—Cecrops, of Athens; Cadmus, of Thebes; Caranus, of Macedon; Lycurgus, of Sparta; Draco and Solon, of Athens.

"*Name the chief Grecian Painters.*—Zeuxis, Parrhasius, Timanthes, Apelles, Polygnotus, Protogenes, and Aristides.

"*Name the chief Historians.*—Herodotus, Thucydides, and Xenophon.

"*Name the chief Grecian Architects.*—Ctesiphon, Phidias, Myron, Scopas, Lysippus, and Polycletus."

A "sketch of the most remarkable events from the Christian era to the close of the eighteenth century," occupies seven pages. The abstract of British biography is very complete, and takes eighty-two pages. To prevent the memory from getting assisted by association of ideas, as it might if chronological order were adopted, the worthies are given alphabetically. Though the list is tolerably complete the author adheres pretty closely to her principle, that the only thing which we really ought to know about great men is their names. Take a couple as they stand:—

"Gilbert Burnet, Bishop of Salisbury, born in Edinburghshire, 1643; died in 1715. He is memorable as an historical and political writer.

"Richard Bentley, born at Wakefield, 1662; died 1742. His literary character as a critic and *divine* is known throughout Europe."

In this last case, the reader will observe that children are taught but little, and that little wrong. Another striking feature about these biographical sketches is, that their length does not vary according to the importance of the person treated of. We find, e. g., *sixteen and a half lines* (space enough in such a work as this for the literary and political history of an empire or two) devoted to Jeremiah Horrox, "who continues to be regarded with admiration."

The sketch of general modern biography takes seventy-three pages; planetary system, two pages; list of constellations, three pages; abstract of heathen mythology, eight pages, etc. I could not give all the subjects treated of without transcribing a greater portion of the work than courtesy or copyright would allow.

DR. WIESE.

As far as literature is concerned, the Reformers [compare pages 211, 212] have been as triumphant lately in education as in politics. Indeed, it seems considered almost axiomatic that he who writes on a liberal education must himself be a Liberal.* Some of these writers hardly justify Mr. Mill's remark, that all stupid people are Tories, and some others, in tilting at the present state of things, endeavor as it were to make up by velocity for want of weight. But there are other malcontents who are not rhetoricians, and who are among the intellectual leaders of our time. We can not afford to neglect protests from men so eminent, and observing from such different standing-points, as Mill, Spencer, Tyndall, Huxley, Seeley, Matthew Arnold. Some of these gentlemen are not merely dissatisfied with English education, but they they have found in Germany a model worthy of our imitation. When they descend in this manner from the ideal to the actual, we Philistines † feel more at home with them. We like to see in a con-

---

* There are a few noteworthy exceptions to this rule, as Professor Conington and Mr. Church, who are both brave enough to defend Latin verses. See *Contemporary Review*, January and May, 1868.

† I hope I shall not be understood as ranking myself among the enemies of light or *Geist* or ideas, still less among the enemies of the "children of light" who are so well represented in this country by Mr. Arnold. I mean merely that I have no pretensions to be of their number, and that I can never aspire beyond being admitted as a proselyte of the Gate.

crete form what the Reformers would introduce, and when we are thus convinced that the change would be for the better, we no longer feel any misgivings in adopting it. But in all such cases we must be very careful that the superiority of the thing to be introduced is clearly demonstrated; and in listening to the admirers of foreign systems we sometimes wish for an opportunity of following out the maxim *Audi alteram partem* [Hear the other side]. Perhaps we remember that in our nursery experiences, the good little boy next door was frequently referred to as presenting a striking contrast with our own unworthiness, while perhaps in the adjacent nursery we were figuring in the same capacity for the humiliation of the good little boy himself. After listening to the praises of the good little German boy who is such a prodigy of learning, and, as Mr. Mathias has shown, is required to pass a harder examination on leaving school than our pollmen are when they leave the University, I take a malicious pleasure in being present (so to speak) at a lecture delivered for the benefit of that young gentleman, in which his failings are freely touched upon in connection with the English boy's corresponding virtues.

I refer to Dr. Wiese's "Letters on English Education." (English by W. D. Arnold, 1854.)* Dr. Wiese is, I believe, a very good authority, and he is referred to with much respect in Mr. Matthew Arnold's report. It is very instructive to compare his remarks on the comparative merits of English and German education with what our own authorities have said on the subject. For

---

*[Another edition, translated by Leonard Schmitz, was published in London, 1877, and though out of print is still obtainable.]

the benefit of those of my readers who have not ready access to the book, I give the following extracts:

"The differences that exist between the objects and attainments of the systems of instruction in use in the English public schools and our gymnasia may be summed up as exhibiting the contrast between skill and science (*Konnen und Wissen*), practice and knowledge. The knowledge of the English scholar is limited to a narrower circle than that of the German; but he will generally be found to move in it with greater accuracy; his knowledge lies in a narrower compass, but generally serves more as a practical power to him."—(p. 59.)

"I am persuaded that they are right who maintain that what the English schools and universities have neglected and do neglect, is amply compensated by that which they have done and are still doing."—(p. 6.)

"I think I have generally observed, that the English public schools, without exception—with all their undeniable shortcomings—yet do know how to guard and to strengthen in the rising generation the germ of future manhood; whereas we are not in a position to repel the reproaches so frequently heaped of late years on our German schools, 'that they have forgotten their business of education, and train up no men for the Commonwealth;' though in making this reproach there is much so utterly overlooked, as to make it, in the mouths of most people, an unjust one. The result of my observations, to state it briefly, is this: in knowledge, our higher schools are far in advance of the English; but their education is more effective, because it imparts a better preparation for life."—(p. 7.)

"The general impression in England is, that the acquisition of knowledge is but the second object of education, and one for which opportunity is continally offering through life, but that to enable a young man to seize upon this opportunity, and to avail himself of it, the first object of education, viz., formation of character, must be obtained early; for that deficiency in this respect is not so easily supplied in after-life. We Germans should reply that it is just in the power of forming character, that the excellence of well-regulated scientific instruction consists; but must we not confess that in numberless cases this result has not shown itself in our young men? Even in Germany most teachers maintain that the main object of instruction is education; but does not their confidence, that this object is best effected by its own means, too soon degenerate into carelessness?"—(p. 50.)

"England has the incalculable advantage of possessing a definite mode of training, handed down from generation to generation, and in all essential points unchanged for centuries; and, above all, the advantages of a fixed central point [Nationality and Religion], toward which everything else radiates: we are involved in uncertainty, and go on looking and looking for something that may remain steadfast: we allow things only valuable as means, to assume the importance of ends, and towards these all the powers we possess are enthusiastically directed. The consequence is, alas! that sooner or later, by the very necessity of things, there ensues a a reactionary movement in exactly the opposite direction."—(p. 79.)

"I have often been struck with the fact that the English are beginning to fear that the heroic feeling of noble manliness is gradually dying out of the nation, and therefore are rather shy of making any great alterations in the old system of education at the public schools and universities in order to meet the wants of modern times; or of making experiments of new systems and subjects of study, feeling as they do how much they owe to the old system for the rousing and fostering of that vital energy. They find that the times most favorable to the formation of strong individual character, were those in which the means of training were simple, and (owing to their small compass) capable perhaps of exercising a more certain influence. Therefore they are in general far from considering the variety of our German plan of study a thing to be envied."—(pp. 55, 56.)

"The ideality of the German mind, and its leaning toward the abstract, makes it feel a respect for knowledge for its own sake, such as hardly exists in England; it possesses for us an intrinsic value. To take a popular illustration, the knowledge that the earth is round, is considered by us valuable on its own account; the Englishman receives this result of scientific research with equal pleasure; but chiefly because he associates it with the thought of being able to sail around it; he asks, 'How does it affect me?' Considerations of profit are doubtless closely allied with this mode of thought; but it would be extremely unjust, were we on this account to reproach the education of the higher schools in England with utilitarianism; it is a cause of complaint in many quarters, that they are not utilitarian enough. The state of the case is pretty much as follows: in England they look to the final object of education, and find this to consist in capability for *action;* even as our own

Wilhelm von Humboldt once said, when he was Minister, that there was nothing which the State ought so much to encourage amongst its youth, as that which had a tendency to promote energy of action. Under this belief the English reject everything from their system of instruction which may tend to oppress, to over-excite, or to dissipate the mental power of the pupil. Their means and methods of instruction would appear to the teacher of a German gymnasium surprisingly simple, not to say unscientific; and so in many cases they certainly are. The English boy, even when his school-training is over, would seem generally to know little enough by the side of a German; and in certain subjects, such as geography, an English scholar is not to be compared with a German who has 'been taught on rational principles,' and the same may be said of physics and other branches of knowledge. With us it is almost a standing maxim, that the object of the gymnasium is to awaken and develop the scientific mind. An Englishman could not admit this, for he is unable to divest himself of the idea, that not to know, but to do, is the object of man's life; the vigorous independence of each individual man is his own life and calling."—(pp 63 ff.)

"In the Gymnasia, Herder warned them against the *luxury* of knowledge: and how frequently we hear the reproach, that their lessons are such as become a university rather than a school; and that consequently the boys are conceited, premature critics and phrasemongers. In England they care only for facts: they reject all critical controversy, and desire by the contemplation of facts to sharpen the faculty of observation. We, on the other hand, too often allow reflection and generalities that cost but little labor, to stifle that spirit of research which fixes itself upon the object and works toward it with scrupulous impartiality. How many a professor has been vexed at finding schoolboys bringing to college so many cut and dried thoughts and views, and so little well-grounded knowledge of simple matters of fact? Godfrey Hermann complained, 'At school they read authors critically, and we must begin at the university to teach them the elements of grammar.' I do not know whether pride of knowledge is so common now in Germany, as it was when Litchenberg spoke of it as 'a country in which children learned to turn up their noses before they learned to blow them,' but this I do know, that all pushing of the powers of thought brings its own punishment afterward. If young men are made acquainted before their time, and without pains on their part, with those results of knowledge which are fitted for a more advanced period of life, they are very likely to use up the stock of enthusiasm, which we all need and have received as a kind of dower to carry with us through life, and which we can best increase by overcoming difficulties for ourselves."—(pp. 66, 67.)

"Thus Dr. Arnold says that the effort a boy makes is a hundred times more valuable to him than the knowledge acquired as the result of the effort; as generally in education the *How* is more important than the *What*. The consequence of this being so often forgotten in German schools, of their not sufficiently guarding against the encyclopædic tendency of their system of study is, that a young man loses not only the natural simplicity and coherence of his idea, but yet more his capacity to observe, because he has been over-crammed; his brain becomes confused and his ear deafened; and after all he is obliged to bestow his labor rather on account of the extent than the depth of the knowledge to be attained. In English schools they have hitherto avoided this danger by confining themselves to very little; students there do not learn nearly so much as with us, but they learn one thing better, and that is the art of learning. They acquire a greater power of judging for themselves; they know how to take a correct starting-point for other studies; whereas our young men too often only know just what they have learnt, and never cease to be dependent on their school-teaching."—(pp. 68, 69.)

"It can not be denied that the maxim, '*non scholæ sed vitæ*' [not for school but for life], is better understood in England than in Germany. All that a school can teach, beyond imparting a certain small stock of knowledge, is *the way to learn*. It is a lamentable misconception of that most important maxim, to suppose that a liberal education can have any other end in view, than to impart and exercise power to be used in after-life."—(p. 76.)

"I am persuaded that we must soon make up our minds once more to simplify our course of study, and the regulations for the last school examination (*Arbiturienten-examen*)."—(p, 77.)

"Were it possible to combine the German scientific method with the English power of forming the character, we should attain an idea of education not yet realized in Christian times, only once realized perhaps in any time, —in the best days of Greece; but which is just the more difficult to attain now, in proportion as the spirit of Christianity is more exalted than anything which antiquity could propose to itself as the end of education."
—(p. 209.)

INDEX.

Accomplishments, value of, 236
Activity stimulated, 191, 263, 321
Actors as good company, 104
Æsop's Fables, 101, 105, 266, 268
Æsthetic culture, 55, 190, 202, 285, 237, 239
Aim of education, 114, 182, 205, 227
A little well learned, 207, 218
Amateur scientists, 231
Analysis vs. synthesis, 46
Andræ, J. V., 58
Apparatus needed, 72, 247
Aquaviva, 18
Arcesilaus, 44
Aristotle, q., 69
Arithmetic, 149, 189
Arnold, M., q., 102, 135, 137, 223
Arnold, Thos., 85, 233, 239, 270, 280, 322
Ascham, 35–42, 45. 67
—and Jacotot, 208, 210
—and Ratich, 52
Attention, securing, 27, 171, 191, 248, 257
Attractive methods (see Learning)
Augsburg, Ratich at, 48
Auschauung, 186
Austen, Miss, q., 217
Axiomatic truths, 301
Bacon
—and Jesuits, 17
—and Comenius, 58, 61, 67
Bain, q., 258
Basedow, 138-155
—and Pestalozzi, 190, 191
Batty and Comenius, 76
Bayle, q., 59

Benevolent superintendence, 184
Bernsdorf and Basedow, 140
Bible as text-book, 51, 73, 101, 139, 150, 284
Biography before history, 272
Bluntschli and Pestalozzi, 158, 163
Bobadilla, 19
Boileau, q., 135
Books for the young, 271
—only supplementary, 243
Borgia, 19
Bowels, regular action of, 88
Boy at nine years, 274
—at twelve years, 112, 131, 178
Browning, Oscar, q., 53
Bulwer, q., 176
Burgdorf, Pestalozzi at, 173
Burke, q., 222
Caecilius, 58
Cambridge tripos, 212
—vs. Oxford, 213
Campanella, 58
Campe, 153
Canisius, 19
Carlyle, q., 252
Cat as a model, 118
Change at twelve years, 131
Character from companions, 85
—of teacher, 277
Checking of children, 91
Childhood sacrificed, 115, 178
—vs. youth, 178
Children as children, 150
Christopher and Alice, 167
Civil government, 106
Class matches, 23, 288
Code of the Jesuits, 18

INDEX.

Co-ercive teaching, 50, 95
Colet, 35, 292
Comenius, 56-80
— and Jacotot, 208
— and Locke, 92
— and Milton, 79
— and Pestalozzi, 75
— and Ratich, 52
— summary of principles, 68
Committing to memory, 49, 104, 120, 209
Composition exercises, 104, 221, 267
Compulsion in occupation, 95
Concrete to abstract, 46, 246
Cowley, q., 297
Criticism, premature, 322
Curiosity fostered, 133
Dancing, importance, 94
Davies, Emily, q., 86, 93
Declamation, condemned, 120
De Geer, Lawrence, 66
— Lewis, 62
De Morgan, Prof., q., 312
De Quincy, q., 85, 282
Descartes, q., 17, 62
Desire for knowledge, 123, 133, 216
Dessau, Basedow at, 143
Desultory reading, 311
Dictation lessons, 266
Didactica Magna, 59, 63, 68, 75
Dion Prussaeus, 41
Disciplinary studies, 211, 212, 215, 225, 252, 257, 318
Discipline, 90, 93
Division of hours, 152
Double translation, 40, 52
Drawing, 106, 120, 190, 202
Drummond, q., 286
Dull teaching defended, 252
Dupanloup, q., 102
Early teaching, 176
Edgeworth, q., 246
Editions of books, 53, 57, 80, 136, 166, 167, 194, 197, 254, 317
Education through play, 72, 120
— in suffering, 129

— of a gentleman, 82
— of opinion, 286
Elbing, Comenius at, 63
Elizabeth, Queen, 41
Emerson, q., 285
Emile, 108-137, 135
Empirical to rational, 247
Emulation and rewards, 23, 72, 288
England, Comenius in, 60
English ed'l theory, 213
— literature, claims of, 216
— Schools vs. German, 316
Enigmas given, 72
Enthusiasm of humanity, 182
Equal capacity for learning, 198
Erasmus, 35
Ernest of Weimar, Prince, 48
Eton Latin Grammar, 214
Evening Hour of a Hermit, 165, 305
Examinations, 72, 137
Exertion encouraged, 191
Experiment and analysis, 50
Fables and allegories, 72
Facts to be learned, 216, 321
Familiarity with subject, 218
Fellenburg and Pestalozzi, 174
Firmness, 129
Formal religious teaching, 284
— teaching, 281
Franklin, q., 265
Fred's Journey to Dessau, 147
Freedom from restraint 111
French, importance of, 100, 146
— methods, 146, 198
Froude, q., 287
Functions of a tutor, 96, 116
Fundanius, 64
Generalities vs. facts, 321
Genesis of knowledge, 247
Gentlemen's education, 82
Geography teaching, 217, 273
Glaumius, 58
Goethe, v., 209, 270
— and Basedow, 141
Gogmagogs, 212
Good breeding, 94

—spirits in teacher, 281
Grammar, 102, 221
—and literature, 300
Greek, importance of, 45, 106, 241
Grubé Method, 195
Guillard, Achille, q., 223
Gymnastics, first use, 152
Hack's *Winter Evenings*, 274
Hamilton, 81, 181
Handelschulen, 230
Hands and voice, 74
Hartlib, 60
—and Comenius, 64
—and Milton, 53
Head-master's influence, 85
Health of pupils, 29
Helps, q., 232, 286, 310
Helvicus, q., 47, 48, 58
Hermann, Godfrey, q., 322
History teaching, 217, 234, 235, 256, 268, 271
Hoose's *Pestalozzian Arithmetics*, 195
Hope, A. R., q., 282
How vs. What, 322
"Human" vs. material, 300
Idleness indulged, 112
Indefinite to definite, 246
Indifference of teachers, 193, 253, 256
Industrial education, 107, 135
Influence of leading boys, 283
Innocence hazarded, 83
Innovators, the, 45, 54, 101
Instruction, definition, 217
Intellectual education, 186, 240
—vigor, 132
Independence of facts, 219, 311
Interest aroused, 257, 270
—essential, 259
—of the teacher, 192
Jacotot, 196-223
—and Hamilton, 210
—and Spencer 209, 212, 214, 217
—and Vogel, 264
—his paradoxes, 198
—his rules, 219
—his special work, 222

Janua Linguarum, 59, 66, 68, 73, 75 78, 80, 303
Jesuits, 17-34, 45
—and Comenius, 71, 75
—and Jacotot, 204, 208
Johnson, Dr., q., 36, 299
Jonson, Ben, q., 282
Jouvency, q., 24-27, 32
Juvenants, 19
Kant, q., 140
—and Basedow, 153
Kingdon, R. G., q., 24
Knight's *School History*, 272
Knowledge and power, 215, 323
—for itself, 320
—vs. power, 211, 212, 215, 225, 252, 257, 318
Known to unknown, 242, 263
Köthen, Ratich at, 48
Kromayer, 52
Krüsi, 173
Lainez, 19
Language lessons, 102, 187, 221
Large vs. small schools, 282
Latin, importance, 26, 31, 45, 48, 54, 69, 100, 146, 214, 229, 239, 241, 255
—methods, 35, 37, 51, 54, 70, 73, 76, 100, 101, 146, 148, 201, 217, 245, 289, 290, 292
Lavater and Basedow, 141
—and Pestalozzi, 158, 167
Learning disparaged, 98
—made attractive, 32, 46, 50, 54, 69, 71, 95, 98, 151, 191, 249, 250
—the Index, 269
—vs. development, 276
Leisure, part of education, 235-237
—value of, 282
Le Maire, 62
Length of school-hours, 25
Leonard and Gertrude, 165, 166
Leopald of Dessau, Prince, 143
Lessing, q., 202
Leszno, Comenius at, 58, 65
Letters on Early Education, 195
Lewis of Anhalt-Köthen, 48

INDEX.

Liberty as a panacea, 127
Lily's Grammar, 35, 100, 290.
Litchenberg, q., 322
Little, but thoroughly. 49, 132, 264, 312, 320
Little learning dangerous, 231
Locke, 42, 81-107
—and Pestalozzi, 190, 191
—and Rousseau, 88, 135
—notion of education, 97
—on sugar, 251
—summary of principles, 107
Logic disparaged, 105
Long, George, q., 36
Love-Letter of Pestalozzi, 160
Lowe, Mr., 124
Macaulay for boys, 270
Mangnall's Questions, 179, 271, 313
Manual training, 135
Marcel, q., 301
Maternity, instruction in, 149
Mathematics, memory in, 218
Matthison, 158
Maurice, Prince, 47
Mayor, J. E. B., q., 36
Medecines avoided, 88
Memorizing, 49, 104, 120, 209
Memory, value of, 216
Menalk and Pestalozzi, 161
Mental discipline, (see Disciplinary.)
Merivale, Herman, 135
Mersenne, 62
Methodology, truths of, 301
Methodus Linguarum Nov., 65, 68
Mill, J. S., q., 229, 234, 238
Milton, John, 53-55, 67
Mind and memory, 74;
Model boy, Rousseau's, 112
Modelling, 191
Money-getting education, 229, 238
Montaigne, 42-44, 45, 67, 130, 132, 202
—and Jacotot, 209
—and Locke, 89
—and Rousseau, 109

Moral behavior, 116, 125
—and religious education, 276-287
—tone of large schools, 282
—training, 185
Moravian brethren, 57, 58, 65
Most critical period, 111
—reckless innovator, 109, 110
Mothers as teachers, 183
Motion and noise, 151
Mozart, 204, 218
Mulcaster, 45, 293
Music, value of, 106, 120, 190.
—methods, 202
—in religion, 283
Natural instruction, 46, 49, 69, 72, 110, 124, 144, 147
—philosophy, 106
Naturalness in teachers, 278
Near things first, 124, 260
Negative education, 111
Neuhof, Pestalozzi at, 159
Niederer and Schmid, 175
North, Thos., q., 273
Nothing to be forgotten, 210
Object lessons, 117, 144, 171, 177, 188, 261
Observation and reflection, 187
One thing at a time, 49
Open-airiness, 86
Orbis Pictus, 59, 66, 68, 79, 80, 142
Originality encouraged, 31
Oxenstiern, q., 62
Palmer, q., 164
Pansophiae Prodromus, 58, 60
Painting disparaged, 106
Paradoxes of Jacotot, 198
Parental education, 232,
Parent's part in education, 72
Payne, Joseph, q., 196-223, 313
—editions of *Lectures*, 196, 197
Pedagogy only from teachers, 224
Penmanship, 99
Pestalozzi, 156-176
—and Jacotot, 208
—and Ramsauer, 308
—and Spencer, 247, 261
—root of his system, 182

Pestalozzianism, 176-195
Philanthropin, 138-155
—description of, 147
Physical education, 46, 228
—vs. training, 238
—training, 55, 86, 107, 111, 180, 190
Pictures valuable, 261
—maps, models, etc., 72
Playing into spelling, 99
Pleasure a means, 259
Plutarch's *Lives*, 273
Poetry, value, 104, 139, 237, 266, 304
Pope, q., 298
Popularity of Jesuits, 30
Prayer in schools. 286
"Preparatory schools," 179, 283
Primary teachers, 180
Private vs. public education. 82
Prodigies of learning, 123
Psychology important, 240
Punishment, 29, 72, 130
—corporal, 92, 91, 139
Pupil's influence, 84
Quaalen, Herr von, 138
Quadrivium, 45
Qualifications of a tutor, 96, 116
Racine, 135
Ramsauer, q., 172, 308
Ratich, 46-52, 67
—and Comenius, 57, 58, 63, 73
—and Jacotot, 208-210
Ranke, q., 31
Raumer, q., 45, 51, 139, 175, 194
Reading, 220, 262, 265, 310
Reading-books, 264
"Real" knowledge, 101
Realists and idealists, 278
Reasoning with children, 96
Reflection, 219
Reformers as a class, 108
Reiner's *Lessons in Number*, 195
Relative value of knowledges, 227, 239
Religious differences, 45, 48, 57, 66, 67, 139
—instruction, 99, 146, 284

Repetition, 27, 49, 219
Repression, 94, 117
"Rewarding" effort, 260
Rewards, 94
Rhenius, 58
Ritterus, 58
Robinson Crusoe, 126, 153
Robinson, R., q., 267
Rousseau, 42, 108-137
—and Basedow, 110, 122, 139, 144
—and Jacotot, 209
—and Locke, 109
—and Pestalozzi, 110, 117, 136, 157, 159, 163, 1 6
—and Spencer, 130
Routine teaching, 280
Sacchini, q., 29, 32, 33
Salmeron, 19
Salzman, 153
Saros-Patak model school, 65
Schmid, q., 19, 29, 185
School-building pleasant, 72
School-teaching a failure, 257
Schummell, Herr, q., 147
Science of education, 240
Science teaching, 103, 117, 132, 202, 230, 238, 241
Seeley, Prof., q., 216, 245
Self-denial cultivated, 90
Self-dependence, 185, 248
Self-direction limited, 201
Self-government, 130
Self-instruction, 46, 197, 201
Self-preservative knowledge, 228
Seneca, 88, 130
Sense-instruction, 46, 71, 116, 118, 144
Service in schools, 285
Sheldon's *Object-Lessons*, 195
Simple to complex, 242
Skyte, John, 62
Smith, Sydney, q., 181
Socrates, 44, 223
Special education, 100, 184, 230
Spelling, 23, 221, 288

Spencer, 87, 177, 202, 224-254
—follows Comenius, 75
—principles, 242
—summary of criticism, 238
Stadius, 57
Stanley, Lord, q., 117, 215
Stanz, Pestalozzi at, 169
Stephens, James, q., 311
Sturm, 45
Subjects made interesting, 259
Sweden, Comenius in, 62
Sympathy with children, 116
Systematic education, 70, 311
Systems of schools, 74
Teaching definitions, 199, 200
—narrows, 280
—too long, 281
—what one does not know, 199
Telemaque, 198, 206, 210
Text-books, attractive, 265
Thing before attribute, 50
Things vs. representations, 122
—knowledge of, 45, 101
Thoroughness, 28
Thoughts and suggestions, 255-275
Tom Brown at Rugby, 271
Tonic Sol-Fa, 120
Tout est dans tout, 206, 219
Tracing in penmanship, 100
Travel for education, 74, 107, 234
Trivium, 45

Tutors, private, 82
Tyndall, 75, 202, 253
Unconscious tuition, 277
Uniformity of method, 49
Universities, English, 30
" Useful Knowledge," 273
Variety of methods, 266
Verification of knowledge, 220
Vernacular before Latin, 45, 46, 73, 103, 139, 245, 298
Verse-making, 104
Vices in public schools, 84
Villa Dei, A. de, 35, 289
Virtue and reason, 90
Vitality in childhood, 117
Vogel's system, 262
Waking children gently, 89
Walmisley, Prof., q., 218
Weise, q., 316
Williams, David, q., 135
Wilson, M., q., 133, 197, 202, 205, 206
Wolsey, q., 35, 36
Work of a tutor, 97
Words and things, 45, 54, 70, 72, 121, 134, 209, 296-301
—unintelligible, 122
Wordsworth, q., 258, 280
" Young ladies' " schools, 217
Youth in teachers, 116
Yverdun, Pestalozzi at, 174

www.ingramcontent.com/pod-product-compliance
Lightning Source LLC
Chambersburg PA
CBHW021205230426
43667CB00006B/573